Galloper Jack

BROUGH SCOTT

Galloper Jack

A GRANDSON'S SEARCH FOR A FORGOTTEN HERO

MACMILLAN

For Janet

First published 2003 by Macmillan
an imprint of Pan Macmillan Ltd
Pan Macmillan, 20 New Wharf Road, London N1 9RR
Basingstoke and Oxford
Associated companies throughout the world
www.panmacmillan.com

ISBN 0 333 98938 4

A CIP catalogue record for this book is available from
the British Library.

Typeset by SX Composing DTP, Rayleigh, Essex
Printed and bound in Great Britain by
Mackays of Chatham plc, Chatham, Kent

Acknowledgements

Research for this book has been headed up with great industry, ingenuity and scholarship by my son, Charlie Scott. It is a matter very much of professional as well as paternal pride to leave the acknowledgements to him . . .

Much of this book may read like fiction but only occasionally is it a product of pure imagination rather than fact. The joy, the challenge, and, sometimes, the despair of writing about Jack Seely is that you absolutely could not make him up.

The quest which has resulted in this volume may have begun with my father on his mother's knee but it has gone on from there; through all of Seely's self-congratulatory books, through all the parodying of his sort, to more recent revisionist ideas close to the Jack Seely path. Once we undertook this project the journey continued on through diaries, letters and photos to libraries, archives and battlefields way beyond the horizon.

All this searching would be for nothing without Brough's Uncle David. The current Lord Mottistone and Jack Seely's sole-surviving child is an astonishing fountainhead of detailed family knowledge. This is still a family history, but thanks to his concern for fact and his collating and discovering of much long-forgotten material, we believe his father's story can now be presented to a modern audience.

The fading mountains of fact and myth which were once built around Jack Seely have been further quarried by Cath Cooper, the retired history teacher whose 200-page, originally-sourced thesis on Seely's public life deserves a much wider readership.

From this foundation on the twin stones of family and academia we have searched on. From Isle of Wight downs to the High Veld of South Africa, indeed from Westminster's halls of power to the killing fields of northern Europe, there has been a very physical aspect to this research. The first steps may have been along the stormy coast that so coloured our hero, but the paper research began at the Nuffield College Library in Oxford. There rests the Jack Seely archive under the friendly and helpful care of Dr Victoria Child and her team. My work necessarily began with asking for their assistance.

The fingers of this history stretch out from there. To the record offices in London and the Isle of Wight, to what were once Seely strongholds around Nottingham and Lincoln and then Harrow. There the first portrait, the schoolboy's cricket team photo found by Rita Gibbs in her owl-like eyrie above Harrow School.

The Royal National Lifeboat Institute was always central to his character, as indeed would be newspaper reports of his heroism. They began in 1892 and would only end with obituary references in 1947. The British Library's Newspaper Library in north London catalogues all this, his rise from notices in the local paper to front-page leads on the nationals and the fade back.

The National Maritime Museum, New Zealand's national archives, the Wellington Museum and the New Zealand Shipping Company website helped add substance to the 1892 trip. The characters of Tom Conolly, Lord Burford and even Te Kooti were enriched by their descendants. The Internet was essential for the latter but many thanks are due to Patrick Conolly-Carew, Charles Beauclerk and Doug Rawnsley for trying to bring some reality to our recreation of the young bucks' journey.

There is no better way to understand than to retread the same ground. This was easy enough on the Isle of Wight and around London, but to appreciate Seely's Boer War we received the exceptional input of Petro Maartens and her family. Her enthusiasm, hospitality and networking was well beyond anything that might have been owed us for Seely having spared her grandfather's life a century before. Through her contacts, the official histories and everything from newspapers and maps of the time to modern videos, sense could be made of that extraordinary conflict. The politicizing of our young yeomanry officer was only to be revealed by his recently rediscovered diaries. But riding his trail would require the inspiring help of our mounted guide, Jennifer Russell, who conjured life, and death, from the battlefields.

And so to Parliament and to the pursuit of each strand of his endeavours and those of his remarkable contemporaries. A pursuit that has depended on many official papers and biographies, on many histories and essays, but particularly on those of Winston Churchill, F.E. Smith and Maurice Hankey, our key witnesses. The modern account is Cath Cooper's and her work was an immeasurable help as we tried to match up Seely's own footnote in history with the man the family remembered and with the Edwardian caricature his own books and many critics portrayed. Any success we have had owes much to her and also to the generous welcome of the staffs at the many libraries and archives.

The First World War is still such an integral part of modern life that any attempt at a catalogue of sources seems futile, but we have had incomparable support from the staff and archives of the Imperial War Museum, the National Army Museum and the British Library in London, and from the Canadian War Museum and the Canadian National Archives in Ottawa. Jack Seely's own accounts in books, speeches and diaries are nothing until balanced with other contemporary sources. Those official war diaries from the general to the specific take you back to the trenches and to the horse-lines, to the movements of the Canadian Cavalry Brigade and its composite regiments. The characters and their beliefs and motives also come alive through the diaries, correspondence and other writings of Seely's comrades-at-arms from Churchill and Foch to Sally Home and Geoffrey Brooke, indeed from Sir Alfred Munnings to Lieutenant Freiherr von Falkenstein. Yet above all these rises Luke Williams, whose account of his time in France with the Strathconas still has pride of place on this desk.

Hindsight has been wondrously supplied by writers as diverse as the Marquis of Anglesey and the Comtesse de Paris, through Lynn MacDonald, Gary Sheffield, Paddy Griffin and Stephen Badsey, through Terraine and Gibbs to the wider sweeps of Gilbert and Liddell-Hart and into the close focus of Major McNorgan's work on the Canadian Cavalry Brigade. Mike McNorgan is still with the Royal Canadian Dragoons and his welcome when we got to Ottawa was as whole-hearted as it was instructive. Besides the scholarship behind his and John Grodzinski's official study of the Canadian Cavalry at Moreuil Wood, Mike set us off on a river network of sources: the Fort Garry Horse's Gordon Crossley in Winnipeg, the Royal Canadian Horse Artillery's Clive Prothero-Brooks at Shilo and Lee Ramsden and his colleagues at the Lord Strathcona's Horse's museum and archive in Calgary.

Others who need thanking include the Hookey family and Rita Gibbs at Brooke, Tony Cripps and Sir Charles Nicholson at Mottistone, Martin Woodward of the Bembridge Lifeboat, the staff of the Bloemfontein War Museum, Michael Orr, Andrew Orgill and Stephen Badsey at the Royal Military Academy at Sandhurst. Also Nick Lyell, Mike Gow, Mark Fletcher and Tim Hailstone gave generous input to the text and Patrick Seely helped hugely with pictures and other documents.

Eddie Bell was a great encouragement at the start and John Tagholm has been urging this project on for more than twenty years. The delight of finishing this book has only been matched by completing the film *Fear, And Be Slain*, which John has produced and directed about the same Seely saga and in which the Moorcroft Racehorse Centre's Mullintor played a starring role as Warrior. Forgetfulness will have led to many omissions from this list for which we crave forgiveness, as we do for all those Jack Seely stories inflicted on so many through the years.

If you have come with us on our journey, can we close by giving thanks to friend and agent Jon Holmes for getting Macmillan in on the act, to their team of Jeremy Trevathan, Stuart Evers, Philippa McEwan and Georgina Morley for helping us through and to their peerless pair of editors, Tanya Stobbs and Talya Baker, whose firm but sensitive encouragement was an education, to designer Alison Padley and proofreader Ruth Carim, to Cherry Forbes for keeping some semblance of order in the office, to colleagues at *Racing Post*, *Sunday Telegraph* and Channel 4, not to mention the family, for their forbearance. We can only hope you found the voyage worthwhile.

Charlie Scott, February 2002

Contents

CONTENTS

CONTENTS

List of Illustrations

Plate Sections

Preface

He was just an old man in a dressing gown, one of those red and blue silk paisley things as I remember. He had a hook nose, a rheumy kindly eye and was sitting taking sips from an oxygen cylinder. He pointed to a black box on the wall and said, 'That is called a "Division Bell". When it rings we have to get up and rush across to the Houses of Parliament to vote.' It was 1947. Jack Seely was seventy-nine. I was only four. My grandfather didn't look like running very far.

He died later that year and, hard though I have tried, I cannot conjure up any other memories of one of the most flamboyantly heroic figures this country, let alone this family, ever housed. So on my mother's knee I was told tales beyond the wildest storybook imaginings. How her father had swum a rope out to a stricken ship on the Isle of Wight's stormy west coast when the Brooke lifeboat could not be launched. How he sailed to New Zealand a year later and met a naked Maori princess out swimming with rather pleasant consequences. How he and my grandmother (not the afore-mentioned princess) dined with Queen Victoria two days before he left for the Boer War with his white horse Maharajah now dyed brown for camouflage. How, after many amazing, bullet-ducking sagas, he came back two years later to discover he had been elected MP, by his wife going round in a horse and trap with a sign up saying, 'Vote for Jack'. How his political career was locked on to that of his friend Winston Churchill, who came down to his home at Brooke to bully and inspire my mother and her sisters into building the biggest sandcastle ever. How Jack Seely rose to Cabinet

alongside Churchill but then, in the so-called Curragh Mutiny of
1914, became not the first nor the last Minister to crash over Ulster.
How later that same year he and his famous horse Warrior were
first off the boat to France and then survived the most astonishing
front-line adventures before both celebrating Christmas back at
Brooke in 1918.

For the small, trusting, privileged boy, here was the shining, old-
fashioned hero we used to find in those 'Boys behind the bugle'
novels of G. A. Henty. An impression only reinforced when I began
to read his own 'How I Won the War' books, *Adventure, Forever
England* and *Fear and Be Slain*, with its magnificently uncompromising opening line: 'Safety first is a vile motto.'

But moods change and by the time I went up to Oxford in 1961
to read history (although most of my terms were spent rushing off
to stables and racecourses trying to become a jockey) the age of the
unimpeachable British upper-class hero was over to the point of
ridicule. I had drunk in the lyrical nightmares of Wilfred Owen and
Siegfried Sassoon, had swallowed the general condemnation of
French and Haig, later to be personified in Alan Clark's *Lions Led
by Donkeys* and, worse still, had looked up plenty of derogatory
references to Seely in other biographies. After reading such asper-
sions as 'stupidity' and 'braggadocio', it came almost as a relief to
find a comment as cryptic as, 'This man is nearly as brave as he says
he is.'

Any remaining sympathy for one's forebear was hardly helped
by the revelation that in the 1930s he became a member of von
Ribbentrop's Anglo-German fellowship and, although far from a
Mosleyite, had met both Hitler and Mussolini on his travels. It did
not need the long line of bitterly hilarious pieces from *Oh! What a
Lovely War* to 'Blackadder' to suggest it might be imprudent to
disinter my grandfather from his memories.

Yet as years passed, curiosity began to return. Before she died in
1996 my youngest aunt told of her own arguments with her father.
How, working for British Intelligence, she knew things that the old
man could not understand. But how, also, her love and admiration for someone she still considered a truly remarkable person

remained undimmed. The urge to look again at this figure from another age started to grow. Even allowing for his customary exaggeration – he is supposed to have recommended his driver (or in some versions his horse) for the VC with the simple citation, 'He went everywhere I went' – here were stories, here was an attitude to make you shake your head in wonder.

Here most of all was an age not so much forgotten as cast into caricature. Harrow, Cambridge, the Bar, Yeomanry, the Commons, Great War general, and finally Lord Lieutenant stiffen the image into cardboard. But prejudice can be an enemy of understanding, can shut your eyes to the fascinating actuality of how it was, can block your heart to admiration of values from other times. Here was Seely as the ultimate Victorian. British Imperialism may have got itself a bad name, but whatever its manifold faults, at heart there was a collective energy and belief and determination at which it's facile to simply sneer.

So we went to look. I had already been to New Zealand but, aided by my own son, went to Harrow, South Africa, Canada, Westminster, the Western Front and above all to the downland and beaches of the Isle of Wight where Seely as a Cabinet Minister still rowed in the lifeboat, and from where as Lord Mottistone he took the title as which he was supposed to make the division-bell journey from that Westminster flat to the House of Lords.

Our own journey caused us some trepidation. We knew there were dismissive doubters already, but what sort of scandals might we discover if we started rooting around in the old man's cupboards all these years on? We would tell it as it came.

Casting off my own comfortable cloak of a sports journalist and Channel 4 racing presenter, I have tried to imagine a world that now seems not one but many centuries ago. Actually, as a matter of horseracing fact, Seely and the future Duke of Devonshire did make a fortune backing the 1889 Cambridgeshire winner at 66–1, and the wide-open vista of Newmarket Heath is one of the places unchanged enough for the eye to still travel to this other age. Once there we found an extraordinary set of stories.

What emerged was a much bigger and wider tale than the

initially sceptical grandson might have imagined. He may not have been a Prime Minister or Commander-in-Chief, but Seely was a hands-on witness to major moments in history. He was also symbolic, not just of another age but of another set of values. Not for nothing did the great lawyer F.E. Smith, Lord Birkenhead, call him 'as gay, as gallant, as debonair, and often as rash as D'Artagnan'. Some of these values may seem almost absurdly jingoistic to our minds. But others challenge us for very different reasons.

They dare to suggest that a simple unswerving devotion to a high ideal may still have its merits. These are values that take us to the very roots of courage, eternal in their application. They question the wisdom of taking just the faults of another era as its most important legacy. They insist that here was a life it would be both dumb as well as dull not to re-explore. In 1947, some months before my single infant memory, Hollywood film director Bill Cowen brought his own son Garry over from Canada to see the 'General'. Garry was ten and has a shining recall both of the old, still upright Seely and of his own splendid father, who once had the night-time nerve, when stuck on wire at Cambrai, to get himself freed by two approaching enemy through the simple daring expedient of cursing them in fluent German for not helping an officer out.

'Those men,' said Garry in 2001, himself a distinguished figure wistful of an age that is gone, 'had such a certainty about them.'

Brough Scott, April 2002

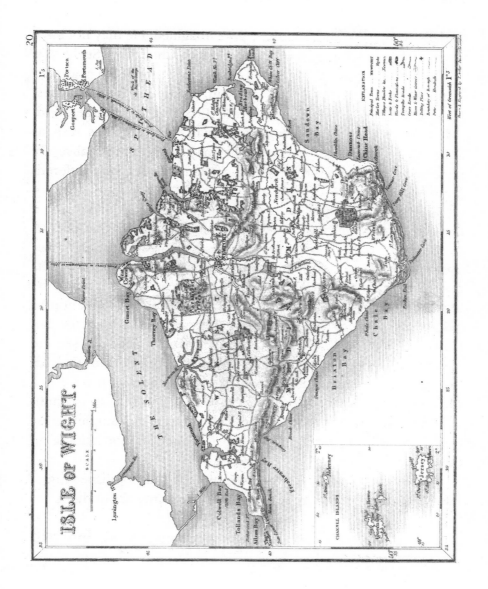

Jack Seely was brought up at Brooke on the wild south-west coast
where his experiences in the local community and with the lifeboat
were very much the making of him (Mary Evans Picture Library)

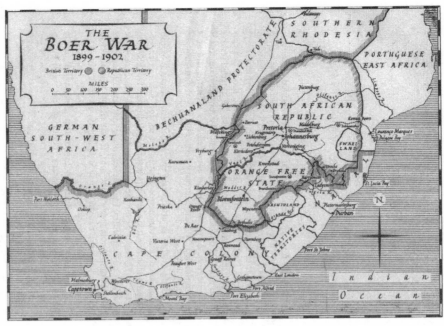

South Africa during the Boer War, 1899–1902 – Seely was based in
Harrismith and his experiences there and throughout the land
politicized him to such an extent that he returned to Britain as a
vociferously critical member of the Government

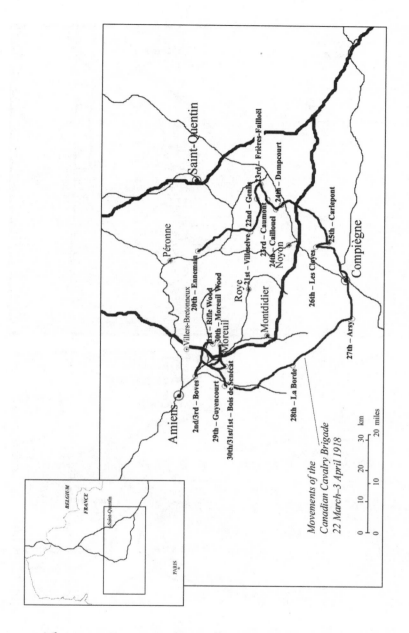

The 1918 German spring offensive split the British and French armies and almost won the war. The fighting retreat of Seely's Canadian Cavalry Brigade reached its 'supreme moment' on Easter weekend against the arrowhead of the German attack

I. GILDED YOUTH

22 March 1918, the Road to Amiens

Jack Seely had never been so certain in his life: certain that this was it.

On the rainy evening of Friday 22 March 1918 Jack Seely was a lean, intense, overcoated figure in a big khaki staff car heading out over the Calais cobbles for Boulogne, Amiens and the Fifth Army HQ at Noyon. At 6 a.m. on Thursday 21st the Germans had launched Operation Michael with the biggest artillery barrage in history. In twenty-four hours they had busted enough holes in the Allied lines to inspire that famous scene of the Kaiser dancing down the platform at Berlin station saying, a fraction prematurely, 'The war is over.'

Worst hit was the line in front of Saint-Quentin, with thousands of casualties and a general retreat. Five miles east at Ennemain lay the 2,700 men and horses of the Canadian cavalry of which Kitchener had put Seely in charge early in 1915. The Canadians were about to be thrown into the furnace. But Seely wasn't with his team of officers including Patterson, Macdonald, Connolly, Cowen, Williams and Harvey, the Irish rugby international who in March 1917 had won the VC at Guyencourt. 'Galloper Jack' wasn't riding Warrior, the horse on which he had become an almost centaur-like inspiration. He was in the car.

The car had been innocently awaiting its owner, but Seely and his ADC Prince Antoine d'Orléans-Bragance had taken it. That was typical Seely. Back in 1900 when there hadn't been a ship to take his Hampshire Yeomanry down to the Boer War he had gone to his Uncle Frank who ran the Union Castle Line and said, 'You have a ship – right, we'll have it – the War Office will pay.' Eighteen years on the situation was much more critical. And once again Seely had a hungry need to get where the action was. He would be fifty in May 1918. If he lived that long.

We laugh now at how gung-ho this all seems. But it shouldn't be that unfamiliar. Every paper, every day, has sports sections sounding off about players 'putting themselves on the line'. For someone like Seely, the opposition wasn't some pumped-up rugby or football team, but uncompromising German shells and machine guns that had already killed millions of his fellow soldiers, including his own eldest son at Arras in April 1917. The cause wasn't just the tribal passions of club and team mates, it was the whole doomed, quasi-religious King-and-Country, 'sword of sacrifice' belief with which he had been inculcated from birth. Yes, hurrying back from an unwanted trip to London and dinner with Prime Minister Lloyd George, it seemed that this really was 'it'.

Looking back eighty-five years we forget how the Germans nearly won the war in 1918. How the Allies nearly lost it. How all that terrible sacrifice at Ypres, the Somme, Passchendaele and the rest might have been in vain. Seely lived another twenty-nine years. In later writings he put an old Empire-worshipper's rosy tint on many things. But he never forgot how close it was in 1918. How could he? On the pivotal Easter weekend of 30 March to 1 April 1918 he and his astonishingly disparate bunch of ranchers, expatriates and Native Canadians (Red Indians) played a key role in two days as crucial as any in the war.

Jack Seely, more than anyone, had known that the war was coming. As a Cabinet Minister up till 1914 he had tried to prepare England for it, and he had then somehow cheated death for four years in and out of the front line. Now everything was desperate once again. He would have taken a long pull on his ever present cigarette, and looked down at the spurs glinting on the heels of his wrinkled, but still highly polished brown boots. He was a cavalry general, 150 miles from his Canadian cavalry. He was in Calais, not

Saint-Quentin, and stuck in a car, rather than on a horse. Deep inside, Seely would have known that this German attack meant that the end game was upon him.

Heavens! Hadn't he been through enough of it? He had been banging away about army preparedness ever since he had come back from the Boer War in 1901 and immediately harangued Parliament over the inadequacies of the British army. He had been on the Defence Committee since 1910, and had been Secretary of State for War from 1912 to 1914. When he had resigned in March of that year over Ulster, he had stayed on the committee, but when war broke out, Minister or no Minister, thoroughbred or no thoroughbred, he and his horse Warrior had been first on the boat. He had been ducking bullets practically ever since. Correction, Seely never ducked.

When Geoffrey (later Major General) Brooke had joined the Canadian cavalry as brigade major in 1917, he had been standing by a low wall with Seely, Prince Antoine and the giant machine-gun commander 'Tiny' Walker when a German sniper opened up. Brooke threw himself on the ground, only to find the other three continuing their conversation quite unperturbed. Brushing his clothes off, he got up and respectfully pointed out a bullet hole on the edge of Walker's trousers. The trio grudgingly moved behind a higher wall.

Only the week before the 1918 offensive, Seely had flown over the German lines and seen the huge black shapes of the new ammunition dumps. From what he had heard in London, the opening barrage had put quite a hole in the Fifth Army just in front of where his Canadians ought to be. And here he was at five o'clock on Friday 22 March, just back across from Dover with the road out of Calais already dark and wet. It would take until late on the Saturday to get down to headquarters at Noyon to start picking up the bits. What on earth had the Canadian Ministry been playing at in summoning him and General Currie, the man responsible for all Canadian forces in France, back to London that Wednesday, when everybody knew that the balloon was going up?

It was a good job he had Prince Antoine with him. When Seely saw the crowd on Victoria Station that Friday morning it was obvious that even his own general's uniform was not going to be an easy passport. It had been hassle enough persuading the boat to sail from Folkestone to Dover and across. And once at Calais, Antoine immediately got the picture. Who cared for whom that row of cars had been intended? They had taken the likeliest one and instructed driver Corporal Anthony to get on with it. Harry Smith, the Hampshire farmer's son who had gone with Seely to the Boer War and had stayed as batman or butler ever since, packed the bags into the boot. When a French official had protested, Antoine withered him on the vine. Yes, Prince Antoine d' Orléans was the smartest aide-de-camp anyone ever had.

The big upright barouche would have been one of the Crossleys used as staff cars since the war began. It had a hood and flaps you could pull up and fold across the front to give the back-seat passengers a little capsule of protection. In the right-hand panelling, equally important for a long cold drive, it had a little flip-open draw where a decanter with a bit of 'inner heating' could be stored. You can bet Antoine d'Orléans would have found it. At five foot eight he was a good couple of inches shorter than the lean, aquiline Seely and, at thirty-five, some fourteen years his junior. When Antoine frowned, his lantern-jawed face could look severe below the pere-grine nose of his royal Bourbon ancestors. But most often it was open and teasing. Grandson of the Emperor of Brazil and great-grandson of Louis-Philippe of France, you could understand why back at the stately Château d'Eu near Abbeville they said the Prince was 'aimé de tous, mais adoré des dames'. The ladies certainly loved him.

Luckily the guys did too. How long before Antoine popped out of the staff car at some of the shiniest doorknobs in Amiens to call up 'Mademoiselles' for General Jack and the other officers as he used to? In the two years Antoine had been with the Canadians, everyone knew him as a star long before his extraordinary feat of lying out all day in no-man's-land sketching a map for the big raid next night. The car bumped forwards. Whisky or no whisky, this was going to be a difficult and wearisome journey, the road choked with reinforcements and supply wagons going one way and ambulances and fleeing civilians the other. Heaven knows where Seely's men and horses had got to. Prince Antoine, his maps and his occasional 'Je suis Antoine d'Orléans' would be needed every inch of the way.

It was dark ahead. The Crossley had electric lights run from a battery in the bonnet, but there was already plenty of traffic coming back from Boulogne: cars, buses, carts creaking along. It was slow going. Anthony kept honking the horn. He was a cool one too. Jack Seely had been lent him by Sir John French, the Commander-in-Chief. 'Best driver I ever had' – was the little field marshal's comment. And Seely had lent Warrior to French in return – 'Best charger I have ever ridden.' The old chief had been replaced by Haig in 1916. But Warrior was still there. God knows how he had survived that last shell, which quite literally cut the horse beside him in half. Ever since Seely had led him off that first boat into Le Havre in August 1914 Warrior had kept his own and his soldier's spirits up. By Sunday Seely and Warrior would be deep in this together.

Seely never lacked belief. 'Fear and be slain, believe and live' had been his motto. And on land and sea, sky and mountain it had served him well. But now even his legendary optimism was under strain. However much Anthony honked and Antoine dealt, he stood no chance of hooking up with his Canadians before Sunday morning. From what he had heard on Thursday things didn't look too rosy around Saint-Quentin. If the situation was really bad, his Canadian cavalry (three regiments: Lord Strathcona's Horse from Calgary, the Fort Garry Horse from Winnipeg, and the Royal Canadian Dragoons from Ottawa) would have had to send most of the horses away and go up to the line on foot. There would be many more dying cries of 'mother' echoing that poor fellow on the next stretcher to Seely at Cambrai in 1917.

But life in France for the officers was not all mud and bullets. Only a week earlier Seely had described his headquarters in the Marquis de Bargemont's chateau at Davenescourt as 'my very own Musée des Beaux Arts'. Alfred Munnings was doing Prince Antoine's portrait on the terrace at the same time as William Orpen painted Seely's in the upstairs salon. That the official war artist despatched to the Canadian cavalry only that February should be the future Sir Alfred Munnings, the greatest equestrian painter of the twentieth century, was a coincidence typical of the colourful Seely story.

After dinner at the chateau that Tuesday night, 19 March 1918, Antoine had played the piano and Munnings had sung one of the narrative ballads which were his speciality. They had toasted the future in champagne. Seely knew that the storm was coming and that it was going to be the most terrible yet. The long, proud, but rather sad-eyed and weary face caught by Orpen's brush may have been flushed red with the drink and the weather, but he was ready. Ready for everything except the telegram that came registered at 10.23 next morning.

'Minister desires see General Seely London least possible delay', it read. No matter that the Minister had long been trying to replace Seely in order to push home his Prime Minister's 'Canadians should be led by Canadians' message. Or that to insist on a meeting on the eve of the biggest battle in history was petty to the point of perversity. Seely wanted to stay with the men with whom he had already been to hell and back, but he and the dome-chested, entrepreneurial General Currie were on the Dover boat that afternoon.

Twenty-nine Chester Square was Seely's London address. A fine six-storey building in Belgravia to which Prime Minister David Lloyd George and Cabinet Secretary Maurice Hankey had been happy on Wednesday 20th to accept dinner invitations for the next evening. But an awful lot had gone under the bridges by the time they got to the table. And that's an understatement.

For a start, Seely had got no joy out of the Canadian politicians. A Canadian in charge of Canadians it had to be. The most they would concede was that Seely could nominate his successor. Bypassing strict seniority, Seely had opted for the Winnipeg rancher and paint magnate, Bob Patterson, who was already in charge in his absence. By general agreement Patterson became a great success, but if Seely had been a man to hold grudges, an image of those politicians would have been worth a pin or two.

By the evening of Thursday, 21 March 1918 there were more pressing matters. When Lloyd George and Hankey came round to Chester Square the full enormity of what was happening in France had begun to come through by telephone and telegram. 'It must have been the shortest dinner on record', noted Seely of what was presumably a somewhat mumbled, mouth-full, prime-ministerial briefing on the opening of the great German offensive. Early next morning, whilst Lloyd George was preparing to brace Parliament for the perils ahead, Seely, Currie and the ubiquitous Prince Antoine (we can only guess where he was the night before) were in full uniform, stamping their feet at Victoria Station.

As explanation of Lloyd George and Hankey's dinner date it's worth remembering that Seely was alone among their former senior Cabinet colleagues to be fighting in the front line. Winston Churchill, Jack's great friend, was actually in France on 21 March as Minister of Munitions and as a direct correspondent for the PM, but he would be back in London by the weekend. By then Jack would be down beyond Amiens in the thick of it. And this time, surely his luck would run out.

If you liked Jack, as Lloyd George and Hankey did, you would drop anything to talk to him, if only to say goodbye. Comparisons are often erroneous as well as odious, but try to picture a front-rank politician in the present day who four years after being in office would be four years into a real-life war with the only 'spin' coming from a shell about to blow everything to smithereens.

But Seely had been on the train, on the boat, and was now in that car. His nature would allow him nowhere else. Perhaps it would be easier to understand if we called up the typical, blimpish caricature of a First World War general. But we are talking about a man all too aware of the blunders of war. A man who on the night before he left for France in August 1914 said that the conflict 'would be long and bloody'. A man who had flown over the Somme battlefield in July 1916 and predicted the slaughter. A man who had fired from a whole trench front of bodies at Ypres. A man who had been sucked into the mud at Passchendaele. A father who had lost a son at Arras.

Seely was in that Amiens-bound car with Prince Antoine, Corporal Anthony and batman Harry Smith because he cared more for his own men and the cause than he did for his life back home. Sure, he had loved women and men and music and horses and the sea. He had a second wife and six remaining children whom he adored. But he had got this far – had walked with kings, rowed in storms, worked in slums, debated in Parliament, fought alongside heroes – with a clearly marked ticket. It said, 'My country, right or wrong.'

And this time Seely had reason to be certain. For that ticket had taken him not only to the ends of the earth but to the very edges of his existence. From cliff top to wave trough, mountain slope to river bed, stricken plane to machine-gunned trench, he had cheated death's falcon of its prey.

It was not nine lives he had used up; at the last count it was at least fourteen.

2

The Storms of Seely Island

If Jack had a guardian angel, it must have had the most overworked pair of wings in the loft.

The sharp-eyed youngest son of MP and Nottinghamshire coal-mine owner Charles Seely was always into risk. As a nine-year-old staying at Brooke House, his grandfather's Isle of Wight home, he found it. The cliff edge between Brooke and Atherfield gave way with seventy feet of salty air between Jack and certain destruction on the rocks below.

But he lived. Walk along there now and it's easy to imitate. Every day the incoming waves gnaw at the cliff base on this western shore. At every storm they savage it. The road my parents travelled towards the white cliffs of Freshwater and Tennyson Down and the Needles after their wedding at Brooke Church in June 1924 has long since succumbed to the sea. But the tides, in their hunger to eat into the present, have now revealed an unmatched bounty of the past – fossil footprints from 150 million years ago. This has become the 'Jurassic Coast'.

Brooke Bay, the rocks around Hanover Point and the cliff edge going south-east towards the distant St Catherine's Lighthouse with Ventnor just around the headland, have become a Mecca for searchers into prehistory. In 2001 BBC Television did a two-week daily television series on a massive dinosaur dig along the cliff side. Next to the coast road at Atherfield there is now a permanent museum with 'work-in-progress' palaeontologists restoring and piecing together the most recent finds. It was near to this that young Jack's story almost stopped before it began.

The turf is what deceives you. It so tightly carpets the earth right to the cliff edge that you can be entirely unaware that you are standing on a lip so thin that it might be your own diving board to eternity. Jack Seely was a protected, privileged boy, but he was a free spirit. That morning freedom took him a step too close, and in mid air the spirits seemed set to claim him on a permanent basis.

Only for the angel to save him. Well, let's not get too silly about this, since you sometimes see the odd cow wandering sore-headed along the beach after slipping over the edge and surviving, and whether or not angels look after bovines is rather extending the metaphor. But the cows have usually had their fall broken by the undercliff. Young Jack's salvation was more extraordinary, for he claimed that the crumbling earth curled under him and together with the gooey clay at the shoreline, cushioned the fall enough to give only fractures and concussion.

There were to be many other 'death-in-the-face' moments. But however exaggerated this early memory may be, it is important for its context. It happened on the Isle of Wight coast, and the comfort afterwards came from his favourite uncle, Colonel Harry Gore Browne VC. It is hardly advanced psychology to notice the impact of the place and the man on what young Jack became.

In the 1870s, to have won a Victoria Cross was an equivalent of scoring a goal for England in the World Cup Finals. The newspapers would carry banner headlines and dip the pen in purple, the great and good would queue to shake your hand, the 'glitterati' would send the carriage round. Harry Gore Brown had won his VC at the Siege of Lucknow during the Indian Mutiny in 1857.

Jack Seely had been born, the seventh of nine children, on 31 May 1868 at Brookhill Hall on the Derbyshire–Nottinghamshire borders, a place his father had rented to be near the collieries the family owned. Harry Gore Browne had gone to the Isle of Wight to manage the Seely estates at Brooke, Mottistone, Brighstone, Gatcombe, Calbourne and far afield. He lived with his second wife, Charles Seely's sister Mary, at Pitt Place between Brighstone and Mottistone, just five miles from Brooke. It was to there that the battered little Jack was taken after his cliff fall drama in 1877, and ever after his uncle's stories became a touchstone of physical courage.

Apparently Uncle Harry was a sweet old man in his Isle of Wight persona, but if you were unlucky enough to be an Indian sepoy trying to aim a cannon at the attacking forces at Lucknow in 1857 you might not have been that pleased to see him. According to the VC citation, Harry Gore Browne clambered up the walls to the cannon, somehow despatching everyone in his way. Whilst Seely never got into quite such a killing spree, you can see some of the origins of his own motto: 'Fear and be slain.'

'Death or dishonour' may sound blood-curdling to us, but to a nine-year-old listening to old Uncle's glory days, it was absolutely the thought he would take to his dreams. One hundred and thirty years ago, to serve the country, to be honoured by the Queen, to wear the VC's crimson ribbon with pride, was a small boy's fantasy. It is significant that in all later tales of his own and others' derring-do, Seely still seems to give those original Lucknow stories pride of place.

Mercifully the need to serve also had a less bloodthirsty application. Harry Gore Browne had come to the Island in 1872 to administer what was little short of a private fiefdom. The Seely estates stretched over most of the spine and coastline of the West Wight, almost a dozen villages owed their livelihoods to this ever burgeoning Nottinghamshire tribe. A family of fabulous new wealth which in its Victorian way tried to embrace some of the responsibilities of their good fortune. Every dependant household was given a ton of coal at Christmas, 'Seely Libraries' were built across the Island to bring books and reading to the poor, and mains water was installed in all the cottages on the estate.

The family had come a long way since Jack's grandfather, the first Charles Seely, had walked along Brooke and Mottistone Downs as a fifteen-year-old in 1818 and uttered the prophetic cry, 'When I make my fortune, all this will be mine.' To understand the boldness and energy in Jack Seely's nature requires a closer look at this miller's son from Lincoln who became a millionaire, an MP, and the bane of his Queen, whose summer home and widow's retreat was Osborne House, just across the Medina River from Cowes on the north of the Wight.

The teenage Charles had come to the Island to recover from a chest infection and stayed with an aunt near Godshill in the southwest. The south of the Island also had Keats and Shelley amongst its visitors, but it seems that young Charles had lucre not literature on his mind and was soon well enough to walk the length of the Downs from the southern tip to the Needles in the west. Being a prosperous Lincoln miller was never going to be enough for Charles Seely. He wanted power and position, and he didn't have too many scruples about how he got them.

His first plan was to become the local MP. This was duly achieved in 1847, but by the time he reached Westminster enough 'irregularities' had been found in the Lincoln vote that Seely was barred from the Commons before he took his seat. No matter; like many small, determined men, the first Charles Seely had an air of irrepressibility about him. He could not yet make his fortune by 'fixing' things at Westminster, so he reverted to a more accessible stage. He bought a farm and, as it turned out, not just any old farm. Sherwood Lodge in Nottingham (now a police headquarters) might have resembled any 2,000-acre estate that an upwardly mobile Lincoln miller might buy to elevate himself into the county gentry, but beneath the surface was the nineteenth-century equivalent of an oil well. It was to be part of the Nottinghamshire coal field.

It could have been luck. But with Seely's eye for the main chance it seems much more likely to have been a piece of well-informed opportunism. Either way, the purchase led to the development of Babbington Colliery, which was to remain in Seely hands until nationalization in 1947. By then the family fortunes had dipped alarmingly, but a century earlier there had been no stopping the little miller on the climb. Not only did he finally become the MP for Lincoln in 1861 (and remain so for nearly thirty years), but he had already hit upon a money-making scheme which gave him both a nickname and fat stipend for life. He sold pig iron to the navy.

Pig iron was specially smelted flat pieces of iron laid inside the hulls of naval sailing ships as ballast. It was very important in the first half of the nineteenth century, and Seely did well to win the contract. He did even better to get a clause in the agreement which happily overcame the somewhat major problem that with the coming of steel hull warships, pig iron became utterly redundant. Seely had the contract written for fifty years from 1850. Not for nothing did he for ever after carry the nickname 'Pigs' with pride.

In the 1860s when the Admiralty introduced 'ironclads', they no longer needed pig iron and asked Seely to terminate his agreement. He refused and continued to deliver the worthless smelter and draw the money till his death. Some flat 'Seely's pigs' were still lying around in Portsmouth Dockyard as late as 1940. Legend has it that on one of his trips to Portsmouth, Pigs looked across the Solent to the Isle of Wight and remembered his teenage vow on Brighstone Down. Whatever the truth of that, the facts are that by 1864 he had developed Brooke House near Freshwater into a home stately enough to receive crowned heads and notables from any land. In April of that year, much to the irritation of Queen Victoria, it became a five-day resting place for the Italian revolutionary hero Giuseppe Garibaldi before he moved on to London, where half a million people gave him a reception never accorded to a foreign statesman before or since.

The Queen was not amused. She was 'half-ashamed', she wrote, 'of being head of a nation capable of such follies'. And even when assured by Prime Minister Lord Palmerston that Garibaldi was being given advice to abstain from further action, she still complained grumpily that 'the Government should have lavished honours usually reserved for Royalty upon one who openly declares his object to lead the attack upon Venice, Rome, and Russia', all three supposed allies of Britain.

As a matter of conjecture, Garibaldi's welcome to Brooke House may have even strayed beyond warm to sexily smouldering. Sir Charles treated him royally enough, taking him to visit the poet Tennyson at Freshwater and welcoming Lord Shaftesbury and Giuseppe Mazzini, Garibaldi's original mentor, to Brooke. He also planted a sapling in his guest's honour, which became the 'Garibaldi Oak', standing for a century huge and heavy-branched on the drive.

But it was his wife Mary who may have taken the 'treats' a bit too far. It could, of course, have just been her writing style, but the letters to Garibaldi suggest a bit more than 'Viva Italia'.

'Beloved General', she wrote, 'When, alas, you left me yesterday, my heart was full of anguish. I went to take another look at your small bed and, full of emotion at the place where your noble head would not rest again for a long time, I stood contemplating it with a heavy heart when I noticed near the bolster the kerchief which you used. Oh, my dearest General, what a comfort it was to me.' Maybe it was the way she wrote, and let's remember that Garibaldi was a lame old goat of fifty-seven, but just imagine if that letter had made today's tabloid press. As a great-great-grandson, I can only be happy at the buzz old Giuseppe must have brought.

Queen Victoria's displeasure with Pigs continued right through until her Golden Jubilee in 1887 when Seely was chosen to give the loyal address from the steps of the town hall in Newport. By now he was a distinguished, silver-haired figure, the longest-serving MP in the House; and in the Isle of Wight such a big landowner that he could walk the seven and a half miles from Brooke to Newport without ever leaving his own property.

'There were times, Mr Seely,' the Queen said in response to the flattering words of the loyal address, 'when our relations did not seem quite so cordial.' To which the old hustler crinkled up his face and said cryptically, 'Yes, ma'am. As we get older we get wiser.'

Today the Garibaldi Oak has finally been gathered to the fire. Brooke House is divided into flats, its gardens into retirement bungalows. But walk down through the village past the red-brick Seely Hall and you soon see the white-crested waves and hear the roar of the sea just as Pigs and his sons and grandsons would have done.

Walk left along the crumbling cliff edge and it's all too simple to relive the moment when the earth gave way and young Jack had his first close encounter with fate. Look out to sea and it's not hard to imagine the inspiration for an energetic and questing boy when he realized how lucky he had been. Boldness was in his genes, glory was the quest, service the price to be paid for privilege. In the house was Nelson's portrait. No boy of Jack's type could look out at sea and not repeat the great admiral's Trafalgar message: 'England expects that every man will do his duty.'

The deal was that you had to be ready to risk your life for others. And for Jack Seely in the Isle of Wight, that meant the lifeboat. Long before his most critical moments on the battlefield he had been proud to be part of the thirteen-man crew of the Brooke Lifeboat, an extraordinary, structured yet utterly democratic and entirely selfless institution, which in many ways was the making of him. It was one thing to listen to the 'death or glory' stories of a fire-eating uncle, but this was courage in the local community – farmers, labourers, carpenters, blacksmiths, carters and thatchers all too literally 'in the same boat'. It was the humility of man against the sea; it was, as he later wrote in *Launch!*, his book about the lifeboats, 'the ideal of service in the common cause of humanity'.

There could be no 'after you, sir' deference to the young master when a big swell was running and a ship was in distress. A man had to prove his worth in the crew and accept orders from the coxswain or else all of them would drown. These were 35-foot pulling and sailing lifeboats, with ten oars for close shore work and a sail for hoisting further out in the bay. They had buoyancy tanks which made them unsinkable and self-righting. But it was a long call from today's helicopter-directed air-sea rescue heroes, their cork waistcoats, bulky tweed and oilskins a heavy contrast to the high-tech warm and waterproof equipment of today.

When a ship foundered in a storm, the gun would be fired, a dozen farm horses bridled, the men gathered, the lifeboat hauled down to the beach, the crew embarked. Then, at great risk, the launch would be attempted, every able-bodied man, woman and child, some sixty in all, pulling together on the two ropes that propel the boat from its carriage into the sea whilst the ten oarsmen time their first heavy stroke in the flood of the wave and then heave straight out through the rollers towards the wreck.

That wind-battered west coast of the Isle of Wight was a graveyard in the days of sail, and even today it is none too safe in bad weather. For any boat hugging the coast in an attempt to creep north-west to the Needles risked getting stuck on the ledge of rocks that run half a mile out from the shore. Once caught, the waves would rip a timber ship apart in hours and then the Royal National Lifeboat Service would have to confirm its reputation as one of the finest of all Victorian institutions. This had been a smuggler's coast, with fishermen trying to get brandy past the excise cutters. But if a ship foundered, the villagers would put to sea. As a local badge of merit, nothing got anywhere close to being in the lifeboat crew.

My mother was born at Brooke House in 1902, and lifeboat stories were her speciality. She was the second daughter and fourth child in a large Georgian house with a full retinue of servants run in true *Upstairs Downstairs* fashion by 'Smith' the butler, who was married to 'Rose' the cook, that same Smith who doubled as Jack Seely's batman through both South Africa and France. By all accounts young 'Miss Irene' was something of a tomboy compared to her short-sighted older sister Emmy and her quieter brothers, Frank, the eldest, and John, who at five was already building doll's houses in anticipation of a future career as an architect of renown.

Irene Seely loved the rawness of the West Wight with its great hump of downland on which she and her horse would gallop beneath the scudding clouds with white specks of sails in the Solent to the north and the endless expanse of the Channel to the west. She was good at English and the piano but in those un-emancipated days her education was limited to governesses and music teachers and that famous primer *Reading Without Tears*. Little wonder that her greatest love was the utterly ungovernable wildness of the ocean at the door. When the wind blew hard enough to rattle the slates on winter nights, she would put her gumboots and coat and sweater at the foot of the bed. The way she told it, the memory of those thrilling, fearsome nights and the thought that this might be the time when the gun fired and her father and the others would have to put out to sea, never dimmed.

By his own admission, nothing in all Jack Seely's own eventful days was ever more challenging than those lifeboat sagas when, for pure, unselfish reasons, men, women, children and horses would gather. And thirteen men would launch to face the furies of the deep. Those moments gave him a tiller to steer through whatever threatened in the years ahead.

3

School Days and High Days

First he needed to survive the foolishness of youth. Of all the stupid things, it was a hold-your-breath dare in the school swimming pool at Hawtreys Preparatory School, then near Wimbledon, now part of Cheam School near Newbury. Jack stayed too long under water and blacked out.

'I have the most vivid recollection', he wrote later. 'Suddenly all the strain of holding the breath was gone. I was in a land of sunlit green fields and church bells.' Similar sensations, he claims, have been reported to him by others rescued from drowning, but luckily in a whole lifetime spent whenever possible on the sea Seely did not test his theory a second time.

Hawtreys seems to have been typical of the harsh, bully-rampant establishments to which the ruling classes felt obliged to send their sons to fit them for the Empire. Surprisingly, considering his later energy and eminence, Seely does not seem to have cut a particularly impressive swathe at either this first school or at Harrow afterwards. But he did give a bully his comeuppance.

At one particular stage a reign of terror cowed the little boys of Hawtreys. The big bully would have them trembling like rabbits for every waking moment. Seely organized them into a unit and persuaded them of the power of numbers. At the appointed hour the trap was sprung, the bully head-butted in the stomach and then sat upon by his Lilliputian opponents. It was a huge success. Except that Seely got the blame.

In standard Victorian fashion the headmaster seems to have been a tyrant too. And when matters began to deteriorate again

Seely led a mass breakout, only to be hunted down by a master on a galloping horse. Back at the school, a public flogging was prepared. The pupils were gathered, the cane was flexed, no doubt the head's face shone with fury. But at that moment Seely's angel appeared in the shape of his grandmother, her carriage crunching the gravel on the drive. The head was replaced and when Seely moved on to Harrow he had progressed enough academically to enter the sixth form a full year ahead of his age.

It was an era when there were instructors other than school-masters to shape a boy's knowledge. Of all the teachers Seely mentions, pride of place goes to the Reverend Ashworth, the chaplain of Newstead Abbey, north of Nottingham, to where Jack used to ride his pony for tutoring in the Classics during the holidays. 'He taught me more Latin and Greek than I ever learnt at Harrow or Cambridge,' says Seely, before adding, 'but in the intervals of his instruction he also taught me much about ferreting rabbits, the strange ways of foxes and badgers, and something of that most mysterious of British animals, the otter.'

Summer 1878 and a little ten-year-old trotting on his black pony from the big house to the abbey to learn about Achilles, Agamemnon and all the rest from the rural reverend in the study. For me, the grandson, it's a scene from a television series, which on closer inspection gives way to a sense of guilt at wondering about other ten-year-old boys who, if they got any education at all, would soon be joining their fathers down the mines on which the Seely fortunes had been built. But it's hard to blame either the chaplain, who also tried hard with mining children, or Jack for that. One gave and the other received a classical Christian and country education. I hope history doesn't judge the chaplain's efforts entirely without merit.

By 1882 Harrow had already been alma mater to five Prime Ministers including Palmerston and the luckless Spencer Perceval who was assassinated in 1812, and Seely started life there as fag to a future sixth in Stanley Baldwin. 'He has been kind enough to say I made rather good scrambled eggs', Seely recorded uncontroversially, but it was at Harrow that he became involved enough in

politics to shed real blood for a cause. It was also at Harrow, albeit
when he returned a term after leaving, that he first set sight on a
pudgy little ginger-haired boy in the 'ducker' (swimming pool) who
was to have such an effect on his and on so many lives – Winston
Churchill, who would become the most famous Old Harrovian of
them all.

The famous 'School on the Hill', looking down from above
Northolt towards London in the east is not necessarily a place you
associate with radical politics, peopled as it was and is by the sons of
the privileged. By today's standards Seely could hardly be described
as left of centre, but in 1885 he was made to recite a Georgic (Latin
verse) for reading Gladstone's Home Rule Bill aloud in class, and
when he supported Milner as the Liberal candidate for Harrow, he
was in a minority of one and got a black eye and a thick lip for his
trouble. His support had a personal inspiration. How could a
questing teenager not fall for the merits of the Irish Home Rule Bill,
even though his own family distrusted it, when the great statesman William Ewart Gladstone came to tea with the headmaster?
'Gladstone completely captivated me', he wrote. 'It was impossible
to be with the man without seeing that here was one with immense
learning and experience, coupled with boyish enthusiasm for the
matter in hand.'

There were plenty of other inspirations nearer home. His father
and grandfather were MPs at the same time, for Nottingham and
Lincoln respectively. They were influential as well as wealthy men,
and the family house in London had leading politicians, lawyers,
inventors and academics welcomed to the table. Young Jack,
sensitive enough to burst into baby tears the first time his mother
took him to a Beethoven piano recital, ''cos it's so bootiful', clearly
drank them all in. At a later age he may have caricatured himself as
a fire-eating man of action, but the picture that emerges from these
early days is of a bright, self-confident, rather indulged younger son,
more dependent on brain than brawn.

Climb the spiral staircase to the owl-like eyrie which houses the
Harrow archives and the only Seely photos to be found are of him
in the House football and cricket teams. The face is oval and almost

delicate but the eyes stare very directly at you across the years. Here was someone who was ready to live life to his own tune. In its own way that tune was radical. But, to judge from his worst recorded Harrow offence, a long way short of revolutionary.

On the day of Queen Victoria's Golden Jubilee in 1887, Seely and his great friend Tom Conolly decided that Harrow ought to be livened up. Goodness knows what two young 'radicals' would try today. These two kids were into daring, pure and simple. Seely was adventurous but Conolly was every bit a match for him; a year younger than his soulmate, the freckle-faced young Irishman was already a star in every sport. Tom and Jack climbed right up the inside of the 100-foot spire of the parish church of St Mary's on the very top of Harrow hill. Once there they unfurled the Union Jack to wave boldly at all the circling, spangled counties from Sussex to Buckinghamshire. Yes, very different times.

At Trinity, Cambridge, the picture hardly changes. True, Seely was academically able enough to target Tripos in both Classics and Law, and some of the surviving essays read intelligently enough. But this was a sybaritic existence, a nineteenth-century print of young gentlemen at play brought to life. Consider the October day in 1889 when he and his friend Victor Cavendish (the future ninth Duke of Devonshire) decided to ride over to Newmarket with ten pounds (as much as five hundred pounds in today's terms) of betting money with advice from the Trinity College head porter to put the lot on the favourite for the Cambridgeshire, the big race of the afternoon.

Once at the races they spotted Victor's uncle Lord Hartington, and the future duke is despatched to quiz the family pillar of the turf as to what to back. Ten minutes later the young swell returns with the news that the favourite's odds were too short, and that it might be more interesting to have something on the outsider, Laureate. With the unbeatable élan of youth, ignorance and inherited wealth, Victor had plonked the whole stake with an accommodating (and no doubt lip-smacking) bookie at 66-1.

You can guess how this story ends, but the first buzz must have been in the watching of it. No climbing into the stands and long-distance looks via binoculars or big-screen television. It might have been the century of steam, but at Newmarket the horse was still king. To watch the races one cantered down towards the start and galloped back alongside. Seely and Cavendish's ponies kept them close to the runners until they got to 'the bushes', the little clump of hawthorn two furlongs from the finish, after which the racecourse sweeps away downhill before the final upward climb.

At that stage the favourite, Primrose Day, was still moving as easily in the lead as a favourite should. The chestnut Laureate was going well enough, but there were plenty of others looking stronger in the pursuing pack, including that year's Oaks winner, L'Abbesse de Jouarre, owned by Winston's father, Lord Randolph Churchill. As the 21-runner field thundered away towards the baying of the crowd and the finishing post, the two young riders would have shrugged off their lost 'tenner' as 'experience'.

Even when they themselves reached the finish, they would not have known what had happened. There were no public-address announcements, electronic signs, big-screen replays. But there had been a rather muted note to the cheering, and now a strange buzz ran through the crowd suggesting a surprise result. Cavendish gave his pony to Seely and ran across the course to find out. Ten minutes later he returned with his eyes bulging nearly as much as his pockets. Laureate had won. The tenner had been transformed into £660. And in 'readies' too.

Getting back to Cambridge must have been a bit risky. No small sum, back in 1889 £660 would have been worth some £33,000 in today's RPI conversion. That was an enormous amount even for the sons of wealthy houses who would have gaily run up extravagant debts as undergraduates. Seely records that after locking the money in his desk back at Trinity they hastened to open a joint account at Mortlock's Bank next morning from which they paid out all their creditors and, in the argot of the times, 'That night we entertained our friends to dinner in my rooms, and there was much rejoicing.'

It's a happy, if very 1880s, scene. But it's the reaction of Seely's parents that is worth recording. Seely had written to his mother the night of the big win. 'I made it a rule to tell my mother everything,' he said, 'the only wise rule of life that I have ever consistently followed.' Much as she loved him, the family was clearly not into uncritical indulgence. Two days later there was a letter in his father's handwriting on his breakfast plate. 'I was always rather afraid of these letters', writes Seely, 'for although my father was a most generous parent, I had recently tried him rather high in the financial line.'

Such worries proved correct:

'My Dear Jack,' the missive began. 'I happened to see the letter you wrote to your mother in which you told her that you won £335 by betting on a horse called Laureate. You know my views about gambling, so I can only say that if you insist on endeavouring to make a living by these means you cannot expect me to continue to contribute to your support.'

The parental disapproval rings authentic down the years. But so too does the affection between child and parent. Amusingly enough, Victor Cavendish had written to his mother and got a rather more forceful letter from his grandfather, the then seventh Duke of Devonshire, which included the superb line, 'I am constrained to write and tell you at once that betting on horses has more than once nearly brought our family to ruin.'

The experience seems to have cured Seely of gambling but certainly not of risk, and in the summer vacation of his second year the Trinity days came to a violent and almost tragic halt. Up till then Tom Conolly had been a good friend to spend the holidays with, usually at the magnificent family seat at Castletown, on the River Liffey just upstream from Dublin, which remains as the best example of a Palladian house in all of Ireland. Tom's grandfather had been Speaker Conolly in the Irish Parliament, the last man to hold that post before it was dissolved and all control reverted to Westminster.

Although Tom and other Conollys were educated in England, they were not the absentee Anglo-Irish type of family who caused such resentment. Indeed, as late as 1930 Tom and Jack's former headmaster, Dr Whelldon, by then Bishop of Durham, was writing to Jack about how much Tom might have done, had he lived, for

Anglo-Irish relations. But in September 1888 Tom and most of the
Conolly clan were absentees all right, ensconced in a villa near the
lake at Davos in Switzerland.

Once again the memory invokes a period piece. The muscular
Christianity of the Victorians marching around in their plus fours
and tweed caps. The coming of the railway had opened up the Swiss
towns with their prospects of sweet air and healthy exercise, the
perfect antidote for the prevailing bronchial conditions that so beset
metropolitan dwellers in Britain. A Mr Thomas Cook from Yorkshire had even taken a first bus load down there. Davos and its lake
soon had casino, baths, restaurants and theatres like any other
European resort. From there all sorts of intrepid mountaineers set
off to conquer the nearby peaks. Most of these were British, but they
included such magnificent obsessives as the American academic
William Augustus Brevoort Coolidge who climbed both the Eiger
and the Matterhorn, accompanied not just by his aunt but also by her
pet dog.

It was a perfect setting for our daring duo, and for two weeks
Seely and Conolly were busy climbing and chamois hunting up the
Weissfluh and Hüreli mountains that rise steeply on either side of
the lake. Conolly's mother and younger sister Catherine were
constantly worried at the risks being taken, but it was only after
Tom had gone back to England that Seely got hurt. It was ironic
that this most serious of all falls should happen out hacking with a
child. But anyone who has ridden knows the illogicality of injury. As
a steeplechase jockey for ten intense and exhilarating years, I had
my share of moments when the world capsizes and the earth comes
up to eat you. Yet despite my standard list of fractures and con-
cussions I never had a single hospitalization to compare with the
shattered hip joint my son got at sixteen when falling off the porch
roof of a holiday cottage.

On a horse accidents can be just as arbitrary. You can walk away
unscathed after your animal has done a horrendous somersault in a
steeplechase but wait in agony for the ambulance when something
has slipped up on the road at a gentle trot. For Seely taking twelve-
year-old Catherine Conolly up one of the mountain paths for what

the French describe as a 'promenade au cheval', it was simply the jerk of the horse's head as it was mounted that proved to be the problem.

For while Catherine was on a quiet little pony Seely's hireling was a fractious thoroughbred 'weed' who was prone to panic when mounted. However, once started, they had a good ride up the mountain paths to a little roadside inn where they got down, bought two glasses of milk and admired the spectacular view of the setting sun. But as Seely swung into the saddle for the descent, his horse threw its head violently in the air. The bridle had yet to be untied and when the attached rope broke it took the bit out of the horse's mouth in the process. One of all riders' worst nightmares had begun.

A runaway horse is a bad thing to be sitting on. There are just three options: throw yourself off, just let it run or try an extreme yank on its mouth to break its momentum. Gathering pace on a tall and narrow thoroughbred down a precipitous mountain pass, Seely did not fancy the first option, faced certain death with the second, and his chances on the third had been shattered by the broken bridle.

There was a precipice on one side and a narrow wooden bridge crossing the gorge ahead. Forget the escapes from the cliff fall and the prep school 'drowning'. This time Seely looked set for heaven and an early bath. Just before the bridge the horse crossed its legs, crashed down and broke its neck. Seely fractured his skull and was dragged away from the chasm's edge by Catherine following up. By some miracle she was soon joined by a doctor coming back from delivering a baby at a farm up the mountain. But for his arrival Seely could have had no safe return.

As it was, a long rehabilitation was needed. Jack's elder brother Frank travelled over and took him home, head packed in ice, on a steamer down the Rhine. Any idea of a dual Tripos at Cambridge was abandoned but eventually, at least according to Seely, a complete recovery was effected.

Others were not so sure. On listening to this tale some twenty years later the Conservative leader Arthur Balfour gave a benevolent smile and said, 'My dear Jack, that explains it all.'

4

Recovery, Rescue and Recuperation

Energy attracts. And when his head finally recovered from its Alpine fracturing, Jack Seely crackled with energy from top to toe. His charm was in the smiling delight with which he would take on anything, and then tell you afterwards just how wonderfully well he had done it. In later life the repetition and exaggeration could become a little tedious. But as a young man the sheer élan of his derring-do was irresistible.

At Cambridge he did not just risk his already lucky neck out hunting, he did it on a horse called Pride of Kildare, who had come third in the 1878 Grand National. In an era when the racehorse could way outrun the automobile, this was the equivalent of driving a top rally car in a forest. As a young subaltern in the Hampshire Yeomanry, to which he repaired for training after Cambridge, Seely did not just beaver away at making the Isle of Wight troop the best in the land. No, he had larger and longer-term ambitions. At Aldershot he impressed an instructor who, as Sir John French, was to become one of the most successful soldiers of his generation.

In two years Seely would return, but not before he had been through the most heroic and dangerous moments of his youth. The heroism came at Brooke in October 1891. Seely was awake when the lifeboat gun went off that morning. No one could sleep with 'a wind of such velocity that the windows rattled like pistol shots, and our old stone built house, with walls three feet thick, shook in the violence of the storm'. Brooke House is up to the left of the single-street village, which clusters around the rectory and the farmhouse before a couple of fields take you over the coast road to the cottage-lined green from which you reach the cliff top. It was there that Seely joined Ben Jacobs, the giant black-bearded fisherman whose writ, as coxswain, ruled the lifeboat. Through the blinding rain they could just see the problem. Three-quarters of a mile out to sea a smallish three-masted ship was in desperate straits. She was the 450-ton *Henri et Léontine*, trying to battle home to Nantes but now being blown relentlessly towards the ledge of rocks at Brooke.

The weather had been terrible for days and the *Henri et Léontine* and her sister ship, *Plombec*, had run for shelter in the natural harbour at Ryde Roads. But the evening of the 18th had seemed calmer. That dawn they had weighed anchor, aiming to round St Catherine's at the Island's southern tip and then steer south-west down the Channel for Nantes. With what had been a steady south-easterly breeze on the beam to port (left-hand) they kept their course, but towards 7 a.m. the wind picked up violently and veered round to the south-south-west. They had to change tack and as the weather now lifted to almost hurricane level, they were incapable of making any headway against the wind blowing them so relent-lessly to the shore.

'She will strike the ledge in a quarter of an hour,' said Ben Jacobs, and he and Seely went down to the sheltered side of the lifeboat house to join the men already gathered there. Listening to the storm whilst they waited for the ten horses from outlying farms to join them was something that made even Seely quail. 'The noise of the breaking seas is so deafening', he wrote later in a tribute to his local villagers and to lifeboatmen everywhere, 'that the few words one speaks have to be shouted in one's neighbour's ear. Over and above the continuous roar there are occasional blasts of wind which shake the stone structure of the lifeboat-house as though an angry giant had hold of it.

'More awe inspiring is the great wave', he continued. 'There is a lull in the continuous roar: one's heart seems to stop, and then – crash; the great wave breaks and one sees the water and foam rushing right up the creek and the road alongside it. Of all the experiences that I have gone through in peace and war, I give pride of place to the nerve shattering effect of the great wave while waiting to launch a lifeboat.'

But launch they must. The tide was high that October morning, so they pushed the lifeboat bow on and launched her directly into the sea. With coxswain and all ten oars ready they got clean away into the foam from the launch. But within thirty seconds the first big wave caught her, lifted the bow end up like a plaything and then brutally tossed the whole craft back sideways on to the beach of the cliff. Mercifully none of the crew were either injured or thrown into the sea. But the tide would have to ebb before a relaunch could be attempted. And the Frenchmen were foundering out there in the surf.

'I did what any other swimmer would do', said Seely with very British understatement. Maybe, but the fact remains that he did do it and none of his many other heroics ever bettered this early feat. He tied the end of a rope round his waist and set off into the breakers to try to save the doomed seamen on the rocks. Somehow he made it through the rollers, got aboard, and went below to see a very strange sight indeed: the captain with half his head hanging off.

When the ship had gone aground the captain had been thrown so violently against the spinning steering wheel that a great lump of his scalp had been taken off. 'I thought for a moment that I was looking at a decapitated man', said Seely, before going on to describe emergency measures you won't find in many medical books.

> Above his bunk was a medicine chest. And in it I saw a bottle of Friar's Balsam. I took this and poured the greater part of it on top of his head in the hope that it would stop the bleeding. This it did in the most miraculous fashion, for the oozing blood stopped completely. I then took his scalp, fitted it on to his head, tied my handkerchief from the back round his chin. It was rather elementary surgery but the doctor who attended him afterwards said that it saved his life.

Presently Tom Hookey, a fisherman and Seely's closest village friend, also got aboard and as the tide went out and the heavier waves began to retreat the two young men were able to get the head-tied captain ashore by an improvised breeches buoy. He was taken up to Brooke House where it was some bedridden weeks until he was well enough to return to Nantes. Not all of his fellows were as lucky.

All four members of his own crew survived but it was the sister ship, *Plombec*, whose troubles proved fatal. She had been the first to 'put about' (turn round) and try to get back round St Catherine's on the starboard (right-hand) tack rather than aim out on the port reach for the Needles. But like the *Henri et Léontine* she just could not make headway against the combined might of wind and wave. By the time she got to Blackgang, six nautical miles down the coast from Brooke, she was at the mercy of the sea. And when the end came it was pitiless.

The coastal shelf is deeper there and the *Plombec* had been blown to within three hundred yards of the beach when gigantic waves began to smash her to pieces on the rocks below. The coastguards fired a rocket line over what remained, more in hope than expectation. Incredibly a figure did catch it and slowly and laboriously they hauled it up the cliff. By the time they pulled him to safety, he was actually unconscious with the rope line anchored in his teeth.

Meanwhile Seely had been testing his French on the Brooke survivors and had come up with a heart-rending tale from the mate of the *Henri et Léontine*. It appeared that the two crews were closely related and that the mate of the *Plombec* was this one's brother. The news had come through that *Plombec* had struck the rocks five miles down the coast but that only one soul had been saved. Could that be the brother? Seely, soaked and battered from his lifesaving swim, but imbued with that Victorian sense of duty, had of course to ride over and find out.

The journey is lonely enough even now, especially in winter, with the light fading as it would have been that wild October afternoon. The white lodge gates are still there at the end of the Brooke House drive. After changing into dry clothes, off he would have gone through the little hamlets of Hulverstone and Mottistone, the horse snorting with effort as it took the sharp rise of Hulverstone

Chute. Trotting and cantering, you can get to Brighstone in twenty minutes.

But once he reached there, the villagers said the ship had disappeared. The pub and store and church are all clustered where the coast road splints off this main route to Newport. Imagine the frowns and rolling Vectis vowels as the locals and Master Seely pondered the mariners' fate. Most of them would have predicted the worst.

He pressed on another five miles to Blackgang. There they told him the story of the unconscious rope-gripper, and said he had been taken over the hill to St Catherine's Lighthouse. Seely admitted to becoming a little weary, subsequent examination showing that the impact of getting aboard the *Henri et Léontine* had damaged his ribs enough to poke one of them into his lung. But he had a letter from the rescued Frenchman at Brooke. And if this survivor was the brother, there might not be much time.

So Seely rode on over the hill. St Catherine's Lighthouse still stands proud and resplendent on the edge of the shore, winking its heavy Isle of Wight warning to wary sailors in the Channel. It's all automated now, and the cottages are rented out to Heritage lovers with a hurricane fetish. But the mind wings back easily to the dying embers of 19 October 1891.

'By this time it was dark and I was nearly done', wrote our hero. 'I tied up my horse; the lighthouse keeper met me at the door and took me to the little room where the unfortunate man was lying. His face was terribly battered and many bones were broken. Against every probability he was indeed the mate's brother.' But a happy ending there was not to be. Seely had with him a message which the first brother had written on a card. It read, 'Très cher frère. Nous sommes tous les deux dans le malheur, mais comme moi, j'espère vous êtes sauve.' Seely tried to show it to the fading mariner but apart from a muttered 'le bon Dieu', he didn't seem to register. By next morning he was gone.

Seely wasn't in any great shape either. He had been up since dawn. He had been through a rib-busting shipwreck. It was dark and cold and he had ten miles to ride home. Forty years later, on reading about himself and others in Seely's autobiography, *Adventure*, Fred Harvey, the Canadian cavalry VC, wrote of his general, 'He does, to put it mildly, exaggerate a little.' That needs to be taken on board for all Seely statements, but even after pruning away the 'adjectivals', 19 October was an astonishing day for any man, any time.

So were the consequences: two plusses and a minus. The first plus was that the French Government awarded him their top civilian medal, 'La Médaille d'Or d'Honneur', for his part in the lifesaving. The framed citation hangs alongside the *Henri et Léontine* figurehead in the hall at Mottistone Manor. The minus was that Seely's ribs and lungs were in a horrendous state after the battering by sea and timber. The need for recovery led to the second plus: Seely plumbs new depths of understatement. 'I was told', he writes, 'that a long sea voyage was advisable.' He went to New Zealand.

'The land of the long white cloud' is far enough away even in today's world of long-haul flights, deep-vein thrombosis, Lonely Planet guidebooks, mobile phones and Internet cafes. Think of it then. For in October 1892 Seely and two friends, the ubiquitous Tom Conolly and Charles Burford, a Nottinghamshire neighbour and the future Duke of St Albans, blithely embarked at Southampton for Cape Town, Hobart and Wellington on what was billed as a 'recuperation cruise'. No one could have guessed the adventures or the love affair to come.

5

The Voyage of the Kaikoura

The *Kaikoura* was a 3,000-ton steam and sail ship. She was rigged as a barque – that's with a little mizzen mast and two main masts and spars. She was supposed to be ready for anything. That October, 1892, she would have to be. Jack Seely had come aboard. Could drama lag far behind? The leg to Cape Town passed with uncharacteristic calm. The *Kaikoura* was owned by the New Zealand Shipping Company and plied this Southampton–Cape Town–Hobart–Wellington route up to three times a year. The voyage would take a month. Some passengers would get off and new ones embark at each stop. The three young bucks were to go all the way.

What's wonderful is the apparent nonchalance with which this adventure was undertaken. Even today young people planning a trip to as far as New Zealand find a certain amount of hassle – passports and injections and contact numbers. And of course finance. Nothing could better exemplify the power of the British Empire and of its ruling class at their zenith than the implications of Seely's description of what he did when told 'a long sea voyage was advisable'.

'Accordingly', he wrote, 'I made a plan with Tom Conolly and Lord Burford to go round the world. Our benevolent parents fell in with this view, and we set sail for the Cape, Tasmania, New Zealand, Cape Horn, Rio and so home.'

This was a time so vividly described in Jan Morris's *Pax Britannica*, when a British gentleman could go into any large town and say 'Barclay's Bank' in a loud voice and know all would be well.

New Zealand might seem impossibly far away and unexplored but it was part of the Empire. You only needed an introductory note and you would be welcomed into the family. Seely's team had what must have been one of the greatest laissez-passer notes in history. At this crowning era of the 'Empire on which the sun never sets' Charles Burford, or to give him his full fig Charles Victor Albert Aubrey de Vere Beauclerk, future eleventh Duke of St Albans and therefore a direct descendant of Charles II and his orange peeling days with the blessed Nell Gwyn, had an impressively crested letter saying, 'This is my beloved godson, I trust you will give him all the assistance he needs.' His godmother was the Great White Queen herself.

The round ticket, excluding drinks, cost £52 10s which doesn't sound too bad until you do the conversion – £3,000 in today's terms; the average wage of a postman in those days was sixty pounds a year. But the assorted families could well afford it and whatever ailments were afflicting Seely and Burford (he claimed to have a bad foot), the former's appeared to have been well cured by the time *Kaikoura* got to Cape Town. By then Seely was in the rigging.

To be exact, Seely and Conolly had accepted a bet for five pounds to twenty-five pounds to work the rest of the voyage as able seamen. The bet was laid by what was described as 'an amiable gentleman of considerable wealth who was taking the voyage for his health'. History does not relate exactly what prompted the wager, but if you were a rich man hoping for a restful voyage and suddenly found yourself with the hyperactive 'deadly duo' rushing up and down the deck, fifty pounds might have seemed a small price to get them out of the way.

There appears to be some confusion as to Burford's role, or lack of it. On arrival at Wellington he announced to an awed newspaper reporter that he had been working 'up aloft'. Seely gives a rather more cryptic version. 'Burford,' he says, 'who was afraid of nothing, never got over the dizziness that comes to some people at considerable heights.' Certainly Charles Victor Albert Aubrey does not seem to have been involved in the bet, or in the drama that ensued.

For a while the trip southwards seemed to be going very well, albeit with two jolly young chaps in the rigging. 'We were allotted our watch and our stations aloft and we were treated in every way as ordinary members of the crew,' says Seely with that enthusiastic innocence of his, before entering a somewhat significant rider, 'being allowed however, to retain our cabins, and have our meals in the saloon so long as our duties as Able Seamen were not interfered with.'

The route to New Zealand goes south and east, coming round the base of the globe to dock at Hobart in Tasmania off the south-eastern tip of Australia and then going on across the Tasman Sea to Wellington at the foot of New Zealand's North Island. The direct flight path is across the ice-locked Antarctic Circle, so the further south a boat goes the quicker, though more iceberg-prone, the trip. What's more, the prevailing westerly winds will blow you there, as they don't call them the Roaring Forties for nothing. As our boys were going to find out.

It's the size of the waves that is so alarming. Ten days out of Cape Town the wind, which had been bowling them along fast enough to have 'negative slip', that is out-running the propeller, increased to gale and then to storm force. Nowadays we have all seen documentaries of great storms; back in 1892 the waves were just as strong: 'Such great mountains of water were an awe inspiring sight, towering higher and higher astern,' writes Seely, 'apparently the height of the top gallant yards. It appeared certain that each one of them must break on the ship and send her to the bottom; yet all except one passed under the taffrail as she lifted to the oncoming sea.'

The 'except one' nearly finished things. It was at night and Seely was in his cabin, mercifully fully clothed from his duties aloft, when the giant wave broke: 'I woke to find myself under water with my head against the cabin roof. In another moment I found myself swept out of the cabin and floating on the sea with the ship sliding along below me. I managed to clutch the port after-rigging with both hands, and in a few seconds, which seemed like an hour, most of the water drained away and I jumped down on deck.'

The rogue wave had broken over the stern at the same time as the wind had veered, flattening the ship into the water and tearing some of the sail away. The need to get the remaining sails stowed was paramount. The boatswain's whistle was blowing and the orders were for all hands aloft. Young Jack obviously fancied himself as quite a tough young gentleman. He was not yet tough enough.

'I climbed up the ratlines on the weather side for about twenty feet; then the violence of the storm was such that it blew me against the rigging so hard that I could not push myself away to take a further step. The sailor, just below, bawled out to me to get on. When I said "I can't", with his knife he pricked the calf of my leg which angered me so much as to give me sufficient strength to push my body away from the rigging and continue the upward climb.'

The image is vivid, so too is the humility that the ocean forces on even the proudest heart: 'He was a splendid fellow, this seaman,' says Seely in his, to us, old-fashioned way,

> and a great friend. My place on the yard was next to his and I am sure I should have fallen off if it had not been for his help. I reached the top gallant yard all right and started to climb along it as I had so often done before. But it was much more difficult than I had ever known because of the angle at which we lay.
>
> However I got to my place and we got to work to stow sail. Truth compels me to relate that although our wealthy friend paid the bet I certainly did not earn it that night – I just fixed my legs between the yard and the footrope and held tight on to the jackstay. I did hand my neighbour a gasket or two, but beyond that I was of no use. The wind was terrific, the darkness was intense, there were scurries of snow and sleet, and being wet through, I was shivering with cold.

For his fellow amateur the ordeal was to prove even more perilous.

> The only head-sail we were carrying was a small fore-gallant staysail, in which the skipper was a great believer in rough weather as it helped in steering the ship in a heavy following sea.

While we were aloft this sail started to flap with a noise like
thunder, and all at once was blown clean out of the bolt ropes. I
see it now like a white ghost floating away out over the sea. The
release from pressure caused the mast to whip in an extraordinary
way, and my friend Tom was shaken off the yard. He had a truly
memorable escape.

No five-pound bet can ever have felt less worthwhile than Tom
Conolly's as he was flipped into the raging black night and sure
oblivion. Seely continues:

He was well out over the sea at a height of one hundred and
twenty feet, without any possible chance of rescue if he fell in; no
ship could round-to in such a sea and hope to live. But when he
had already fallen some fifteen or twenty feet he clutched a
swinging rope. If it had been a taut rope of any kind of course he
could not have held on at the speed he was falling. But it so
happened it was a buntline, which gradually eased up as he held
on. Finally he was left suspended at the end of about forty feet of
rope. As the ship rolled he caught the ratlines on the starboard
side and held on.

Captain Crutchley was an old sea dog who had seen many things
and when dawn came up, the weather eased a fraction and the
pumps were getting the water level back down, he knew the
remedy. He had Seely and Conolly to the cabin, produced a bottle
of gin, and told them not to put the cork back in the bottle. At full
light they could see how lucky they had been:

At the after end of the ship there was a poop deck, about six feet
above the main deck, which had accommodation for about
twenty men and was supported by four rows of iron standards
about as thick as one's wrist. This deck had been smashed
absolutely flat down on the deck below, the iron standards being
twisted into corkscrews and other fantastic shapes. We had
shipped a great deal of water, and although the pumps were
holding their own, the situation was still of some danger.

It was not over yet. As the captain and his two gin-skinned assistants scanned the horizons they began to pick up the great flat-topped shapes of icebergs on the port beam to the north of them, far further north than they should usually be expected. The gin had certainly not depressed Captain Crutchley. 'What a lucky thing I took a southerly course', he said. 'We shall leave all the worst of the ice to our port hand.'

The captain was correct. 'As the afternoon wore on it cleared up, and from the crow's nest we could see about twenty miles in all directions. To our left was a continuous row of icebergs. The loom of more ice could be discerned to our right. But ahead of us lay a great lane with not a berg in sight.'

Hobart was made, the Tasman Sea was crossed and Wellington must have seemed the most welcome end to an unprecedented adventure. Instead, even more colourful ones lay ahead.

6

Te Kooti across the River

As the ship came round the bay into Wellington harbour, the city awaited. Although boasting only 5,000 inhabitants, it was proud, organized, cathedral-dominated, Empire-outpost respectable. But the rest of New Zealand would make rural Isle of Wight look like Piccadilly.

Great tracts of North Island were either wholly unpopulated or were shaded on the map as 'Maori Land'. Captain Cook may have got to Poverty Bay in 1769, but Samuel Marsden, the first missionary, did not get to New Zealand until 1814 and *Aurora*, the New Zealand Company's first settlers' ship did not dock at Wellington harbour until 1840, the same year that the Maori chiefs signed the Treaty of Waitangi ceding sovereignty to the British crown.

Since then there had been problems, notably the land wars of the 1860s, with the local Maori chiefs rebelling at what they considered unreasonable exploitation by the land-hungry settlers. But by 1892 the British writ was accepted, at least in theory, in most parts of the island. The least secure was King Country, the area west of Lake Taupo to which the Maori King's supporters retreated in the 1860s. That, naturally, is where Seely's team were headed.

The three 'swells' made the papers. Burford was the star name. In those royalty- and aristocracy-worshipping days, here was the future Duke of St Albans in their midst. 'Tall and fair', reported the *New Zealand Mail*, 'still with a slight limp from an accident at home, Lord Burford, whose father the Duke has 'Grand Falconer of England' amongst his titles, is looking forward to exploring the country.'

The *Mail* eagerly reported the 'noblesse oblige' interest that Burford too had been in the rigging and it is symptomatic that what to us would seem a pretty arduous journey, to ride right up through the island from Wellington via Wanganui and Lake Taupo to the Bay of Plenty on the northern coast, was dismissed as a mere matter of fact. Seely, not shy in telling us if he thinks he has done something remarkable, is equally laconic. 'Our plan', he confirms in a voice ringing back to those Imperial officer days, 'was to ride right through the Island from south to north. We arranged to take with us an Englishman named Park, who had been in the telegraph service, and a half caste guide with a musical Maori name which we abbreviated to Robert: an exceptionally fine rider and athlete, a powerful swimmer, with an iron constitution and muscles of steel.'

This attitude to what in those days would be called his 'social inferiors' is hard for us to balance in these much more open times. But appreciating it is vital to get a full understanding of Seely's most attractive strengths as well as his more obvious weaknesses. Sometimes when he bangs on about rowing in the lifeboat alongside his 'friends' the fishermen and the farmhands, you get close to the famous *Beyond the Fringe* sketch when Peter Cook and Jonathan Miller look at Alan Bennett and Dudley Moore and say, 'We are upper class and they are lower class, but we talk to them just the same.' Yet, as ever, there is sincerity beneath the jingoism. 'Robert' may have been a 'half caste', but he quickly became one of Seely's all-time heroes.

Perhaps it all began a bit too well. 'The five of us started for Wanganui,' he records, 'each riding one horse and leading another as a pack horse. Our way lay through recently cleared sheep land, carrying twelve sheep to the acre, alternating with sandy scrub. The horses went well and we were the happiest people alive.' Who organized what in today's terms would be the ultimate horseback safari is unclear. But as Seely was twenty-four, a couple of years senior to both other boys, and became an inveterate organizer in later life, it's probably fair to give him most of the credit. But a week into the journey, the honours were entirely in Robert's quarter.

After Wanganui, one hundred miles due north of Wellington, the coast continues westwards but our party turned northwards, aiming for Lake Taupo seventy miles ahead. On the second evening they found their route blocked by the river Mangawhero swollen in flood – the only ford crossing just a hundred yards up from a narrow gorge leading to a roaring rocky waterfall.

'Follow me,' said Robert.

'Without waiting for an answer', Seely wrote of their guide, 'he rode down the bank to the river, leading his pack horse, and rode two hundred yards upstream on the sandy bottom in not more than two or three feet of water. Then he turned his horse right handed, rode him in, threw himself off the saddle as the horse started to swim, directing him by splashing his head on one side or the other in the approved cavalry drill book style, and safely reached the other side, about 150 yards down stream.'

The others had followed Robert to the opposite bank without bother. But Seely's horse had never swum before. It got more and more stirred up, finally rearing clean over backwards into deep water. As ever in these circumstances (the same thing, slightly less dramatically, once happened to me in full hunting gear) the horse swims back to the entering side whilst the rider swims and swallows for the other bank before he realizes the problem. This time Seely's problem was reaching the bank at all.

There was a sweeping current, a rising bank, the odd trail of willow branch, and coming ever closer the roar of the waterfall beyond which a rocky grave awaited. Needless to say, Seely made it. And doesn't exactly undersell the tale.

> At the moment when I was most exhausted I managed to clutch the very end of this little leafy bough. Where I caught it, it was as thin as a knitting needle. But I rapidly drew it to me just faster than the current sweeping me down until finally I had to take a strain when the bough was about as thick as my little finger. The bough cracked, but it held and there I lay on my back in a twelve knot current, with thirty feet of vertical rock above me. Then I heard shouts and there stood Tom and Robert on top of the rocky

cliff lowering a rope to me. Oh the moment when I clutched that rope and knew that I was safe!

It was all very dramatic but some pretty basic practical problems remained. Seely's horse was still on the other side. For his latest hero, this would be no problem:

> The astonishing Robert was already in the saddle riding upstream. He again swam across the river, left his horse on the opposite side, and ran up the rocky cliff overlooking the river on the side which I had left, where my horse was standing, trembling with fright, up to his girths in water and close up against the rock. With extraordinary ease Robert lassoed him and drew him upstream to the ford, remounted and led mine upstream and across as he had done originally. Robert was almost a superman. The only people to compare with him for that kind of business that I have ever seen are the Basuto who live in the upper reaches of the Caledon River.

They were all safe but soaking wet, and the way they dried themselves when they camped might today suggest some homoerotic undertones to their relationships. 'We made a blazing fire', says the first of three bachelors, two of whom never married, 'and as both the clothes we were wearing and those on the packhorses were equally wet – there was nothing for it but to dry our clothes in the blaze, and run races without even a shirt in the moonlight until we were warm. By that time Robert had made us some tinned soup, which we consumed, also some whisky, then we rolled ourselves in blankets – still wet and slept soundly and well.'

Without any evidence, we might as well let the night keep its secrets. Especially as there were some very different encounters ahead, starting with two days' ride through a forest of ferns, undergrowth and the great red rata tree, endangered today but in those days endemic. 'No noise reaches this deep recess, there is dense silence, broken only from time to time by the Bellbird's clear notes – more beautiful than any bell – in three cadences – first, two major thirds in descending scale, then a minor third, all three in quick succession.'

Out into the open with Lake Taupo only a couple of ridges away, they noticed 'the towering bulk of Tongariro in fierce eruption to the west of us', but did not realize they were about to meet an old volcano of the human kind.

They had not seen any sign of human habitation for days. But suddenly Robert came back with an ashen face and whispered the words 'Te Kooti'. It was the most notorious name in the whole Empire. Te Kooti had finally been pardoned by Queen Victoria, but he remained New Zealand's most fabled outlaw because of the fearsome slaughter that he was supposed to have carried out at Chatham Island and Poverty Bay in 1867.

As Seely understood it, Te Kooti had refused to submit to British rule, so he had been tried and convicted of rebellion and sentenced to transportation to the wilderness of Chatham Island three hundred miles east in the Pacific. After sentence he took a Bible and through an interpreter swore a thunderous oath that 'at the place where I land I will kill every man, woman and child until justice is satisfied'. The courtroom chilled with foreboding and it was right to. At Chatham Island, Te Kooti swam out to the guard boat, climbed up the cable, killed most of the crew and compelled the remainder to sail him to Poverty Bay, where he went ashore to club to death every man, woman and child in that little settlement before escaping to the hills. It had been two decades earlier, but across the Empire the legend of Te Kooti's vengeance still frightened little children at bedtime.

Needless to say, one man's terrorist is another's freedom fighter and in reality Te Kooti was a lot more than just a bloodthirsty brigand. He did indeed escape from Chatham Island on the *Rifleman* but he brought two hundred men and women with him. He did murder the magistrate and many others in the Poverty Bay district of Matawhero but that was only after he had been harried by the magistrate's forces. And when he did finally renounce arms in 1873 he founded the Ringatu Church based on visions he had experienced on his prison isle.

Whatever Te Kooti's story, and he was to die in 1893, he must have been a formidable figure for these young imperialists to meet.

Coming towards us was this redoubtable man. He was old then with a wrinkled face and grizzled hair, he wore a blanket tied round his neck and falling over his shoulders, otherwise he was quite naked, except for one spur on his bare right foot. I am bound to say that even if I had never heard of him I should still have trembled at his ferocious aspect.

Park spoke to him in Maori and when he demanded to be told exactly what we were up to, Park told him we were 'very great English noblemen with a message from Queen Victoria' and what business was it of Te Kooti to ask us what we were doing.

At this the old volcano rumbled. 'Te Kooti appeared very angry at this: then all at once he burst out laughing and held out his hand.' 'I still wonder whether I did right', says the normally over-generous Seely. 'I have only twice refused to shake hands with a man, and Te Kooti was one of the two. On the other hand I have shaken hands with a man just before his execution for murder. But in this case the remembrance of the massacre of Poverty Bay was too much for me and I turned aside.'

The shadow soon passed. A few miles further on they came over the ridge and there, 'stretching as far as the eye could see was the great Lake Taupo, glittering like a sheet of pure gold in the sun'. The ultimate safari was far from over yet.

7

Cupid among the Kiwis

Swimming rivers and refusing to shake hands with outlaws was all very well, but by the time our party reached Tokaanu on the shores of Lake Taupo, they needed something else. They needed permission to continue.

The Maori chiefs may not have been in open rebellion, but up here they preferred to be left alone with their own customs and had also introduced an alcohol ban to avoid the whisky-hooked exploitation that had so debilitated the natives in America. This was a pretty empty place. It was only in 1892 that the first steamship company began operating up the Whanganui River from the coast to Pipiriki. Lake Taupo was a further fifty miles north. So far the only white men that Seely's team had met on their journey were a surveying party. These men were trying to go north-west, but the chiefs had politely but firmly refused to let them through.

So it was time to call a meeting and to play their cards. Reading Seely's report, that old sense of certainty rings through. This was what an English milord's upbringing had prepared him for.

We thought the letter which Burford had secured from Sir George Grey [the then Governor of New Zealand] might secure us a free passage. Also I had a letter from Mr Bowen, the Senator, conveying a message from the Maori representative in Parliament. Moreover, Burford was a godson of Queen Victoria and she had sent him a very kind message wishing him 'bon voyage.' Park accordingly arranged for a party of the petty chiefs to have dinner with us at the inn, and about a dozen of them turned up. They listened in respectful silence to the message from Sir George Grey and the Maori representative, but at the mention of Queen Victoria they burst into loud guttural applause.

One of the party had on a pair of trousers, another a valuable Kiwi mat, but the rest were in blankets, worn like an Italian officer's cloak. They ate a large meal and the innkeeper allowed them about a tablespoonful of whisky each, but no more. The old chief who sat next to me was a man of about 70 years of age. The Maoris had quite given up cannibalism, but it had been practised in his lifetime. He opened up the subject to me through an interpreter, and amused me by the emphatic way in which he denied that any Maori had ever eaten human flesh for any purpose of greed! It was, he said, purely a sacred rite in order to show complete victory over a fallen enemy. I have been told that what he said is quite true, at any rate I am sure it was so in his case. At the close of the banquet we all drank Queen Victoria's health, the assembled company bowing, after which they facilitated our journey into the unknown land.

If only all Victorian journeys could have been as innocent as this. No land-grabbing, no killing, no attacks on the native language or customs. But there was to be an unexpected danger round the corner: the breaking of hearts. The day after the banquet our team left their horses with the innkeeper with instructions, duly carried out with no fuss, to deliver them to Taupo, at the north-east corner of the lake, some thirty miles round the un-roaded shore. They had a new means of transport. They took to canoes.

The idea was to travel up to the western side of the lake and then go inshore to the land of a chief who was prepared to accept them. They arrived late and next morning Seely went to the river for a swim by himself, and without anything so fancy as swimwear. What followed, in every sense, must have been quite a sight.

As I stood poised on the rock with my hands above my head ready for the next dive into the glorious pool I distinctly heard the sounds of silvery laughter. I dived in, swam as fast as I could to the opposite bank and ran up the sandy slope. With little screams

of pretended fright, there fled from the bushes half a dozen little
girls, followed by one much taller. Taken with the fun of the
thing I ran after and started to overhaul them. Then the tall girl
who was shepherding them, suddenly turned and, standing very
erect, with head held high, lifted a warning right arm and fore-
finger. It was the most beautiful thing – animate or inanimate
– that I had ever seen, like the most perfect Greek statue, with the
poise of Raphael's young St John the Baptist in Florence.

One hundred and ten years later, the images he conjures for me are
a bit fleshier than a boy's statue in Florence:

'So we stood facing each other', he continues. 'She had been
swimming too, for beads of water shone in the sunlight like
diamonds in her hair, and on her body. Then she stamped her little
foot. I bowed and obediently walked away wondering how so
marvellous a creature could be found in this distant land. I could not
resist turning my head to have a last look at my new found goddess.
As I looked she turned and gave me an indescribable smile, a toss of
her head and the wave of her hand.'

This was all a bit more exciting than deck quoits with Conolly
and Burford, or being fished out of the river by the mighty Robert.
A couple of hours later Seely had dried off, got dressed and
presented himself with full respects to the local chief, a handsome
young man whose grandfather had been one of the signatories of
the Treaty of Waitangi in 1840.

After the civilities were over the young chief called out for his
only sister to come into his hut to be introduced. Ducking through
the doorway, her glistening body now draped completely in a cloak
of kiwi feathers, was the vision herself. She bowed to Seely with
stately lack of recognition and said how glad she was to meet her
first Englishman. When she said goodbye she did not seem to
understand about shaking hands, so Seely, ever gallant, took her
fingers in his own, raised them to his lips and kissed them. She
smiled. It was the smile he had seen by the pool.

Quite how much more she gave him is lost in the mists of
cupid's memory. For several days she 'showed him the forest': the

birds, the hot springs, the wild boar. She taught him Maori – even late in life he could say, 'My soul is filled with respectful adoration.' She switched from her kiwi-feather cloak to 'ever changing garlands of flowers and leaves'. It was a full-blown infatuation. Back in King Country the official reaction was hardly surprising. 'After a few days the chief came to see me and, quite politely but bluntly, asked me my intentions.'

In terms of the opposite sex, Seely seems to have led a sheltered life. Now he was badly smitten: 'This girl of seventeen', he wrote,

> though some would have described her as an untutored savage, was without doubt the most beautiful creature that I had ever seen. Moreover, though she could run and jump like a gazelle, and swim like a salmon, she had the manner and bearing of a queen; thoughts and ideas of unbelievable charm and beauty. I had often heard people making speeches about cementing the Empire and the union of hearts. Here was a union of hearts if ever there was one.

He insists that but for Tom Conolly he would have married and stayed. Conolly played the killer card. He said it would break Seely's mother's heart. 'As she was the most adored and adorable mother in the world it was a hard thing for me to answer.' What followed has the authentic tone of true Victorian battle between romance and the cold shower.

> It was decided we should leave the next morning and we duly went down and embarked in 6 canoes. The others went on ahead, and I was left to say goodbye to the chief and his sister and embark in his own war canoe, manned by twelve strong natives with uplifted paddles. I shook hands warmly with the chief and then turned to say goodbye to my princess. I put my arms round her and kissed her, no rubbing of noses in native fashion, but a kiss from one to the other. She burst into tears and so, I confess, did I as I jumped into the canoe and in a moment shot into the stream under the deft blows of the twelve well wielded paddles.

Just before we rounded the bend I looked back and saw her standing hand in hand with her brother. She waved farewell to me and I never saw her again.

But he never forgot her either.

8

New Zealand to New Horizons

Duty is a heavy word. In 1892 it was also a far-reaching one. Within a couple of weeks it had snuffed out the continuing travels of our intrepid trio. Maternal duty had ended Seely's romance amongst the kiwi feathers, regimental duty was to pull Conolly back to England, and familial worries would have Burford on the next boat after him. The wonder is how well the communications worked. What happened to Tom Conolly was just the same as happens today. When you get back to a reasonable-sized town, you go up to the communications centre and try to send or receive a message.

In Tom's case the town was Rotorua. The team had taken the canoes and paddled across to Taupo where 'we met our horses again, which had been sent round the lake by the innkeeper in charge of three natives, thence we rode to Rotorua to see the hot springs and the remains of the Pink Terraces which had been blown up in the great volcanic eruption a few years before. It was here that Tom received a letter summoning him to take up his commission in the Scots Greys, so off he went, alas, by the next coach to Napier, en route for Wellington, to join the first homeward bound ship.'

Message sent, message received, action taken. If you accepted those certainties, the long arm of the Empire would activate you even at the other end of the earth. Seely's team may have gone into the far beyond but they duly checked in at the post office as all expeditions should, and the two remaining English milords were greeted with a smile almost wherever they went:

New Zealand was deliciously primitive in those days. There were few railways, few roads, and very few bridges. But you could go almost anywhere on horseback, and wherever you went you were sure of a very warm welcome from whites and Maoris alike. The hospitality of the British settlers to a stranger was unbounded. They were a deeply religious people, and at the same time full of the joy of life. The charm of the inhabitants, added to the marvellous beauty of the country, made a combination unique in the world.

Burford was the next to get the call, but not before he and Seely had been through the excitement of hunting wild horses on the Taupo plain near Opepe. An exploring party had been massacred here some years before and their horses had bred in the wild just as happened in Argentina when the fleeing Spanish turned five mares and seven stallions loose outside Buenos Aires in 1534. Forty-seven years later the returning conquistadores found 'the whole plain was swarming with horses'.

In 1892 there were certainly plenty in the Taupo region and the pursuit was popular with the local Maori tribe because they were on a promise for half the catch, even if this proved to be a lot more difficult than envisaged. Seely and Burford had done lots of lassoing practice but needless to say when it came to the real thing it needed the redoubtable Robert to play the cowboy part. Even then the prize catch, the little black stallion who was the leader of the herd, pined so badly in captivity that they had to turn him free. The Maoris kept a handsome mare, and the Seely party took the other stallion to sell in Napier where Burford found his letter.

His father, the tenth Duke of St Albans, wanted him home because of family illness and so the Wellington steamer was taken next day and Charles Victor Albert Aubrey de Vere Beauclerk passes out of our story. His limp was better, but despite all those names and ancestors one cannot say that his future was that glorious. He had brief stays in the Nottinghamshire Yeomanry and the Scots Greys and his main claim to fame is the rather dubious one of being certified insane after shooting the chef on board his family yacht in Portsmouth. It was 1898, he had just succeeded to the title, but would spend his thirty-two-year tenure in a specially built annexe of a lunatic asylum in Kent.

So Seely was on his own. 'But the people at Napier were more than kind, bought all the horses at a good price, put me up at the club, and then took me out to a famous sheep farm to see the way in which an elaborate farm should be run.'

His clock too was beginning to tick, but if the round-the-world voyage with Burford and Conolly was over, he hadn't come this far only to leave without seeing something more of the Antipodes. His plan of action appears to have been another masterpiece of Empire organization and his briefest of descriptions a superb example of assuming that the reader completely understands how an active young gentleman of means would handle things as 1892 gave way to 1893.

'From New Zealand I crossed to Australia, where I shot many duck and made many friends, returning to England completely restored to health, in time for my yeomanry training.'

Empire connections and enthusiasm to use them could put Puck's girdle round the earth. Re-routing from Napier to Sydney, across two thousand miles of Tasman Sea to a place and people he had never met, would not be a problem. Letters of introduction, notes of credit to the bank, and in a day or two it would be a close call if the duck population north of Sydney liked him less than he liked the swarms of man-eating mosquitoes which shared their watery habitat.

Gentlemen had to use their leisure, but the deal, and at this time it was the best deal ever devised by man, also involved this concept of duty. That meant Seely doing yeomanry training in readiness for some day when Queen and Empire might need defending. But in his case the deal also meant him getting some sort of qualification for a job.

The law appeared to be the chosen profession. But whilst the connections were typically impressive, his first taste does not seem to have been that thrilling: 'On the advice of Sir Richard Webster, then Attorney General, I went to the office of Field Roscoe, solicitors in Lincoln's Inn Fields to learn conveyancing. It was indescribably dull but I learnt a great deal. Moreover, Blackburne taught me to play chess at Simpson's Divan where I often lunched. He was the most famous living chess player of that time, thinking nothing of playing several games simultaneously, blindfolded.'

If that sounds heedless – and when you think of the slums across the river and the official estimates that one in four Londoners lived 'in abject poverty', it does – the only defence plea is that Seely was a product of the time and, at twenty-five, he was a young man not afraid of doing his bit. At Brooke in January 1894 the lifeboat gun went at 2.30 in the morning; the challenge, once again, had come from the sea.

Despite his medal-winning heroics with the *Henri et Léontine* three years earlier, young Jack had not been around consistently enough to be an official member of the lifeboat crew. But when everyone mustered in the foggy early-morning darkness on this occasion, one of the crew was ill. The steamer *Ossian* had run hard on to the rocks. Seely was put in to row stroke on the port side. The boat was launched, the waves overcome, seven men were rescued and the mighty Ben Jacobs, the coxswain, proposed 'Master Jack' as a permanent member of the lifeboat crew.

Down by that stormy coast there was no higher honour, and there is no doubting the sincerity of Seely's later tribute: 'I can truly say that of all the posts that have been given to me, this fills me with the greatest joy.' Yet the accolade did not come without cost. There were no fatalities this time, unlike six years earlier when Second Coxswain Reuben Cooper was tragically swept overboard in the *Sirenia* rescue, but Seely got sick after his soaking. He contracted pneumonia and pleurisy and lay so near to death that he claims to have heard a nurse say, 'I am afraid he has gone, a nice sort of boy too.'

He was to recover, but someone very close was beyond recall. Victorian families are often presented as stern and unloving. Not this one. 'It was not a very happy time for me for quite a different reason. My mother had fallen desperately ill, and shortly afterwards she died. She was very gentle, beautiful and kind.' Mother and son was much more than just a dutiful relationship. For the luckiest young man in the Empire, it was a warning that the sun would not always shine.

9

The Loyal Blade

Another illness, another on-board recuperation. Not as far as New Zealand, this time the boat was a 'dahabiyeh' sailing up the Nile. Once again the indulgent father had footed the bill for his apparently beleaguered youngest son. Once again the recovery was complete.

'The effect of life on the Nile was quite miraculous. I stepped on to the dahabiyeh a very sick man who had been told by the greatest living doctor [Sir Andrew Clark] that he must give up all hope of an active life. Within a week I was better. In a fortnight I was practically well. In three weeks I was as fit as I had ever been. Such is the effect of constant sunshine.'

It may not be a total surprise to the reader to learn that one of Seely's posts in later life was that of a director of top travel agent Wagon-Lits and Thomas Cook.

What is amazing to our hustling, workaholic world is the actual amount of time such vacations involved. If Seely really was 'as fit as I had ever been' after three weeks, what about the remaining month and a half described in his diaries? There was lots of shooting of duck and quail, a trip to the Temple of Philae and a four-day camel excursion taking bags of gold to subsidize (and nearly getting knifed by) a supposedly friendly Arab tribe.

On this trip he had a late-night conversation that was to have a profound effect on the way he handled the horses on which at times his life would depend. He was sitting out in the sheikh's compound under the stars: 'Only the bark of a dog, the grunt of a camel, and the weird little sibilant noises from innumerable smaller beasts broke the tense silence of the calm North African night. Every now and then there was the loud whinny of a horse (that most mysterious of sounds) for we were surrounded by Arab horses.'

The sheikh was a young man of natural dignity and complete understanding of the equine psyche. 'Your people', he said quietly to Seely, 'treat the dog as your friend and the horse as your slave. With us Arabs it is the other way round. Ours is the better plan.' Seely queried whether you couldn't be close friends with both horse and dog. But the sheikh was adamant: 'No. Every man should have one horse he cares for beyond anything else. If he makes friends with the dog the horse will know, and he may lose the friendship of the horse.'

While this sounds rather extreme, for Seely it was to prove prophetic. Five years on he would be spending weeks on the veld with his horse Maharajah with not a dog in sight. By the time they sailed back to England, they had a link that even the sheikh might envy.

This Nile trip might have been a wonderful holiday, but on Seely's return home he achieved success of a more lasting nature. He found himself a wife and 'the beginning of 18 years of unalloyed and unbelievable happiness'. It may have been a Victorian marriage, with the husband often away on first military and then political service, but all of what evidence we have, including my mother's recollections, are of a happy union, a real partnership.

Emily 'Nim' Crichton, was the tall, bold, dark-haired and affectionate daughter of Sir Harry Crichton, Colonel of the Hampshire Yeomanry, a shipping magnate and owner of Netley Abbey, which stares handsomely out at the entrance to Southampton Water. Sir Harry was a son of the Earl of Erne, one of the leading figures in Northern Ireland, with a castle overlooking Lough Erne. He also had a land agent, Charles Boycott, whose name is immortalized in the language. In 1880 when the Erne estates refused to lower its tenants' rates, Charles Boycott was the target of the systematic shunning policy organized by nationalist Charles Parnell, and the 'boycott' was born. In short, the Crichtons were frightfully grand and felt themselves able, according to my mother, to look down on the Seelys as being (mills and coal mines) 'in trade'.

By that standard young Jack was moving up a notch, because not long after his marriage (in Winchester Cathedral on 7 June 1895) he was called to the Bar. Quite how he fitted all this in between yeomanry training, lifeboat rowing and Nile exploration is not fully explained. Far be it for a grandson to suggest that there might have been any short cuts taken, but somehow to the Bar he was called, a member of the Inner Temple he became, and the Midland circuit had a colourful new player in its ranks.

It also had a fount of splendid if sometimes apocryphal stories with which men like F.E. Smith (the future Attorney General) could tease their friend. 'It is reported', F.E. wrote of one legendary Seely exploit, 'that he once defended, but without success, a man accused of murder. As the unfortunate man was removed from the dock, his counsel is said to have assured him with great earnestness that "It will at least be a satisfaction to know, before you face your Maker, that everything which forensic ability could contribute has been done on your behalf." '

Seely disputes such disparagement, claiming that by the time the South African war and then the House of Commons closed his legal career, 'I was really getting on quite well and had a considerable number of briefs.' He did, though, admit to having been 'a little unfortunate' with his first case.

He was to prosecute in an apparently open-and-shut case of assault and battery, two men having got involved in a fight, one nearly killing the other. Unfortunately Barrister Seely's appearance in court was not totally conducive to focused arguments. On the eve of the case he had borrowed a horse from his brother Frank to go hunting, had taken a mother and father of a fall and been carried home concussed and covered in blood with his top hat stove in like one for the opera.

'The doctor came, stitched up the cuts and covered my face with plaster. Next morning I was in court with a wig which felt much too tight and a splitting headache. The case was called and I stood up to open the attack. The judge, with a smile, said these awful words: "Is this the prosecuting counsel or the prisoner?" '

The laughter took a long time to subside and it is an undying tribute to the jury system that Seely got his conviction.

He was now married to the daughter of his yeomanry colonel, practising (a touch idiosyncratically) at the Bar, had a child on the way and had already won a lifesaving medal with his local crew at Brooke. Yet something was missing. For the indulgent but ambitious Victorian parent in Charles Seely, the next step was clear as day: he and his father had both been long-serving Members of Parliament. It was time for young Jack to do his bit. For Sir Charles Seely in the Isle of Wight in 1895, arranging this was not a problem.

In confidence, Sir Charles had discovered that the local MP, Sir Richard Webster (Conservative), was to leave the Commons to become Master of the Rolls. It was therefore arranged that Sir Richard would come to Newport, announce his resignation to the Conservative Association and recommend young Jack as his successor. But there were two snags: no one had told Jack; and he was a Liberal. The resulting scene is such a perfect period piece that it is best told in Seely's argot of the day.

My father drove me into Newport in an old fashioned landau with a pair of horses and on the way explained the situation to me. I protested that I did not want to stand as a Conservative. Here was a difficult moment. My father had given his promise on my behalf, never thinking that I would take so strong a view. I hear the horses now trotting along under the elms at Swainston and my father saying: 'Don't be ridiculous, there is no difference between the Conservatives and Liberal Unionists' – The reply: 'But you are a Liberal Unionist'.

'Yes but I was a Liberal Member for twenty years before the Home Rule split, and my father for twenty years before me. You are starting afresh. With the situation as it is, there is no difference now.'

'But I have always been a Liberal. You probably don't know that I was the only boy who supported Milner when he stood as the Liberal candidate for Harrow in 1885. And what is more, that I was condemned to write a Georgic as a punishment for reading Mr Gladstone's Home Rule Speech aloud in the middle of form.'

'But that is not quite the same thing.'

'Ah but I think it is.'

At Newport, much family embarrassment was saved by the arrival of a telegram saying that Sir Richard's elevation had been postponed at the last minute and he would therefore be remaining as MP. So my father and I drove back to Brooke crestfallen but the best of friends.

They don't make politics like that any more. Nor do they have, except perhaps amongst the most diehard of palace courtiers, many monarchy worshippers of the Seely type. In the summer of 1897, at the close of the Diamond Jubilee celebrations, Queen Victoria drove round the main towns of the Isle of Wight receiving their local tributes and 'loyal address'. The Hampshire Yeomanry rode escort and at the close Captain Seely was invited to a dinner party at Osborne House where worship could be done in person. His report does not disappoint.

> We went to the drawing room where we were all introduced in turn to Queen Victoria. My turn came and I made my bow. The Queen was ever so gracious, she seemed to radiate an air of majesty and sympathy, her voice was not only a command but a caress. She thanked me for all the numerous escorts which I had provided and conveyed her thanks to the men. She asked for details about the man whose horse had slipped up on the stones and begged me to go and see him next day.

As the carriage trotted Jack and Nim back to Brooke that night, few people in history can have faced their thirtieth year with quite such happiness at their own good fortune or such confidence for whatever lay ahead. But all this yeomanry training was required because the Empire was an ever expanding force and the Queen Empress and Pax Britannica would need fighting for. And when Seely's turn came he would have his first lessons in the brutal unromantic truth: that real conflict costs misery and blood.

II. CUTTING THE TEETH

The Cape, Churchill and the Gun That Lowered

He was ready for a fight.

Yes, this able, charming, popular thirty-year-old father of Frank, John and Emily was prepared to risk his life not only for the lifeboat but also for the Crown. And it was on a lifeboat trip that the readiness bubbled over.

The expedition was honourable enough. In 1898 he had been elected a member of the Lifeboat Institute and in typical hands-on Seely fashion decided to visit all the south-west lifeboat stations as one of the inspectors. He was even prepared to make an unusual sacrifice to pay for it. 'I have always been rather hard up', claims the millionaire's son a touch unconvincingly, so 'my wife and I sold our dog cart [lightweight two-seater trap] to the local doctor, and with the proceeds went off on this delightful holiday'.

It must have been hard work as well as instructive. They launched a different lifeboat every day from the Isle of Wight to Land's End. By the time they got to Cornwall Seely must have been getting weary. Maybe that was his excuse for intemperance. More likely it indicates just how strongly devotion to the Queen Empress, the 'my country, right or wrong' ethic, had taken hold.

> We had launched one of the Cornish boats for practice in rather a heavy sea. There was no wind so we had to pull all the way. When we were about three miles from land, all rather hot and tired, the inspector told us to take in the oars and have a rest. He started a conversation about the possibility of war in South Africa. These splendid Cornish lifeboatmen, who have saved ever

so many lives, had many relatives among the miners engaged in the South African Goldfields and one of the crew produced an eloquent argument, with which we afterwards became familiar from the speeches of Sir Henry Campbell Bannerman, Lloyd George and others, to the effect that the Boers were a fine and sturdy people, that we had no right to their country, why should we lose a single man to help a few millionaires, and so on and so forth.

Somehow or other this filled me with unreasoning rage. I was near him in the boat and announced that if he said it again I would hit him. He did say it, and I hit him. Of course he then hit me back much harder. We were promptly separated and continued the exercise. Fortunately my opponent was not a teetotaller, and we most effectively healed our quarrels that evening.

So one of the ultimate imperial follies gathered momentum. And to someone like Seely any dissent was little short of blasphemy. How dare the Kaiser send a congratulatory telegram to South African President Paul Kruger after the collapse of the Jameson Raid at the beginning of 1896. Was he not talking about the mightiest empire the world had ever seen? How could loyal Englishmen doubt the correctness of Foreign Secretary Chamberlain's demand that the Boers guarantee British interests. It was all gung-ho stuff and Seely's opening reaction was typical: 'I well remember that when the troops embarked for South Africa, the one fear of everyone concerned was that they might not get to the scene of the war before it was over. Then came the disasters of Natal, and everything was changed.'

Kimberley, Ladysmith and Mafeking were being besieged. The wicked Boers were trying to twist the Imperial Lion by its tail. All the more reason for gallant yeomanry to get stuck in. This was Seely's chance. Volunteers were called for, 'and of course,' he says, 'my own troops from the Isle of Wight volunteered to a man'. Another troop from the mainland completed the Hampshire Yeomanry squadron and a squadron from Surrey joined them to complete a boatload. Then there was a slight hitch as to whether he or a Major Hervey should be in command (no prizes for guessing who got it) Seely had already got himself one of the most important of all volunteers. He had hired Harry Smith.

An officer would need a batman. Harry Smith was a 25-year-old farm labourer's son from King's Somborne, five miles west of Winchester. He had volunteered for the Hampshire Yeomanry as a diversion from the inevitable path which rural life would allot him either in the field or on his mother's laundry round. Working for 'Captain Jack' sounded like an adventure. It was. For thirty years as batman in war and butler in peace Harry Smith became one of the great support figures in Seely's life. Cool, discreet, tough, organized, he was Jeeves with attitude.

So stage one was complete for the Hampshires, but there was a lot more to do before the Dutch farmers could be taught a lesson under that distant African sun. The squadron moved to barracks at Christchurch, got themselves together and eventually were declared fit to travel. But there was a hitch.

Cue for one of those Seely moments fiction could hardly create. Imagine the scene down at Christchurch at the very beginning of 1900: five hundred eager yeomanry under the vigorous Colonel Woods, all present and correct, ready to 'teach Johnny Boer a lesson' but landlocked for lack of a ship.

> I decided to try and charter one from my uncle Sir Francis Evans, who was chairman of Union-Castle Line. I went to see him and said, 'Uncle Frank have you got a spare ship?' He said 'Yes.' I replied, 'then I want it.' He smiled, 'Who is going to pay for it?' My reply was: 'Never mind about that. If you produce a ship the War Office is bound to pay.'
>
> He then and there sent off a sheaf of telegrams ordering the *Goth* to be got ready forthwith. Then I went to the War Office, where my friendship with Lord Wolseley stood me in good stead. They said that it was a most odd and irregular proceeding, but under the circumstances they would agree and would put another squadron of yeomanry on board which would just fill up the boat. I returned to Christchurch with the good news, and

much was the cheering when I announced to my little band that we should be sailing within a week.

Embarkation was not without its problems, leave-taking not without both honour and regret. For Seely the trouble began with a horse – his own horse, to be exact. Maharajah was a smashing-looking little Arab gelding, almost white and hardly measuring fifteen hands. He was neat and hardy and had been brilliant during yeomanry training. But when Seely rode him up to register at the docks, the clerk looked up and said, 'Sorry sir. No white horses. New army orders. Bad for camouflage.'

In vain did the ship-producing commanding officer protest that this was his best horse. Army orders prevailed. Maharajah was going back to Brooke. An idea flashed into Seely's head. He took Maharajah round the back of the docks and called for several gallons of a dark brown dye called Condy's Fluid. Maharajah was duly doused and when he dried off – presto! – Captain Seely had a fine new strawberry roan charger. He even had a photo taken to prove it. A fine pair they make. Seely, lean, tall and elegant in the saddle, a leather-gloved right hand hanging to his side as proof of winter. Maharajah, ears cocked, head bent intelligently, bridle and halter and tether rope neatly combined with gleaming Pelham bit in best cavalry fashion, the black bedroll tied across the saddle above the rider's knee.

Maharajah's change of colour proved to be a lot more than an amusing bending of the rules. One of the greatest disasters of the Boer War was the realization that the British had the wrong sort of horse. The officers were raring to get their big, strong, corn-fed, stable-sheltered hunters to chase those Boers off the veld. There was even a company raised in Dublin who called themselves the Foxhunting Battalion. But the dry, stony, arid conditions soon reduced big upstanding hunters to limping wrecks. The army could not get them enough food, nor any cover. Horses died by the thousand. The much sneered-at lean and hungry, live-off-the-land Boer horses turned out to be exactly what was needed. Maharajah, with his iron legs and hardy constitution, was one of the very few who survived to sail back to Southampton eighteen months later.

By then so much would have changed and, most significantly of all, the Great Empress herself would be no more. So Seely's final meeting, a dinner party at Osborne two days before he sailed, had history in it.

There were only seven people at the table: Queen Victoria, her daughter Princess Beatrice (the Governor of the Isle of Wight), two courtiers, a lady-in-waiting, Seely and his wife. 'It was a very different dinner party from the one I had attended two and a half years earlier', he reports, 'and the Queen was very grave and sad.' He describes the arrival of a telegram with the Boer War casualties writ in large letters so that the short-sighted old lady could read them herself. Of how the Queen took Nim for an audience afterwards and 'kissed and comforted her' when my poor grandmother burst into tears at the thought of Jack leaving her and the children for such an uncertain future. Then it was Seely's turn and obsolete though such monarch-worship may now seem, the authenticity of the emotion shines through:

'It was the same penetrating, commanding, gentle voice; but slower, softer, sadder. Again, as before, she begged me to thank my men for having volunteered for the war, and she wished them with all her heart success in battle and a safe return. I confess that I was deeply moved, and as I kissed her hand, longed that I might see her again. Alas, it was not to be, for a year later, while we were still in South Africa, the great Queen passed away.'

It takes three weeks to sail from Southampton to Cape Town. The *Goth* seems to have been a good enough ship, although relations of poor Trumpeter Denham probably wouldn't think so. He died of fever on the way out and had the flag and musket-ball privilege of a burial at sea. Seven horses also got fed to the sharks, but that's a small percentage of the 300 on board, and proof of the policy of walking them round and round the deck every day.

Once ashore there appears to have been an element of clubiness in camp. 'I found the Duke of Marlborough with the Oxford Yeomanry and many other friends.' But it would not last long, even when Tom Conolly rocked up to visit. Perhaps it would have been better if he hadn't. For whilst together, he and Seely made a vow that neither of them would ever surrender unwounded. Within six months that vow would cost Conolly his life.

For Seely, the great awakening was soon to begin, for the news from the north was not good. The disasters of Spioenkop and Vaalkrans up by the Tugela River while General Buller made his laborious progress towards breaking the siege at Ladysmith had underlined to everyone the hostility of the terrain and the mobility and effectiveness of the enemy. To beat the Boers was going to hurt. Seely was hurting soon enough.

He and his company were first entrained two hundred miles north up to De Aar junction and then had to march in great heat the sixty miles north-east to Britstown where the commander turned out to be the formidable General Kitchener. 'We all admired him and most of us feared him.' The Avenger of Khartoum was an exhausting commandant to report to at any time, particularly so if, like Seely, you have inadvertently 'borrowed' his two Indian cooks en route.

They survived Kitchener but only just survived his orders, which involved a forced march fifty miles up to the Orange River, and back again. By this time the weather had broken, 'the veldt was white with water', horses from the accompanying 7th Dragoon Guards who had come straight from the ship 'were dying in large numbers' and the tired City of London Volunteer whose rifle Seely carried spoke for most of his colleagues with his repeated groaning epithet: 'Never again,' he kept muttering, 'freedom [each volunteer had been given the Freedom of The City of London] or no bloody freedom.'

Knowing what was happening and where the enemy was proved to be perennial problems. When they had reached Dewets-dorp Winston Churchill, now the highest-paid journalist of his day at the then astonishing terms of £250 (almost £16,000 in today's terms) a month from the *Morning Post*, arrived with news of an elaborate attack to be made on a ridge next morning. When the operation began there seemed surprisingly little opposition until

Seely and company suddenly spied a lone horseman riding the ridge and waving his hat. It was Churchill, who had discovered that the Boer forces had left in the night. It was used as the opening scene in the film *The Young Winston*.

Young Jack's information, or lack of it, nearly ended everything a little later. His company had trekked seventy miles north, up to Senekal. He, Harry Smith and an orderly called Dyer were riding ahead of his troop towards what they had been told was an empty kraal. Seely had dismounted when Dyer was suddenly surrounded and both he and his horse were shot. His horse died. Seely looked across and there was another Boer with his rifle aiming straight at him.

'It was a clear sunny morning, and he was within twelve yards of me. It was no good for me to run away, because I realised I could not be missed. So I stood still waiting for the end. Then an extraordinary thing happened. The man lowered his rifle, looked me straight in the eyes, turned round and walked away.'

The guardian angel had come with him to Africa. For another year she would never rest for long.

Sympathy Vote and Cheers for a Train

Back home an angel was busy in his absence. She was called Mrs Seely.

By-elections have long been famed for a touch of originality but the Isle of Wight poll in the summer of 1900 must take the biscuit. The sitting MP Sir Richard Webster (Conservative) had finally been made Master of the Rolls as originally planned four years before. The Conservatives then adopted Jack Seely as their candidate, despite the slight drawbacks that he was both a Liberal and away at the Boer War.

Nim Seely was not abashed. She got out her dog cart, whether a new one or the original one requisitioned from the doctor isn't known, and drove around the towns and villages of the Island with the simple sign, 'Vote for Jack'.

She was much helped by her father-in-law, who made Brooke House a campaign headquarters, and by her brother-in-law Charles Seely of nearby Gatcombe House. By all accounts, Nim was the most charming and energetic, not to say the most heavily hatted campaigner, but cynics might have added the slogan, 'You Know It Makes Sense', to remind the electorate of just how vast the Seely holdings were throughout the Wight.

But on the eve of polling day Nim's campaign had an unwanted surge in sympathy support. Rumours were rife that Jack had at the least been wounded and most probably killed in action. In those 'sword of sacrifice' days, how could you vote against someone laying his life on the line?

The rumours had substance but not accuracy. There had indeed been telegrams through to the War Office reporting Seely as a casualty but they were based on seeing him fall rather than witnessing any wound. It was Monday 28 May, the day after Trooper Dyer had been shot and wounded near Senekal. Jack's squadron were pinned down close to the Boer position near a hill called Biddulphs Berg. He had personally run back to ask unsuccessfully for support.

'But they had precise instructions to go no further, so I started to return as quickly as I could. Just as I had nearly reached my little party there was a burst of fire, and I thought it best to fall flat on my face and crawl the remaining fifty yards. The party I had just left who were watching me were convinced that I fell on my face a dead man and so reported on their return.'

Imagine the consternation such a telegram must have caused back at Brooke. And even if the actual truth had been known, that Monday and Tuesday had been a long, long way from risk free. Seely's team were hidden in the long grass but so close to the Boers that they could not stand up in daylight.

'Unpleasant fire from front and rear', he records in a diary he kept at this time.

> In about an hour all the rest retired except my squadron and twenty Derbys [Derbyshire Yeomanry] with Power whom I took charge of. Later realized we were left alone. Changed magazine, fixed bayonets, no man to shoot when 25 rounds only in belt – 600 yards from what now find is main Boer position. Their [field] guns opened 5 pm 700 yards range. Men behaved splendidly. 3 wounded – tied up [tourniqueted] one. When quite dark, formed square, carried wounded in centre and started to find camp. After five and a half hours hard work, got whole party safe to camp, to immense surprise of everyone.

Election campaigns are famously exhausting, but events back in the Isle of Wight were a doddle compared to the candidate's schedule. Seely did not get his shattered team back until two thirty that Tuesday morning, but they were called out immediately for a big attack with the whole 8th Division. It was not a success and that evening the relative position of the unwitting prospective MP contrasts starkly with that of his main supporters.

Whilst Sir Charles Seely and his daughter-in-law reviewed the day's events in Brooke House's stately dining room with the Garibaldi Oak standing proudly next to the drive, Captain Jack was adding a couple of rueful notes in his diary while shells landed around him:

'This at sunset – we are covering the retirement and receiving a little long range fire from big guns and Pompoms [mobile 13 mm cannons]. Boers revealed surprising strength and kept their guns in action all day – attack has failed. Casualties are 200.'

By the time election day came, the worry back home was getting desperate and father-in-law Sir Harry Crichton, he of Hampshire Yeomanry renown, got himself to the War Office with the plan of telegramming the latest Seely news to the party on the stump. When the telegram came through, it was mistakenly handed direct to Nim. 'Have no positive confirmation of Jack's death in action', it read, 'but fear the worst.'

With such drama around the Seely candidature, success at the poll had an inevitability about it. He was elected by a thousand votes, quite a substantial majority in those days of limited franchise, when of course no women could vote, despite Nim's central role in the campaign. All that was needed was to tell the new MP that if he survived, the House of Commons and the Conservative Party awaited him.

The news took a fortnight to travel, by which time his squadron were patrolling across the veld near Harmonia, about forty miles south of Senekal, as part of General Rundle's campaign to bottle up the main Boer forces of De Wet and Prinsloo in the Brandwater Basin, an area with Basutoland and the Drakensberg mountains along the south-west and other ridges completing the circle. By then the privations in the field were becoming marked. There were no tents, so after being very hot in the day they had to sleep under the stars in the freezing cold night. What's more, there was a serious lack of food and water. They were first on half- and then at one stage on quarter-rations. How many MPs would record what should be the crowning elation of their election as just part of another not too pleasant day in the field?

'June 9th Saturday. Took out patrol 7-30. Very sharp frost, Shifted camp 2pm three miles on Senekal road. C Heseltine returned bringing news that I am elected for Isle of Wight by 1062. Also bringing warm clothing for men from Nim and, above all, letters from her and her pathetic picture.'

Next day there is a 'wired to constituents' diary note, but through this long High Veld winter the new MP's main ambition was to keep himself and his troops warm and fed and mounted, and to try to push this increasingly 'wearisome' campaign to its conclusion. Lord Roberts may have been doing well further north but Seely's diary entry for 5 June, which had included, 'Official news at 5pm Pretoria surrendered. Great rejoicing', had been preceded by, 'Bought £60 warm clothing for men.'

At a time when the average annual wage for a farm labourer was forty-five pounds, sixty pounds was a fair sum of one's own money to spend on a strength recorded the same day as '4 officers, 77 men, 116 horses', and the extremes of heat and cold on the veld are best conveyed by an incident recorded a little later:

'I actually saw infantrymen laid out in a dead faint from the heat on the side of the track, while my pony was trying to beat a hole in the thick ice in the spruit [stream] alongside the road in the vain endeavour to get a drink of water.'

Seely's voyage to New Zealand on the *Kaikoura* had had its dramas, but there was always a cabin to return to. There had been soaking, freezing moments on the *William Slaney Lewis* (the Brooke Lifeboat) but there was Brooke House on the shore and Lingard, the old butler, to run the hot bath. This was a lot less pleasant: 'June 17th Sunday. Put up tents – first time for just over two months – pouring rain all day – very cold.'

And the horse situation was getting desperate. The inadequacy of the British cavalry's typical English 'hunter' was becoming more and more apparent, his own good fortune in having the hardy and now undyed Maharajah more evident by the day. But for many others, the horses were in trouble. 'Must have more horses and food for them', he had noted at the beginning of May. 'Now have 30 remounts – from pony catching, native chiefs and own kaffirs [native troops].'

But the attrition continued. One morning in June he records supervising the shooting of twenty horses too debilitated to continue and on 15 July there is a significant note: 'Bought Basuto horse £25.' Significant not just for the price, extremely substantial by local standards, but for the recognition that these hardy little Basuto ponies were the conveyance required.

Maharajah had been and was to remain Seely's one constant source of success in South Africa. The long weeks of mutual dependency on the veld formed a bond between man and horse which forever sealed in Seely's mind those desert words about a horse being the greatest ally that a man could have. Not only did Maharajah follow him around like a dog, but the experience of getting so close to a horse was one that Seely was able to replicate with other horses later in life. With Warrior, the most famous of them, that affinity was to be his saviour when life hung in the balance and his future was more a matter of hope than expectation. As for Maharajah, dog or no dog, he was more than a match for the Basutos. And that was saying something.

The Basuto ponies were barely fifteen hands but were magnificently tough and hardy. Their feet did not need shoeing, they could live off the poor grass of the veld, and they could keep up a slow but easy lope for what seemed hour after hour. A hundred years after Seely's experiences I rode a Basuto beneath that Free State sky and once I got used to the slight oddity of their loping gait, I realized that this is the conveyance for the territory.

But in July 1900 events were developing beyond Jack's angel's intercession, and they only brought anger and agony in their wake. The Hampshires had slogged back north on yet another forced march and a full month on their casualties were suffering: 'July 9th Mew and Dyer no better, having been unattended for 3 days – demanded official enquiry.' A new assertive impatience at what he calls 'the incompetent and old fashioned military mind' is beginning to shine through. A week later the news is far more bitter. And the comment after the final entry has a ghastly unwritten poignancy. It is just one long pencil-drawn dash.

'July 16th Monday. Received news Keenan shot dead. Buried by Kaffirs near Boer Lines. Climbed Kopjes. Pratt told me my Tom was killed————'

Tom Conolly had been his life's closest friend. How much now for climbing the church tower at Harrow? For holidays at Castletown, at Brooke and that skull-cracking one at Davos? What use the memory of the *Kaikoura* voyage and all that kiwi feather excitement? How deadly that 'no surrender' vow which the pair of them had sworn in those bull days at Cape Town? Conolly's troop had suddenly found itself surrounded by De la Rey's commando at Nitral's Neck in Natal. It was 'a fair cop'. Hands up would seem the obvious option. But Conolly had vowed. He was fast and tough and Irish and hadn't been two years in the Harrow rugby team for nothing. He shot the Boer closest to him. He got three bullets in exchange.

Seely was a very clubbable man who inspired great affection. But he never quite replaced 'my Tom'. Perhaps it was as well that he had little time to ponder his grief as the campaign to close on De Wet and Prinsloo in the Brandwater Basin was coming to a head.

The locals were getting restive: not just the Boers but the supposedly neutral native chiefs across the Free State's eastern border into Basutoland (today's Lesotho). They had been given nominal independence under British 'Protection' in 1870. They had a fast-flowing river and steep mountains as natural defences. They had few rifles, but with clubs and spears they could make things pretty unpleasant – especially at night. They needed reminding that as neutrals they should not allow Boers passage to escape.

On 24 July De Wet managed to slip through the supposedly tightly drawn net of British troops to the north. But he had a mere 1,500 people with him. Prinsloo had 4,000. He would be Britain's biggest prize of the war so far. On Friday 27 July Seely was based near Fouriesburg, towards the southern end of the basin. Early in the morning a rider galloped up with special new orders. It was feared Prinsloo would try to break out to the east by crossing the

Caledon River and escaping into Basutoland. Seely was to take his 100-strong squadron and stiffen up the local Basuto chief not to allow the Boers through. What followed was, in every sense, a cameo from another world.

The crossing point across the Caledon was down a steep escarpment some fifteen miles to the north-east. The company were as usual sleeping in the open, heads tucked in behind the saddles, the horses tethered up in five 'rings', their heads being linked together, most of them lying down but the sick ones standing up. After weeks on the veld the squadron was like a wild thing, always ready to move.

'There is no packing up to be done,' explains Seely as he describes the urgency of that extraordinary morning,

> officers jumping to their feet; sergeants running around to the men and waking them up; a man running past me with the saddle on his head, his bridle over his arm, his tiny store of personal belongings in one hand and two hard biscuits in the other.
>
> Within ten minutes every horse was saddled up and the men were standing by their horses ready to mount. Then away we went, one troop as advance guard at a canter, with scouts in pairs galloping out to get two or three miles in advance fanwise. The remaining three troops followed at a walk, until the advance guard had got four miles ahead, when they also cantered on in column of troops, with their own scouts a couple of miles distant on either side of them. Following them were Driscoll's Scouts recently attached to my command. I was in the centre of the fan of scouts as was the good custom of the war.

Today there is a tarmac road from Fouriesburg carrying cars and tractors, but the essential raw ruggedness of the terrain, bordered on the east by a steep escarpment running down to the swift-flowing Caledon below, is just as Seely and his local scouts would have encountered it. To the west the land is open, which means that a good rifle shot can give you what the diary euphemistically calls 'a warm time'. It began to get warm as they hacked along that morning.

After a couple of hours they had got clear of the enemy bullets and arrived above the Caledon ford. Then, as now, it was a horrifically steep descent. So much so that a couple of horses tripped and rolled 'like rabbits' down the slope. Halfway down the company halted and took out the telescope. Across the river, the chief awaited.

Seely took just two men with him: his ADC Bobby Johnson, who was later to become Sir Robert Johnson, Master of the Royal Mint, and the ubiquitous Harry Smith. Once across the river it was apparent the reception committee was a large one.

> They were in a great semi-circle grouped around a fierce looking fat man seated on a rock. I rode into the semi-circle, jumped off my pony, advanced to the chieftain sitting on the rock and held out my hand. He looked at my hand as if it were some curious specimen then looked up at me and shook his head. I addressed him in English but again he shook his head. A thousand naked warriors, all armed with spears, and a few with rifles, listened to my words and observed the menacing shake of the head of their chief. There was a murmur – not a friendly murmur – and the semi-circle came nearer to me. I turned about and shouted:
>
> 'Is there anyone who speaks English?'
>
> There was no answer. It was a tense moment, and I did not see a way out, when all at once a voice from the back shouted out in a strange, piping squeak:
>
> 'Moi, je parle le français.'

Salvation comes in many forms, and this one arrived thanks to French missionaries who had originally targeted Basutoland and had taught our friend lingua franca. But while communications had begun to be established, negotiations were anything but simple.

Apparently Seely started off all right: lots of stuff about speaking on behalf of the Great White Queen and how some of her nasty Dutch enemies were trying to escape British forces and if he, the chief, stopped them crossing the river the Great White Queen would smile on him for ever and ever.

The warriors seemed to like this and cheered every mention of the Great White Queen. But the chief was not so sure. Who were these three men? How did he know it wasn't some sort of trick? What if Prinsloo and his 4,000 men came over the hill in a minute? He shook his head and told the missionary pupil to tell them to get back across the river.

Then Seely put his neck on the line. He played the 'I have the whole British army behind me' card he was to use again in even more critical circumstances eighteen years later. He said that if the chief obeyed all would be well, but if he didn't the Great White Queen's vengeance would be awful – 'terrible things would happen and the waters of the Caledon may well be red with your blood'.

The pause while this was translated must have been a tense one. But the trump worked. The chief expanded into a smile. No wicked Dutchman would be allowed across the river. He would be friends. He would send us pigs and food. He would like the message to go to the Great White Queen.

Maybe the message got to Prinsloo. For two days later, on Sunday 29 July 1900, he surrendered all his forces just ten miles to the north, and for Seely's force another set of restive locals became the problem. He was supposed to proceed back through the Golden Gate Pass to Harrismith, accepting surrenders from local Boers on the way. It was a simple order to give. If you are reduced to just four officers and sixty men and holed up in a remote farmhouse with all outlying settlements occupied by your still-armed enemy, it was not such a happy instruction to receive.

The Golden Gate Pass is huge and forbidding even today. Any lookout could easily assess how tiny this 'conquering force' actually was. Any organized group could have picked them off without much delay. But they didn't. Most surrendered arms quite civilly when the Queen's men came to call. Some just stole away. Seely understood. He was beginning to appreciate this 'enemy'. They 'behaved like gentlemen'. It was their land and there should be a settlement rather than dragging on with these forced marches whilst the likes of Botha and De Wet rallied their commandos to a harsher and much longer study.

The man who got back to Harrismith on 10 August and cheered

with his troops when they saw their first train in four months was beginning to question. He was still a fervently loyal subject. He would always remain a believer in 'my country, right or wrong'. But where there were wrongs, he was going to shout about them and within a couple of months he would face a court martial for it.

12

Sickness and Anger

It had been coming for a long time. Seely got to Harrismith at the beginning of August 1900 and the flare-up which led him to face the court martial under General Rundle, the commander of the 8th Division and capturer of Prinsloo, occurred at the end of October. But his anger at the rigidity of the military mind had been building ever since he and his squadron realized how lousy both their new base and new operations were.

Then, as now, Harrismith looked pleasant enough. Set beneath the massive flat-topped mountain of Platberg, it is where the Durban road forks west for Bloemfontein or north for Johannesburg and Pretoria. Then as now it had a fine long main street with a church and a club and a golf course. It was safe from Boer attacks. But for Seely, and for so many others, it was a place of argument and disease.

The first church service did not augur well. There was a new vicar with a poor voice, who blithely announced 'O, little town of Bethlehem' as the next hymn, apparently unaware of the African Bethlehem just fifty miles to the west along one of the most ambushed routes in the Free State.

It was now four full months since they had joined the 8th Division west of Senekal and set off on the endless series of marches and Boer-chasing, bullet-ducking skirmishes towards and across the Brandwater Basin. Throughout that time Seely and his squadron had been in the open, and by turns very hot, very cold, very hungry and, almost always, very tired. It was now a full fortnight since a galloper had come through with the Prinsloo news that, 'The enemy has surrendered unconditionally.' Harrismith was supposed to be heaven. Not hell.

But the devil was doing his work. By the second Sunday the normally so ebullient Jack is recording, 'have not been so miserable before'. The vicar had chosen an 'unpleasantly pathetic hymn'. Jack had sent a long wire to Nim but 'still no news from home'. Worst of all there was a huge wrangle between his young officers, Peacock and Johnson. 'I think everybody is plagued out, hence these rows.' It is his first reference to the biggest killer of the war. By December the War Office would have logged 12,000 deaths, 7,000 of them from typhoid and other diseases. The cemetery at Harrismith was filling up with British dead. Seely would be lucky not to join them himself.

First there was another week, another dust storm, another row. 'Too much drink about – one of my men caught – everything going wrong – if we can't go home, how I wish we were trekking or fighting again. It keeps people together.' On Wednesday 22 August at least that wish is granted: 'Marched 10 am with 6 days rations and secret instructions.' It did not help him for long.

Within a couple of days he was feeling 'very ill'. Within a week he was hospitalized in Harrismith: 'Have got "gastro-entiritis" which sounds so imposing it makes me feel better.' A few days later he was evacuated to Durban. Any study of the mortality rates in Harrismith suggests that the move, a typical officer bonus, almost certainly saved him and it was a month before he rejoined his team. A month that included six visits to the dentist ('rather painful'), a lunch with a lady called Jesse Cooper at 'Sunrise', a move to Howick General Hospital, '3,000 foot up – supposed to be the healthiest place in Natal.' There was riding, golf, tennis, dinners, chess and a cable from Nim to say that he would be unopposed in the upcoming general election.

But there was also unfinished business and with it mounting aggravation. On 7 October he finally caught up with his men a hundred miles north of Harrismith at Standerton: 'found my squadron in camp, almost as pleased to see me as I them'. Two days later they set off south, taking a huge convoy of supplies to the beleaguered garrisons of the veld: 'a great trail of ox wagons and much heavy transport, making us particularly vulnerable to attack'. Days would be difficult, nights spooky, no romance under these stars. It would be exactly three exhausting, dangerous and enraging weeks before the whole operation would finally lumber into Harrismith. With Seely under arrest.

Today this part of the Free State is wide, empty, open farmland with just the odd homestead and native village scattered about. God knows how lonely and difficult it must have been as the long laboured convoy heaved along across that open veld, camping at dark, never sure from where the next Boer attack would come. This was a land made for the mounted guerrilla attack. This was the lair of De Wet.

The territory, while open, has enough undulations running through it to give cover for an aggressor intent on harrying the convoy and its protectors every hour of the day and night. And dotted around the landscape are sharply rising little hills (kopjes) providing the perfect natural lookout posts for the Boers to know exactly how far the slow-moving convoy had come.

The diary of those first weary thirty-five miles from Standerton to the river-crossing, one-street, cattle town of Vrede gives a picture very close to those old film memories of the cavalry guarding the wagon trains in the Wild West.

October 9th. March 7 miles covering advance.

October 10th. March covering rear of convoy. 30 Boers on right flank – a little shooting – no damage.

October 11th. Marched 6 a.m. covering left flank. Went forward 5 miles with three troops to cut off Boers but they were driven the wrong way – Sergeant of IY [Imperial Yeomanry] killed. Boers on left kept trying to get at convoy – we managed to keep them off – a good deal of shooting for some hours – saw convoy safe into Vrede, then retired from our last position at dusk – no casualties.

The next day started at six thirty, included what Seely considered a hare-brained kopje assault and did not return to camp, 'all very tired', until four thirty. 'All's well that ends well', he recorded, 'but such schemes would not often succeed', and the pattern soon emerges of a long and exasperating journey. As the wagon train plodded wearily on towards the red-brick cattle town of Reitz, another sixty miles to the south-west, matters took an uglier turn: 'rest of mounted troops went farm burning – thank heaven I was not there'.

The policy, started by Roberts and embraced by Kitchener, of torching farms anywhere near known Boer activity, upset Seely from both a tactical as well as a humane point of view. Tactically, he argued, a charred farmhouse would provide un-burnable cover for Boer commando rifles as well as an enduring legacy of bitterness against the British. Meanwhile, if you destroyed all the cover and provisions of the farming family you were then duty bound to gather up all the women and children for their own protection, however distressing that experience may be.

It was a situation he absolutely hated, and he wouldn't have yet known how much worse it was to become in the tented prison camps, which proved wholly inadequate for the numbers of women and children involved and for the onset of the worst winter in memory. The attrition rate from disease became appalling, particularly amongst the children, and the term 'concentration camp' added nothing but shame to Britain's name. By 19 October Seely's own morale was at its lowest ebb: 'There will be many suicides', he records, 'if we do not return from Harrismith.'

Next day was no better: 'Marched 5-30 am with Gloucester squadron to meet the GOC coming from Reitz – horses rather done. The whole move a mistake. Returned camp 10 pm.' These are just pencil notes in a diary liable to censorship, but the anger from such a usually sunny character comes burning off the page.

The weather was a mixture of blazing heat and drenching rain. In eight months Seely and his men had become hardened to the conditions and in turn had refined their own rules of operation under fire. Amongst these was that the senior man in any party should be the first to arrive at any position and, if attacked, the last to leave. By Monday 29 October the great convoy had finally creaked, not only through Bethlehem, but to within two days of

Harrismith itself. With one of his men shot through the neck while actually talking to him the day before, the newly elected MP was still in no mood to relax his regulations. Especially not when a big Boer attack developed on the rearguard of the ox wagons and Seely had to quickly get his four troops into defensive positions on the nearest hill. So when the stiff-headed regimental commander came thundering up and said to leave two troops in position and retire the other two further up the line, Seely duly despatched them with his deputy and stayed behind to hold out against increasingly heavy shell and rifle fire.

No prizes for guessing the reaction when the regimental military genius galloped back and cried out haughtily, 'Captain Seely, I ordered you to retire with two troops, leaving two in position. Why are you still on the hill?' The situation was getting ugly in every sense:

'I tried to explain by shouting as best I could to the regimental commander, but shells were dropping about him – one very close – while this argument was proceeding. In a lull I heard him say: "Will you obey my order and retire to the position you are to take up?" I shouted back "No," and returned to the crest of the hill to direct operations.'

There was plenty to direct and it took a fair while and a lot of bullets before the convoy was at last far enough away for safety:

It was a long time before we rejoined the column, and when we did, it took me still longer to canter the whole length on a tired pony in order to report the success of our efforts to the regimental commander. When I found him I was very tired, hungry and thirsty, but, frankly, elated at the complete success of this very minor, but to us, very critical operation. I was going to tell him that we had held on for two hours and had got everyone alive away, including the wounded. In my own mind I was sure he would reply with words of cordial congratulation, thinking that just for once I had behaved really quite well. I reported to him as I proposed. The unexpected answer came back: 'You may consider yourself under arrest.'

He wasn't joking. Captain Seely had disobeyed a superior officer's order and was in it up to his neck. He was under arrest and by King's Regulations must continue under arrest until a court martial condemned or released him. He would be on parole until they got to Harrismith but must meanwhile hand over to his second in command, Geoffrey Heseltine. 'GH says I am between the devil and a VC.' The sympathy was all with Seely, but the betting was on banishment and disgrace.

Two days later the court martial was heard in a little one-storey house on the edge of town. There was the usual long table carrying the sword of judgement. In the chair was General Sir Leslie Rundle himself, the same Rundle who had sent personal congratulations after a separate kopje-storming incident only the previous Friday. Seely was nervous but unrepentant. He had technically disobeyed an order but would do the same again. He was sent from the room.

Eventually the man nicknamed 'Sir Leisurely Trundle' for the slowness of his advance through Natal called the captain back in. The court had considered all the circumstances, accepted the admission of an offence and had decided on a reprimand. But they had also decided to reinstate Seely to his command. 'And I may add', concluded Sir Leisurely 'that they congratulate you, apart from the offence which you have committed, upon the efficient manner in which you conducted your defence.'

The wonders of army justice had somehow come up with a result. Seely galloped back to his unit, hailed by the cheers of the long-tented camp. And it seems the brass hats soon wanted to join in. It was only a couple of weeks later that the news came through, for that order-defying defence of the rearguard outside Harrismith had indeed made him famous. For his bravery and organization under fire he had been awarded the DSO, yet the arguments were far from over and a lot was to happen before the final, merciful embarkation. The new MP would be doing his research.

13

Bad Times on the Veld

Disgruntlement was rife. The moment the cheers had subsided back at the squadron a deputation of men came to Seely. They had volunteered in good faith almost a year ago for a war that was going to be over 'in weeks'. They had nothing to guarantee their legal rights for pay and holidays. They were getting sickened – and not just by the typhoid epidemic which was worsening all the time.

'We agree with them and Rundle with us', is Seely's note and the very next day the General despatched a senior officer to Pretoria 'to state our case to Bobs' (Lord Roberts). The prompt reaction showed that there was some post-court-martial unity amongst those in charge at Harrismith. But as the year wound out Seely's diary is a study in disillusionment halfway to despair.

It was pouring with rain. The fresh horses sent up from the Cape turned out to be 'useless Argentinian remounts', Seely, like so many others, became ill and by 7 November he was complaining, 'things altogether in a bad way – blacks and whites sulky and despondent – somebody must pull things together quickly both here and elsewhere.'

His gripes are now as much about tactics as about conditions. It's been three months since the official stance was that 'the war was almost over' and yet here he was about to be sent off once again round the Vrede–Reitz–Bethlehem–Harrismith circuit with the situation ever more unhappy and uncertain. 'Still more orders contradictory as to Police', he says. 'Orders last night state that a state of war exists and will exist until (1) prisoners of war return, (2) parties of enemy cease to snipe, which is absurd.'

Once out on the veld he found the continuing pillage operations extremely unpalatable: 'Nov 28th . . . orders to stay where we are for two or three days, rounding up and burning – the whole thing is futile – instead of hurting our enemy with mobile columns, we prowl around at two knots burning farms, which is impolitic, cruel and appears to the Boers cowardly.'

After a week back in camp visiting the sick, waiting for letters, ('worried about my Nim'), playing golf ('House of Commons v The World'), and cricket ('18 and a catch'), his squadron was back on the fire-and-pillage trail. Lord Roberts may have left Cape Town on 10 December amidst triumphal celebrations but there was nothing triumphant about the morale on the veld.

'December 11th Split into parties of 200 collecting cattle, sheep, horses, mealies, food of all kinds, also the women from the farms. We take such an infinitesimal proportion of the total that it is all useless – why not find Boer himself and fight him – we know where to find him.'

Harrismith was not a happy place. In Britain twelve months before they had all been buzzing with 'let's go and get the Boer' jingoism. This Christmas and New Year were going to feel very different.

December 25th: Gave Nim's tobacco to the men, also plum pudding – they came to say nice things and cheer – the one bright spot in a most melancholy day.

December 31st Dined with Generals and Doctors – 'absent friends, sweethearts and wives' – all rather sad.

In this mood black humour is often the best resort, and a week later officialdom provided a corker. Seely's squadron and three big columns of troops were involved in what was becoming a dangerous shoot-up with a large group of Boers. Seely's team managed to get themselves an elevated position on the nearest kopje, from where they noticed the great Platberg heliograph flashing above Harrismith at the spot they called 'Kitchener's Chair'.

In the absence of anything but the most primitive of telegram and letter services, this heliograph (a signalling mirror) was visible on a clear day from fifty miles away and was practically the CNN of the Harrismith–Vrede–Bethlehem circuit. The first time Seely and his signallers got their own 'helio' up to communicate, two Boer bullets shot one of the legs of the tripod. It was a dodgy business getting it up for a second go, but eventually they logged on to the distant flashes and began laboriously to write down and read out the weighty message that their masters had decided to send across the skies.

'Lord Roberts', the flashes spelt out, 'landed at Cowes yesterday in order to meet Queen Victoria. He said "the war is nearly over and nothing remains but a few guerrilla bands."'

Down below Seely, three generals were struggling to make headway against the typically well-targeted enemy attack. Up beside him his sergeant turned from where he was crouching beneath a rock, the crack of the last bullet ringing just above his head. If that message didn't make you laugh, you would just have to cry.

'Well, sir,' he said, as sergeants do, 'they may call them baboons if they like, but they shoot bloody straight.'

Lord Roberts's optimism did not do poor old Victoria Regina much good, the sun finally setting for the Great White Queen on 23 January 1901 and the symbolism of the end of an era with so much unfinished wasn't lost on subjects far afield. 'Jan 24th. News of Queen's death. Paraded squadron – great grief.'

The royal passing may have caused sadness but it made no difference on the ground. The weather was beginning to scorch, 2 February was 'the hottest day we have had' and 3 February sounds a horror.

'Marched 6 am. About 200 Boers – had a rather worrying time on the left flank, nobody hit. Why can't we fight these gentry, instead of having perpetually to fend them off – it gets worse instead of better – what has become of Englishmen. Burnt two farms – Took one prisoner – hot and foolish day.'

If Seely's own and his squadron's morale had been tested before, the next month was brutal. He would be beset by bullets, shells, weather, weariness, extreme illness and unwittingly sign two foot-notes in South African history.

First they slogged the hundred miles up to Standerton. On the way they suffered their usual rearguard harassment from Boer commandos, they discovered that typhoid was so bad in Vrede that the whole garrison was being evacuated and Seely nearly got killed by 'friendly fire' when a misdirected shell missed him by inches.

Imagine the relief when they finally made Standerton and Seely was able to tell his men that they had three weeks for rest and refit. He dined with his fellow officers, who included Bromley Daven-port, the man who had carried the official complaint to Pretoria in November and who himself was to later become an MP. They took wine 'to celebrate the opening of Parliament'. In Seely's tent there was a real bed. He told Harry Smith to let him sleep round the clock.

Imagine the groaning, eye-squeezing consternation when he awoke to find Smith apologetically shaking him up at 1 a.m. New orders had come in, his squadron and others were to report immediately to the station to entrain for Newcastle, eighty miles to the south-east. When he writes, 'Great difficulty in getting trans-port loaded', I can hardly bear to think about it.

To make matters much worse, the rains had come with a vengeance. It poured all night – 'Very miserable for men and horses.' It poured all next day and for a full week thereafter. Every-one's clothes were soaking. Seely's reputation had grown enough for him to now have 400 under his command as they tried to march through the mud out of Utrecht towards the Pivaan River. But the damp had finally got his stomach. 'Horrid pains', he admitted, 'under pinafore.'

It was the start of a bout of dysentery which would reduce him, quite literally, to skin and bone. It would be ten days before he finally stayed in his tent and a doctor forced him off to hospital. Meanwhile the rains were making progress practically impossible: 'Every stream a torrent, every river a flood. Both the broad, flat banks of the Pivaan River were so soggy and deep that the oxen sank into the mud until they disappeared, and the convoys could not be got through. The wounded suffered the extremity of misery. They could not be extricated and their wounds gangrened.'

Seely was not at his sharpest and the Boer cause should be eternally grateful. For the whole idea of the Utrecht operation was to try to pin down Louis Botha, the most charismatic of all the Boer generals, the man who had cracked the bull whip to drive his weakening men back into the line at Spion Kop, the man who kept the British at bay right into 1902 and who in later life was to become the first president of the South African Republic. Botha was a very hands-on soldier. So too was Seely.

Both men were in the habit of patrolling their front line at all hours. One night at a place called Lone Tree Hill their paths crossed unknowingly, and the stomach-cramped Seely, normally so deadly with any sort of firearm, loosed off what he liked to describe as two of the most important bad shots in history

> At about one o'clock I reached one of my posts, a corporal and two men, just twenty yards to the north of the lone tree. A fine rain was falling and there was a mist, but the moon was up and one could see a little way. I lay down beside the corporal who said that he had just heard a horse's hoofs. Hardly had he said it when a figure appeared dimly in the mist, on horseback, riding towards us. The corporal was about to fire, but I snatched his rifle from him, whispering, 'Let him come on.' The mist was drifting in swathes over the hill and for a moment he was invisible, while I heard the horse advancing on the stony ground; then for a second I saw a commanding figure silhouetted against the grey mist. The corporal was so excited that he shouted to me quite loud: 'Shoot, sir.' The figure turned and galloped away. I fired, re-loaded and fired again. I ran forward with the corporal but although the range was no more than fifteen yards I had made a clean miss both times.

Eight years later Seely as a British Cabinet Minister and Botha as Prime Minister of the Free State would be dining together at Buckingham Palace. They had become firm friends, but only because Seely had been ill enough to miss the bearded Boer and then lucky enough to have another of his guardian angels rescue him from near-fatal sickness. She was Mrs Graham, the wife of the commandant in Utrecht, and she took him under her roof when he finally yielded to doctor's advice on 2 March. He was in terrible shape. For sheer, consistent privation, it had been the worst four months he would ever endure.

14

The Long Haul Home

Mrs Graham had let a skeleton into her house. Considering that Seely did not even get his first egg down for a fortnight and that when he finally made the comfort of the Rand Club in Johannesburg on 22 March he was a full two stone underweight, it is no exaggeration to say that given normal conditions, let alone normal soldier's conditions, Seely would not have pulled through. But it is typical that he cavalierly rode his luck to make the next six weeks some of the most significant of his whole career. While he was recuperating in Johannesburg he began to dine with the great and good; when he was sent on to Kroonstad to train up new recruits he began three weeks of intense, sixteen-hour-a-day administration. In between he was involved in an incident that remains a legend in South African history. For a budding politician, it would be hard to find six weeks to match them.

Those who met him at this stage would have found an emaciated, enervated, but educated, and now campaign-toughened young man of thirty-two. His twelve months in the field had brought him an understanding of the hardships of friend and foe alike. 'The trouble with you soldiers,' said High Commissioner Sir Alfred Milner after a long session with the young captain, 'is that you all become pro-Boer.'

If Milner had known how Seely would be immortalized by a frieze in Bloemfontein, and by a statue in Hoopstad, ninety miles north-west, of a young boy facing a firing squad, he would no doubt have dipped his rather doleful, academic face in a touch of 'I told you so'. But the story of 'the boy who would not talk' remains one of the most touching in the whole Seely legend.

One night Seely was awakened with the news that an important Boer commando was believed to be holed up in a farm some twenty miles away. While 'the faithful Smith' saddled Maharajah and his own pony, Seely briefed Bobby Johnson to gather twenty men with whom they would try to get to the farmhouse before daybreak. They didn't quite make it and as they came in towards the farmhouse in the dawn light three figures could be seen galloping away into the distance. After a brief ineffectual chase Seely rode back to the farmhouse.

'There I found Bobby, with his men and an extraordinarily good looking Dutch lad of about twelve years of age standing with them. On the way back I had realized that the hunter had become the hunted and unless we could find out where the commando lay, we were almost bound to be intercepted and killed, or, worse still, captured.'

For his own and his men's safety, Seely was desperate to know where the father's commando was based. But all his demands and threats met with clear-eyed refusal. Finally he decided on the last resort. With a whisper of, 'We won't really do this', to the sergeant, he ordered out a six-man firing party, put the boy against a wall and ordered 'Load, ready, aim . . .' and while 'fire' was still unsaid, gave him one last chance to speak.

> Then I saw one of the most beautiful things that I have ever seen in my life. The boy was transfigured by patriotism and devotion. He lifted his head, looked me straight in the face, put his hands behind his back and said in a loud clear voice:
> 'Ich sall ne sag.' [I shall never tell you.]

Seely immediately walked straight over to the boy, shook him by the hand and said, 'I hope one day we will meet again.' When this story was related in Seely's book *Fear and Be Slain* thirty years later, the author appealed for the boy, now man, to come forward. After much peer-group pressure the incurably modest Japie Greyling of Hoopstad finally admitted that he had been through this experience. Seely wrote to him but sadly a meeting never occurred.

A hundred years on, I met Petro Maartens, Greyling's

granddaughter, by the new memorial to Japie's heroism in Hoopstad churchyard. It had been commissioned for the centenary and confirms Japie's place as one of the 'brave children of South Africa', already commemorated in a famous stone frieze on the wall of a government building in Bloemfontein.

Petro Maartens introduced me, as Seely's grandson, to her eighty-year-old uncle, another Japie, who only discovered his father's feat when he read about it in a school history book. To his son's pleadings the original Japie would say only that the whole affair had been very frightening and that that night he lay awake until his mother came into the bedroom and said to him, 'Whatever happens after this, it is never any good to fear or to hate.'

The Greylings and the Maartens are God-fearing Afrikaner families now coming to terms with their place in the new South Africa. They took me to the farm where little Japie's mother was held at the side of the kitchen while her son faced the firing squad. They showed me the 1960 film of the incident, with a villainous Seely sporting (somewhat incorrectly) a long musketeer's moustache.

Exactly how, or indeed whether, our two grandfathers exactly fitted into this isolated scenario will never be solved. But Seely's tribute to timeless courage, wherever it be found, rings bell-like down the years:

> As long as I live, I shall never forget that wonderful moment when the love of father, home and country triumphed over imminent and apparently certain death; nor shall I forget the look in the face of that boy, as with head erect and glistening eyes he said:
>
> 'Ich sall ne sag.'

Seely, like Milner, was due to sail back to England early in May 1901, but not before he went through an ordeal in its own way as demanding and ultimately as beneficial as anything he had been through on the veld. He arrived at Kroonstad on 12 April to see General Broadwood and apparently help out with training new recruits. Next day the general blithely embarked on a trek, leaving

Seely in command of 800 people to train up for service and precious little staff or system to do it with.

To his great credit he attacked this new task with just as much enthusiasm as he galloped at kopjes or argued for an end to farm burning. 'Wish there were 26 hours in the day', he records early. He had no time for church for the first two Sundays, he reorganized training methods and by 23 April there was no concealing the pride: 'sent off 100 men by rail, 65 and 140 horses by road – have housed, trained and despatched nearly 400 men.'

He had also found and been angered by the overcrowding and disease in the local concentration camps which would become a cause célèbre back home. The remarkable Emily Hobhouse would be stepping ashore from the same boat as Milner and would soon begin to horrify Britain with her stories and correct predictions that thousands, mostly children, would die, and babies would have almost no chance of survival. Seely was at last able to go to church on the evening of 28 April but beforehand his conscience was pricking: 'Went to worry the camp people as to their insanitary state for the twentieth time.'

But his own priority was now to make the 700-mile journey down to Cape Town before his boat sailed. He made it with four days to spare, and is it any coincidence that 'wired home to Nim that we sail on Tuesday on *Mongolian*' in his diary is immediately followed by 'went to Cathedral'? After going to church that Sunday he 'walked a long way up the hill at sunset – it is strange to be going home'. Seely's experiences were making him thoughtful.

The voyage aboard the junk bucket that was the *Mongolian*, two full weeks slower than Milner's aboard the *Saxon*, had plenty to make him pensive. The gallant Maharajah got settled and soon had his coat clipped to ease the heat. Seely didn't get sick, but the men soon did. Trooper McCudden died on the 19th, so too did the engines for a while as the crew tried to repair a leak.

Seely taught himself longitude and latitude to keep his mind working, but the hospital bay was full and stiflingly hot. Three more soldiers died before *Mongolian* reached Las Palmas on 30 May and Trooper Watkins of the Manchesters died as they anchored there.

Two more went on the final leg, but in Seely's heart concern for his soldiers was beginning to be overwhelmed by other thoughts rather closer to home.

On 7 June 1901 the man who had bought 'Boer toys for my kiddies' had one more frustrating, heart-aching day to endure: 'Going very slow. Radford and Holland better. 107 miles from Nim.' When they sighted the Needles at 11 a.m. on 8 June this was a homecoming in every sense for someone who had lived and sailed for so long around the Isle of Wight.

Mr Laws, the pilot who would navigate them up Southampton Water, came on board at 12.30. Seely records that Laws prefaced his duties with the slightly comical touch of reciting a greeting in verse. As they came round the Needles the coastguard station at Totland signalled 'Welcome'. Boats were bedecked with bunting off Yarmouth harbour. Best of all and joy of joys, at 1.15 he could see his father-in-law's ninety-ton steam yacht, *Chimera*, and on it Nim waving madly. They docked at 4 p.m. By eight he was ashore at Ryde and into the arms of his beloved Island, with Nim and Frank and Emmy and little John who said shyly, 'Is this my Daddy?'

It may have been a privileged life but it was already a committed one. If four years earlier Seely had actually become the parliamentary candidate for the Isle of Wight as his father had intended, he would have done so as a mere scion of the great. Now this absentee candidate was returning with a great deal to say and experience aplenty. He was a man with a mission.

15

The Club of Clubs

He was a hero in an age that loved its heroes. Within a week he had taken his fill of tributes from his devoted Islanders and entrained to London to tread the stage for them at Westminster.

There was always an element of theatricality about Seely and so he took to the Commons even more naturally than he had done to the veld. His grandfather, father and now his brother had all been MPs, political life had been as much an expectation as an aspiration. Of course, these were very different, much more reverent times, when the return of a war hero could be quickly hailed as proof of the enduring superiority of our island race. But even making allowances for the century which separates us from that June afternoon in 1901, the *Yorkshire Post* description of the scene as Seely took his seat waxes quite ludicrously lyrical:

> Questions over, the eyes of the House instinctively wandered to the bar. There, tall and straight, like a lance in rest, was a bronze-cheeked, fair-haired, blue-eyed man, as fine a specimen of the Saxon as ever trod the floor. There was a warm cheer. The Saxon bowed. Unattended he advanced up the floor. When in the centre he stopped, clapped his heels together, and bowed. He moved to the table, clapped his heels again, and bowed once more. He signed the roll, and when the Speaker stretched out his arm, and with a smile gave the Saxon a handshake, the house cheered again. For this was Captain Seely, Member for the Isle of Wight, fresh from the wars and looking fit, although malaria did bowl him over.

His election experiences are unique. Captain Seely, at the head of a troop of Imperial Yeomen, was one of the first to go to South Africa when there sounded the alarm of war. Whilst away there fell a vacancy to the Isle of Wight because its representative, Sir Richard Webster, then Attorney-General, was raised to the high office of Master of the Rolls. Captain Seely, one of the most popular men in the Island, who a while before had received a medal from the French Government for saving the lives of French fishermen on the Wight coast, was asked by cable to stand as Tory candidate, and his wife would fight the Radicals for him while he was fighting the Boers for his country. The lady took him to the head of the poll with a noble majority. But Captain Seely never came home to sit in the last Parliament. Then arrived the general election. Would he stand again? Yes. But this time no Radical had the courage to face the lady. He was returned unopposed. Captain Seely was still at the front fighting when all the others were taking the oath. But he marched up the floor today as brave and handsome a young Saxon as we have in Parliament, and he got a welcome that must have sent a thrill to the heart of the woman who was watching the scene from behind the bars that shield the ladies' gallery.

It's that sense of certainty once again. As far as Jack Seely was concerned his course was written in the stars. His father and grandfather had been in the Commons for more than fifty years, his older brother Charles was the present member for Lincoln, now he himself would join what at that time was the most influential club the world had ever seen.

He loved it and they loved him. Not just gushing Tory sketch writers who would soon turn against him when they discovered he was actually a Radical in disguise, but MPs from all parties. It says much for Seely that in addition to his established friends from Harrow and Trinity, he was also devoted to such diverse characters as the Irish Nationalists John Redmond and T.P. O'Connor, and was in awe of the Father of the House, the great miners' leader Thomas Burt. These three were hardly the most obvious soulmates for the husband of the granddaughter of one of the great Anglo-Irish Protestant families of Fermanagh, or indeed for the son of one of the richest coal owners in the kingdom.

But the most significant of all the friendships was with the 26-year-old MP for Oldham whom he had last seen galloping to the top of that mountain in Dewetsdorp fourteen months earlier. Winston Churchill had won his seat at the general election and was now at the centre of that group of young, privileged, free-thinking Tories gathered around Lord Salisbury's son Lord Hugh Cecil and so known as 'the Hughligans'. Seely was welcomed in.

Churchill was already a national phenomenon of the first water. The son of the brilliant but ill-fated Lord Randolph, whose biography he was shortly to write, he had become a headline figure himself with his capture and escape in South Africa, not to mention his graphic descriptions of it in the *Morning Post* and in the American lecture tour he undertook to raise funds after the election. The £10,000 generated would represent more than £600,000 today and would allow Churchill the freedom to launch himself into his MP's duties, for which there was no salary until 1910.

Such financial concerns did not of course apply to the member for the Isle of Wight, who throughout this time depended entirely on the support of his proud and munificent father. But what made him attractive to Churchill was his boldness and courage, not his bank balance. Winston was such a many-sided character that he liked to pack his friendships with people to match his various parts. If Hugh Cecil provided an intellectual tour de force and the Duke of Westminster an unwavering aristocratic support, Jack Seely, neither an intellectual nor a blue-blood, was the dashing, fearless man of action to whom Churchill could also directly relate.

In her book *Winston Churchill as I Knew Him*, Asquith's daughter Violet Bonham Carter points up the Hugh Cecil–Jack Seely contrast and, in view of the impact Winston was to have on Jack over the next twenty years of constant meetings, fellowship and correspondence, it's worth looking again at her unique insight into what it meant to be part of Churchill's inner circle.

'His friendship was a stronghold against which the gates of Hell could not prevail. There was an absolute quality in his loyalty, known only to those safe within its walls. Their battle was his own. He would concede no inch of ground, no smallest point against them. In a friend he would defend the indefensible, explain away the inexplicable, forgive the unforgivable.'

To that stronghold Seely brought charm and flamboyance but he also brought unmatched direct front-line experience on the big issue of the day, the continuing conflict in South Africa. And when you consider the fevered reaction in Westminster when even a few hundred British soldiers were despatched to Afghanistan for a few weeks in 2001, it's not surprising that ninety-nine years earlier a man fresh from a war which had already lasted two years and cost thousands of British lives would be listened to with interest.

Especially as Seely did not toe the party line. After all those weeks of danger, disease and frustration on the veld he hadn't come to the mother of parliaments to stay silent. Officially he might be a politician, but from now on part of him would always be a soldier. Listening to fat party hacks at Westminster mouthing away about alleged Boer atrocities and the rationale for farm burning turned him 'blue with fury'. By the end of July he had written his first letter to *The Times*. It challenged a report that the Boers were in the habit of murdering wounded men and for all its formality still carries the firm punch of somebody who knows what he is talking about as well as the softer touch of someone who wants to help the fearful and forgive the enemy.

> I venture to ask you to publish this letter for the sake of those, tens of thousand in number, whose anxiety for their husbands, sons, brothers is great enough already without the addition of this traditional terror.
>
> During the seventeen months that I served in South Africa I had, perhaps, rather exceptional opportunities of learning how our wounded were treated by the Boers. On two different occasions men under my command who were dangerously wounded were attended to by the Boers; in each case they were tended with the greatest kindness and care, and the wounded men

themselves begged me to thank those who had been so good to them; on both occasions the general in command of the column conveyed his thanks, either personally or by letter.

I have spoken to many officers and men who have been left sick or wounded in the hands of the Boers, and in no single instance have I heard anything but gratitude expressed for the treatment they had received.

In the tense excitement of hand-to-hand fighting it may be difficult to differentiate between the wounded and the unwounded; but the relatives and friends of those now fighting can rest assured that Englishmen left wounded on the field will receive from the Boers no less care and kindness than wounded Boers have invariably received from the British.

The point was taken at the very highest level. Colonial Secretary Joseph Chamberlain invited Seely to dine privately and discuss the Boers in general and Britain's farm-burning policy in particular. The young politician, if not cowed, was mightily impressed: 'He was then at the zenith of his power and physical vigour, when it was a high privilege to talk to a man with so penetrating a brain and such incisive speech.'

But while the scene of the sunburnt young tyro and the immaculate senior statesman is a cosy one, the conclusion is interesting:

'It was a late sitting and, I remember, we ate sausages and drank champagne and stout mixed – an excellent drink much beloved by the famous Bismarck. At the end of supper Mr Chamberlain said to me, "Well I wonder if you are right. We shall know some day, in the meantime all you soldiers are what they call here Pro-Boer."'

It was a direct echo of what Alfred Milner had said in Johannesburg. Leaving aside the reference to what we jockeys used to call Black Velvet and drank to keep our morale up and the sweat flowing in the Turkish baths, there are traits emerging in the man that were to provide both the early pillars as well as later cracks in his reputation.

Apart from the already well-chronicled belief in the Empire, what was forming in Seely's public persona was a detailed wisdom on military matters and a love-thine-enemy generosity which, following five years of First World War front-line experiences, finally led him to become an arch-appeaser right up to 1939. While hindsight, of course, can see all the flaws in such a policy it cannot understand what drove him forward at the time.

At heart he was a radical. This gilded hero who at weekends went back from the big house in London to his own and his family's many other homes in the Isle of Wight was actually perceived as left of centre. By the end of the summer the local Conservative Association was already complaining that this new MP was making dangerously radical noises about such things as education, taxes and even (hush, please) the hereditary principle. And when that autumn Seely toured the Island at the suggestion of the senior and distinguished member for Southampton, Sir Barrington Simeon, he claims to have been genuinely taken aback when at the end of two rainswept and windblown weeks Sir Barrington turned to him in the dog cart and said of his speeches that 'though excellent, nobody by any stretch of the imagination could describe them as Conservative speeches'.

Seely was an issues not a party man. He had after all agreed, albeit a touch reluctantly, to stand as a Conservative when he had always seen himself as a Liberal. He was a man of wide and cross-party fellowships. And in many ways the whole point of his destiny in politics was to do his duty as he believed it to be. He needed to justify the Seely life.

And what a life it was, with the Seely homes at Queen's Gate in London, Sherwood Lodge in Nottinghamshire, Brooke House in the Island, as well as Jack and Nim's own house at 29 Spencer Road in Ryde to which the Waterloo–Portsmouth train and ferry service could whisk him back in less than three hours, not much longer than today.

Jack and Nim's family was growing. My mother, Irene, was to be born in the summer of 1902, with Patrick and Kitty to follow, making it a six-pack of children by 1907. In London, political life could be all-involving, but it seems that with Sir Charles so firmly behind him, and with increasing Hampshire Yeomanry activity, Jack abandoned any efforts to earn a living at the Bar. Or indeed to work for money at all.

Back in the Island there was the community of the lifeboat. There was golf at Bembridge, a links course along the foreshore, sailing at Cowes, bathing at Brooke and of course riding over those downs from where the wind blows, the oceans beckon and whenever Seely was given half a chance he would sit down and start composing another letter to *The Times*.

It was idyllic but he was no lotus eater. The Hughligans (or 'Hooligans') were spoiling for a chance to really shake up the government. As the negotiations for the Treaty of Vereeniging finally settled the South African war in May 1902, the Hooligans began to close on a target. They would make the military establishment heed the lessons of the veld, they would put Secretary of State William Brodrick's proposed army reforms to the sword. Seely, to the mounting horror of Isle of Wight Conservatives, was about to make his Westminster name.

16

The Road to the Chiltern Hundreds

It pays to have a specialist subject. Say what you like about Seely, and plenty did, no one in Parliament could match him for recent first-hand experience of the burning military issue of the day.

When in a debate in early August 1902 he attacked the Government for being behind the military times, wasting money on barracks rather than guns, and not having a proper structure to handle new inventions, Prime Minister Balfour himself stood up to respond. Seely had already discomfited Lord Roberts, the legendary Commander-in-Chief. He had attended the newly formed National Service League at the Duke of Wellington's Apsley House and had strongly opposed Roberts's and the League's ideas for compulsory as opposed to voluntary military service. This young man might be charming and well connected, but he was beginning to rub the establishment up the wrong way.

This only appeared to give him energy. He and Bobby Johnson, who had been through so much together in South Africa, got themselves over to Zurich to watch the Swiss army manoeuvres and back home he busied himself with encouraging the volunteer principle in general and the establishment of rifle clubs: 'Every man should be able to defend his country.'

Seely himself claimed that 1903 'marked the real beginning of my parliamentary career' and as so often in life one intense involvement quickly led to another. First up was the attack on the Brodrick army plan. The Hughligans had formed themselves into something called the Army Reform Group. Seely wrote another letter to *The Times* at the end of January and then seconded Ernest

Beckett in the group's amendment to the King's speech, saying that the War Office needed rooting out from top to bottom, that red tape had slowed the war in South Africa and that lumbering us with a much bigger but no less backward standing army 'would end by landing the country in national disaster'.

It was all heady, rebellious stuff and this must have been as privileged a bunch of dissidents as Parliament had ever seen. Beckett himself was to become Lord Grimthorpe, and alongside Churchill and Hugh Cecil there were also the future Lords Rochdale and Wimborne, not to mention Ian Malcolm, who since he had married Lily Langtry's daughter by Edward VII could claim to be a son-in-law (albeit on the wrong side of the blanket) of the King.

By all accounts feelings ran pretty high, and while it is arguable that in military terms Seely was laying up bitterness with the professional soldiers for which he would never be fully forgiven, with his political opponents, however fierce the confrontations during debate, he appeared to return to 'the club house' the best of friends. Witness this recollection:

> All through this time Mr Brodrick and his financial secretary Lord Stanley, retained their good humour and never faltered in defending a policy in which they believed, but which they knew was receiving less and less support from every quarter in the House, and outside. Never were there more honourable antagonists than these two, and I rejoice to remember that on the last night of the army estimates they came to supper with us and vowed eternal friendship, while frankly prophesying continued political enmity.

The attack was a success, the government plans were stalled, Brodrick was moved and Seely and the Hughligans had meanwhile got themselves stuck into another issue which was to generate even more heat. Joseph Chamberlain had come back from South Africa to announce plans for tariff reform and Imperial preference to try to bolster trade within the Empire. These are old slogans now but in that era they were flame to the touchpaper. Liberal thinkers had free trade as, in Seely's words, 'the ark of the covenant'. He thought tariff reform was a return to the bad old days of taxes on basic foodstuffs, of the 'dear loaf' which most affected the poor.

'Both my grandfathers had been prominent members of the Anti-Corn Law League. I had had tea with Mr Gladstone when I was a boy at Harrow and had sat on John Bright's knee as a child. The idea of returning to Protection seemed to me positively wicked.'

Chamberlain announced his plan in the House of Commons on 28 May 1903 and Seely did not hang about. The very next day, with his political confidence high after the army-reform battles, he was booked to address some unwitting members of that staunch Tory militia the Primrose League at Belvoir Castle and took the opportunity to 'denounce the scheme in uncompromising fashion'. The day after that (this gives you a glimpse of the lifestyle) he is down in yeomanry camp at Ringwood in Hampshire but still finding time to write to his closest ally:

My dear Winston,

The more I think of it the more certain I am that we are right and J.C. [Joseph Chamberlain] is wrong. But whether the majority will see it is another matter. Would Beach [Sir Michael Hicks-Beach] be President of a Free Trade Committee? So far no safe man of great reputation has said a word against the scheme. I am very fit and full of parliamentary zeal.

The game was really now afoot. Within a month Seely and Churchill had gathered a meeting of fifty-four Conservative 'Free Traders' into a House of Commons Committee room under the chairmanship of former Chancellor of the Exchequer Lord Goschen. By 13 July they had formed the Free Food League with the veteran Hicks-Beach as president, Privy Councillor Lord Hobhouse as chairman and Seely and Goschen as joint-secretaries. Churchill and Cecil were among the usual suspects and their first aim was at the very top – they wrote to Prime Minister Balfour himself.

The letter was handwritten by Seely and represented a unanimous resolution from the executive committee of this new

1. Jack's schooldays. Seely at Harrow
   in 1887 (centre top)

2. 'The deal was that you had to risk
   your life for others'

3. 'The Queen was ever so gracious. Her voice was not only a command but a caress'

4. Seely at Southampton Docks in January 1900 riding the normally white Maharajah dyed brown to meet camouflage regulations before embarking for the Boer War

5. Seely (with telescope) in the Boer War – 'An endless series of marches and Boer-chasing, bullet-ducking skirmishes'

6. The good news was he got elected an MP whilst away at the war . . .

7. . . . the bad news that he, a Liberal, got in as a Conservative

UNION IS STRENGTH.

VOTE FOR SEELY.

From photo by the Art Photographic Company, Newport, I.W.

THE FAVOUR OF YOUR

VOTE & INTEREST

IS RESPECTFULLY SOLICITED

FOR

CAPTAIN SEELY,

The Conservative & Unionist Candidate,

AT THE

Forthcoming Parliamentary Election, Wednesday, May 23, 1900.

[PLEASE TURN OVER.

8. The Spy cartoon of Seely in the Commons: 'There, tall and straight, like a lance in rest, was a bronze-cheeked, fair-haired, blue-eyed man, as fine a specimen of the Saxon as ever trod the floor.'
Yorkshire Post, June 1901

9. Jack's first wife, Emily 'Nim' Crichton. 'Back home there was an angel working in his absence. She was called Mrs Seely'

10. The Guards Review at Hyde Park, 28 April 1913. Jack Seely, Secretary of State for War, and Winston Churchill, First Lord of the Admiralty. 'Mars and Neptune, both from Harrow School and both ex-Tories as chirpy as two boys from a tuck-shop'

11. Churchill and Seely under pressure from the German threat

12. Seely and Churchill afloat

"WHEN THE STORMY WINDS DO BLOW."

13. Jack Seely, cabinet minister and lifeboatman. 'The ideal of service in the common cause of humanity'

14. Seely, Churchill, Asquith and Lloyd George together in 1913. Colleagues or conspirators?

15. 'Rock-a-bye babies, on the tree top. When the wind blows, cradle will rock. When the bough breaks, cradle will fall and down will come Seely, Asquith and all.'

Cartoons of Seely and Asquith after Seely's
resignation over the Curragh Mutiny, 30 March 1914

16. 'The Es-scapegoat' (above)

17. 'The Penitential Stool' (below)

18. Jack Seely at forty-four, widower
and father of seven with his youngest
child, Louise, in the spring of 1914

Warrior white Star

19. Jack Seely's famous charger, Warrior – the greatest horse in history?

20. 'The Arch Colonel has turned up at Antwerp full of fight and hope.' Asquith on Seely joining Churchill in Antwerp, October 1914

21. The Canadian Cavalry Brigade, 'Seely's Lions', cheer the King

Unionist Free Trade League opposing the principles of protective duties on food. It claimed that every Conservative Government for fifty years had opposed such duties and it also quoted from a recent speech of Balfour's appealing for party unity.

So about a hundred years before it did the same thing over Europe the Tory Party was in the process of tearing itself in two. Seely and Churchill gave a dinner for Balfour but the splintering process was already under way. By the autumn both the Chancellor of the Exchequer and the Secretary of State for Scotland had resigned to go with Chamberlain, and the Lord President of the Council, the Duke of Devonshire, had gone the other way. Churchill and Seely would soon be off in the same direction.

Their original aim had been to win the anti-Chamberlain argument within the party, but even Seely with his often naive optimism must have realized that they were on a collision course. In October Churchill was writing (although it was never sent) to Hugh Cecil with the suggestion that he talk through with Seely the idea of joining the Liberals. In November Seely was giving a long peroration to Shanklin Conservatives which would have made it impossible for him to stay in the party if Chamberlain won the day. In December Churchill and Seely so strongly espoused the Liberal stance at a Conservative Christmas bazaar in Manchester that the Chairman publicly denounced the pair of them from the platform.

Not surprisingly, both of their local associations were soon to disown them but it was in fact Seely who, in the spring of 1905, was the first to cross the floor of the House of Commons. But the reason he did so was not just the free trade issue, on which Churchill continued to be the most brilliant of all speakers in a campaign which, in those pre-radio, pre-television days, used to pack audiences by the thousand into halls all around the country. Seely's reason for going was the plan to import Chinese labour to the Transvaal as mine workers.

The Pretoria Government had announced this in January 1904 and Seely duly took one of his walks on Mottistone Down. The resulting letter to *The Times* opened up the controversy to such an extent that the Miners' Federation distributed copies to fan the flames. Their principal argument was against the taking of jobs from British subjects, but Seely, who claimed he felt more strongly about this than about any other issue in his whole political career, was really more concerned about the honour of the Empire than about the unemployed. For the Chinese labour ordinance, which was subsequently brought to Parliament, entailed housing the immigrants in special secure compounds and deporting them by force at the end of their contracts. This, Seely argued, was little more than slavery. In fact, it was worse than local black workers were treated. It would bring, he said, 'disgrace, disaster and dishonour' upon the Empire.

Seely's main informant was Captain Thomas Creswell, the manager of the Village Main Reef Mine with whom he had talked at length in Johannesburg in April 1901 and who was bitterly opposed to the Chinese plan. Cresswell's aim was for an all-white mining force, to avoid the racial tensions with the black workers. To add Chinese to the mix would be asking for trouble. It was a view based more on pragmatism than principle.

But Seely was on a higher horse and going straight for the government gates. True, he was a long way from what would be a currently acceptable position on human rights, but in that era he was still markedly to the left of centre. 'In the great principle of common respect for the law,' he wrote, 'the right of every man, black, white or yellow, to have a fair trial before a properly con-stituted court, summed up the whole justification for the Empire and if we were to abandon it, or allow others to abandon it, it were better the Empire had never been.'

Parliamentary proceedings came to a head in March 1905. At one stage Seely's older brother Charles produced a paper detailing the objections of the Chinese Ambassador to the labour ordinance and further inflamed the Commons with the uniquely Edwardian rebuke: 'We had come to a pretty pass, when England was reproved by a Chinaman for degrading men so near to the level of slaves.'

The climax came on 21 March. Parliament has often been a rowdy place, but it has rarely been noisier than it was when Seely stood up to speak in support of the Liberal leader's motion of censure on the government's Chinese labour bill. It was almost entirely boos and jeers until a familiar voice very briefly broke through. 'I am quite unable', came the voice of Winston Churchill, 'to hear what my honourable friend is saying owing to the vulgar clamour maintained by the Conservative Party.' More pandemonium and cries of 'traitors' followed. Seely abandoned ship, but when Balfour rose, he too was swept away by a tidal roar from the other side.

Seely, in that most wonderfully antiquated of parliamentary phrases, 'applied for the Chiltern Hundreds', the right to ask his constituency to re-elect him under a different guise. He went down to the Isle of Wight to appeal to his constituents with a little help from the fellow Hughligan whom he called his 'doughty champion during these troublous times':

'I issued an address in which I asked for the support of all parties against this pernicious scheme. Reading it again after 25 years, I see that it was an extraordinarily good address. I can say this without the least arrogance because all the best parts of it were written by Mr Churchill.'

The appeal worked, and he was returned unopposed on 6 April. As promised to his electorate, he duly took his seat amongst the Unionist Free Traders until the Chinese Labour Bill was passed, when he crossed over to the Liberal side.

It had been an impressively impassioned campaign but Seely's almost ludicrous sense of goodwill still won through. 'Throughout this time of acute bitterness my friendship with Alfred Lyttleton [the Colonial Secretary and prime opponent] was never impaired to the slightest degree. We continued to play golf together and dine together in the height of the controversy and I learnt to love and admire him more and more.'

Those are fine gentlemanly sentiments. But Seely's next stop was to an altogether harsher environment. He was to represent the slums of Liverpool.

17

Abercromby

Seely and the slums, on the face of things, it seems almost to be an oxymoron – looking at the pictures of him and Churchill and the others; top hats, gold watch-chains and the rest; remembering all that guff about the 'Saxon' when he took his seat in the House of Commons; thinking of Brooke House, Sherwood Lodge and 25 Queen's Gate – as a baronet's son married to an Earl's grand-daughter makes his way round the squalid blocks and tenements up at the northern end of Liverpool.

Yet round them he went. It is in the long tradition of Liberal politics that there should not be too much hypocrisy in the very wealthy trying to do something about the very poor. Besides, if Seely wanted to win the Abercromby Division of Liverpool for which Herbert Gladstone put him up in January 1905, he would have to catch the poor vote to offset the built-in Conservative majority in the smarter end of the constituency, which included the university, big shipping and other companies, and the residential quarter next door.

In addition, it is a mistake to get too intoxicated with the Westminster image of Seely and the rest of the Hughligans. Sure, he was amongst the super-privileged and worshipped at the altar of the monarchy and the Empire, writing about 'the radiant beauty of Queen Alexandra and the debonair dignity of the King', but he had already proved himself no soft touch either physically or in public debate. He was thirty-eight. He was already, Nim being the classic Edwardian mother figure, the father of four. He had travelled the world, survived sea, sand and bullets, and had most recently stood up to the most hostile verbal onslaught one set of educated men could throw at another. He was ready to meet the people.

Meeting them was one of his talents. When Violet Bonham Carter describes Jack Seely as of 'simple mind', it is not entirely a fastidious Asquithian put-down. For she precedes it with 'dashing man of action, of ebullient courage and robust self-confidence'. Add those qualities to the openness of a 'simple' as in 'straightforward' mind, and you can see why Seely had an almost irresistible genius to get on with everyone. He had shared the perils of lifeboatmen and soldiers just as much as the intellectual rigours of statesmen and judges. John Bright, the great Liberal reformer, had made an impression on his nursery self. His family firm may have sent women and children down the mines but they built homes, hospitals and libraries. In their own Edwardian way they were considered on the side of the poor. Seely wanted to show it, too.

His Abercromby Liberal chairman, Mr Burton Ellis, later Lord Mayor of Liverpool, had hatched a 'cunning plan'. He could see what an attractive, energetic figure Seely was. He knew that the total electorate in those days of limited franchise (no women, no under-21s, no one but householders) was just over 7,000. Seely had probably got the best part of a year before the election. He should put himself about.

> By the time the Election came I had personally shaken hands with about two thirds of the electorate. It may or may not have contributed to my success, but it did have one undoubted effect on my life. I learnt for the first time how really bad slums could be. Those poor people in the Catholic quarter were living in cellars and tiny rooms. Often a man, a woman and three small children in a room ten feet square, almost quite dark except on the brightest day. Consumption and other diseases were rife. The wages of the dock labourers were precarious and often two thirds of what they earned went to the adjoining public house. I made friends with the then Bishop of Liverpool, and the medical officer of health, and together we vowed not to rest until we had got rid of such awful conditions.

Such ambitions have not been completely fulfilled even today, but at the very least Seely's efforts with Bishop Chavasse showed that his heart was in the right place. The question, in a constituency that had been solidly Conservative for the last twenty years, was whether he could steer the votes in the right direction.

It would need guile as well as energy. A few years later a famous cartoon would name Seely as the 'Pavlova of Politics', able to pirouette impressively where he stood without actually going very far. It was this skill that he had to perfect at Abercromby when it came to the Irish Home Rule question. On the one hand, his Catholic voters were tremendously in favour and he had been introduced with the endorsement of the famous Nationalist figure T.P. O'Connor, MP for the neighbouring Scotland Road con- stituency. On the other, he was still not a completely convinced 'Home Ruler' and the majority Protestant forces in the city were intent on highlighting the issue.

Seely's method was to smile and twirl around the subject. At his adoption meeting it seems as if the resourceful Burton Ellis actually turned out the lights when Seely, after wearing down his audience with a long and impassioned diatribe about free trade and Chinese labour, finally got to the divisive Irish Home Rule section of his speech. At an election meeting outside the brewers Stuart and Douglas, he pledged support for jobs, for taxation on land values, for religious tolerance and when asked about Home Rule said he had 'already dealt with the matter'.

Irish Home Rule and its implications were eventually to bring him down, just as it has done so many other British ministers since. But the biggest issue here was free trade, and whilst Chamberlain conducted his 'raging, tearing propaganda' across the country, and Churchill in Manchester led the charge against, there was a battle royal for Seely right in the heart of the Liverpool. For if he had the supportive T.P. O'Connor on one side, on the other he had one of the greatest debaters of that or any other century. The future member for Walton was a young genius of a lawyer, who as the most brilliant 'brief' of his generation was to rise to Cabinet level as Attorney General after long being immortalized as the absolute master of the judicial retort. 'Your speech has left me none the wiser,' complained a judge. 'Not wiser, my Lord,' came his reply, 'but better informed.'

He was eventually to be ennobled as the first Lord Birkenhead and Beaverbrook would say of him, 'he has got the best brain of any man among my contemporaries. If all his other qualities matched his intellect he would be the biggest world figure of our time.' At this stage he was merely the not at all plain Mr F.E. Smith.

18

The Rebel's Route to Government

For the political world, F.E. Smith was a revelation. Even at thirty-three, 'He was,' wrote Seely years later, 'as he is now, the most powerful platform orator in the country.' For Seely himself he became something more – a constant and supportive friend in peace and war right through to his untimely death in 1930.

Not that you would have thought this if you had listened to the pair of them in public. 'We would denounce each other's policy in unmeasured terms from different platforms in the great City of Liverpool, and afterwards we would continue the denunciation over the supper table in the Adelphi Hotel.' It was Alfred Lyttleton and the Chinese labour question all over again. They may have disagreed in politics but they got on as men. 'We liked each other all the better,' said Seely, 'because of the frankness of our disagreement.'

The same forgiveness does not seem to have quite applied to another consistent opponent during that 1906 campaign. The suffragettes were on the march but Seely, like Churchill, was cautious, not to say old-fashioned, about agreeing to Votes for Women. Coming from a large family and with now five children of his own, his real belief was that a 'woman's role was in the home', admitting in later life the slightly odd idea that he had thought suffrage would somehow 'lower rather than raise the status of women'.

But with one particular suffragette dogging his every meeting in search of flushing out a proper statement from the Abercromby candidate, he resorted to the sort of diversion that would have driven latter-day feminists to righteous fury.

SUFFRAGETTE: What about Votes for Women?

SEELY: I am in favour of a tentative measure of Women's Suffrage. (Applause.) But I am sorely tempted to add that it depends on the lady. (Loud laughter and applause.)

The same lady had to be removed from the Sun Hall when Prime Minister Henry Campbell Bannerman came down to speak for Seely on 10 January. But notwithstanding her efforts or those of F.E. Smith, nor the continued dominance of the Conservatives in Liverpool overall, Seely did win the Abercromby Division back for the Liberals for the first time since 1885.

The Tory-supporting *Liverpool Courier* had a moan about Seely's use of cries of 'small loaf' and 'Chinese Slavery' but did grudgingly give him his due: 'Major Seely DSO made people forget how his newly adopted party leader cast slights on our soldiers in the Boer Wars, while his assuming ways and his talent in not telling too much about his politics secured friends and diminished the hostility of opponents.'

Seely, as ever, had friends aplenty. But at thirty-seven and a fully paid-up New Liberal, what he really hoped for was a Cabinet position. He recounts being 'frankly furious' when all his regular dining companions, Churchill, Lloyd George and the miners' leader John Burns, got the call from No. 10 until 'then there was one'. His call never came. He met the Conservative leader Arthur Balfour walking across Horse Guards Parade who said, 'I wonder to what political group you will now belong, perhaps the Outside Left', to which Seely replied, 'Oh no, sir, a more formidable party, the Left Outside.'

Pretty soon he got involved with an incident that looked as if it might result in permanent exclusion. Seely had tabled an amendment for the Government to reduce the size and improve the efficiency of the army and refused to withdraw it even when asked by the Prime Minister himself. The party chiefs were not amused:

The Chief Whip, Mr Whiteley, who was a very blunt man, came and sat down next to me on the front bench below the gangway, just before the debate ended, and held out dire threats of political excommunication and other horrors if I did not withdraw the motion. In his justifiable anger and excitement, he said something about expelling me from the Party, to which I am afraid I replied, in a voice which was heard all over the House, that he could go to the nether regions and take his party with him.

Truculent New Liberal or not, Seely was passionate about army reform – 'getting rid', as he said, 'of the stranglehold of red tape: the provision of quick-firing artillery, more machine-guns, improved rifle-shooting, more mobile troops, the putting of greater trust in the auxiliary forces and in the intelligence of the average man'.

To brief himself better he wangled himself to the German army manoeuvres. Being Seely, it was done in style, taking Nim with him as well as his former Cambridge friend A. C. Hall, 'the owner of 6 Mile Bottom near Newmarket, renowned for its partridge shooting', and his wife. Being Seely, the events that followed also included a cameo which no one else, not even Churchill, an earlier visitor to German manoeuvres, could have got involved in.

Eight o'clock of a September morning, the massed ranks of the Imperial army were drawn up in battle formation across a sandy plain near Frankfurt. The delay was getting tedious. Inquisitive Englishman was heading for trouble.

There was a long wait of about an hour, during which the Kaiser, who was umpire-in-chief, rode from one side to the other with his staff. He said 'Good Morning' to us as he passed, and hoped we had had an interesting time. I employed the interval of waiting in having a look at the Kaiser's spare horses. One was the famous white Arab, given him by Abdul Hamid on the occasion of his recent visit to Constantinople and the Holy Land. I induced the groom, who was in charge of this horse, to allow me to go for a ride on it.

I have ridden horses in almost every country in Europe, and in some countries in every Continent, and I can truly say that this was the most perfect of them all. In appearance, manners, in courage and docility combined, he was indeed perfect. Unfortunately the Kaiser perceived me cantering him in and out of the trees, enjoying the superb manner in which he changed legs at every bend. He rode up and expressed his displeasure in extremely unparliamentary language.

The owner of the world's most famous Imperial moustache was not the first, nor the last, monarch to discover that with Seely you just could not make it up. Mind you, it looks as if Wilhelm's anger was partly through fear of losing his own starring role in the panto-mime. After the most ludicrous of mock battles, which if repeated in real life would cost thousands of lives, a familiar figure suddenly raced into view: 'The Kaiser on the famous white Arab, swiftly changed himself from umpire-in-chief into the cavalry commander of the attacking side. At the head of a cloud of horsemen – the flower of the German cavalry – he swept along the enemy line. At the same moment the attacking infantry dashed forward with loud cheers, and the battle was won.'

For all his flamboyance, Seely had his serious side. On his return from the manoeuvres he wrote Secretary of State for War Lord Haldane a memo prophesying that the Germans would lose hundreds of thousands of men with their style of frontal attacks but that they would learn the lesson in time and remain the most formidable of fighting machines. On his return to Westminster he was busy, first as one of the four chairmen of the Private Bill Committees and then as Vice Chairman to the committee which organized the assorted yeomanry and other volunteer forces into the 'Territorial Army'.

Life in almost every sense was unbelievably good. He kept up his lifeboat duties whenever he stayed at Brooke and always travelled down from London for official practices. In 1906 his father had bought 29 Chester Square in Belgravia for his youngest son, no mean address, to supplement Jack and Nim's basic Island home at Spencer Road in Ryde, and to house a family which, with the arrival of Patrick and then Kitty, was soon to rise to eight without count-ing Harry Smith and the rest of the servants.

Since until 1911 only government ministers received a salary, Seely had accepted his Abercromby nomination with the assurance that he would meet all his election expenses himself, something that could only be done thanks to his father's unfailing generosity. By all accounts Sir Charles Seely was a wise and prudent, if immeasurably wealthy, figure, so you have to imagine the vicarious thrill he must have got from the dashing exploits and growing success of his pride and joy. He had backed him through adventure, war, marriage, politics and home building. His son had repaid him with no small honours already. But in April 1908, in Jack's fortieth year, the dividends reached a new level. Asquith took over from the ailing Campbell Bannerman and asked Seely to come in as Under-Secretary of State at the Colonial Office.

The procedure was for Jack to answer a summons to Asquith's house in Cavendish Square. After all those years of sponsoring his son's career, Sir Charles, now seventy-seven, could not resist being part of the moment. 'My father drove me there and waited at the corner of the Square to hear the result of our interview. Great was his joy when I told him the news.'

The old coal owner deserved his pride. As a politician, Jack Seely had arrived.

19

Energetic Minister, Unseated MP

Fate was to even things up later, but on 12 April 1908 Jack Seely was in the right place at the right time with exactly the right challenges ahead of him.

The most pressing task in the Colonial Office was to get an agreed self-governing union of the four colonial states – two Boer, two British – in South Africa and that country, as we know, was one about which Seely already had expert knowledge. What's more, since the head of the department, the Colonial Secretary Lord Crewe, was in the House of Lords, Seely would have the full ministerial duty of steering such a heavyweight and contentious bill through the House of Commons.

Churchill, now promoted to President of the Board of Trade, had been Seely's predecessor as Under-Secretary and two years earlier had experienced just how high feelings could run on South Africa. At that time the measure was merely a new self-governing constitution for the Transvaal. With the then Colonial Secretary Lord Elgin in the Lords, Churchill too was the mover in the Commons and the target for withering attacks from opponents like Lord Milner, not to mention the *Daily Mail*, whose headline read:

TRANSVAAL GIVEN BACK TO THE BOERS
FRUITLESS SACRIFICES OF THE WAR
22,000 LIVES AND £250,000 FOR NOTHING.

Seely as the future 'Pavlova of Politics' would have to spin for all he was worth. But Asquith had chosen wisely, it was just the job for him. For while no Conservatives could fault the dangers he had braved during the Boer War, his naturally forgiving nature now made a close ally of the Boers, particularly Louis Botha, the first Prime Minister of Transvaal and the future first Prime Minister of the Union.

But there was method behind the clubbiness. Botha may have been keen to do a friendly deal with Britain, but plenty other of the Boers took a very different view. They believed that Germany was the colonial power to which they should be linked, to such an extent that in 1914 a number of them, including the legendary Christian de Wet, actually declared for Germany. Botha and Smuts had then to move swiftly to douse the fire and leave De Wet, the one-time 'Pimpernel of the veld', to die in bitterness and disgrace.

Seely believed that it was imperative to get a settlement, even if that did mean giving concessions to the Boers in granting a Europeans-only franchise. This was in direct denial of what had been understood as accepted by those non-Europeans who had supported the British campaign in South Africa. Amongst these, of course, was a young lawyer turned ambulance corps sergeant called Mahatma Gandhi.

Today such concessions can look like a cynical betrayal which allowed South Africa to march off on the road towards apartheid. And Seely's answer to Labour leader Keir Hardie – 'as to the wishes of the natives, we have taken every step we possibly could to ascertain what their wishes are' – sounds a bit like saying that the turkeys haven't expressed any unhappiness about Christmas.

'Those who want this bill', he said when it finally reached the Commons in July 1909, 'mean to do right and justice to all men and women and all races and creeds in South Africa.' In that statement you can detect the seeds of the over-optimistic good nature which was to lead Seely to the appeasement folly in the 1930s, but at this stage it was tempered by pragmatism. The Shadow Colonial Secretary may have tut-tutted about the Europeans-only franchise, but he agreed that 'the will of South Africa is that this shall be the Bill, the whole Bill and nothing but the Bill', whilst the Tory leader Arthur Balfour went as far as to say that granting equal rights to blacks would threaten white civilization.

So Seely, a Liberal, persuaded the Tories as well as his own party to pass the Union Bill without a division and so avoid what would be a certain mauling in an increasingly militant House of Lords who were refusing to accept Lloyd George's social-reforming budget. To do so he had used his cross-party friendships, made up with old enemies, constantly consulted the King, and even on one triumphant occasion, re-jewelled Queen Alexandra.

She and Edward VII were giving a special lunch for Botha, Smuts, Steyn and the other South African delegates as part of the softening-up process. When Seely arrived he noticed that she was not wearing her part of the Cullinan diamond which Botha had presented to the King on behalf of the Transvaal in November 1907. In its uncut version this thing weighed 3106 carats, five times the Koh-i-noor diamond. Having been cut in Amsterdam, it was now set in assorted crowns and jewels in the Tower of London. Prompted by Seely, the Queen sent a carriage rattling off Thameside and during lunch the glittering jewel arrived to be passed round the table to much guttural approval from the Dutch.

As a member of the Government Seely actually got paid. Fifty pounds a week may not sound much, but it represents some £150,000 a year at today's rate, and at the Colonial Office Seely got something more important than money. He joined a team and within it established one of his own. He took on the highly recommended R.V. Vernon as his Private Secretary in the Civil Service, 'the embodiment of method and caution'. As his Parliamentary Private Secretary he appointed Godfrey Baring, whom we last met as the Liberal opponent to the then Conservative Seely in the Isle of Wight. As his Personal Private Secretary he found a bright young man recommended by the Government Chief Whip, the Master of Elibank. He was called George Nicholson, and his and Seely's lives would become closely entwined.

Seely's official papers at Nuffield College, Oxford, show just how busy the new minister had become; and not just on colonial matters. Asquith had also appointed him to the newly formed Committee of Imperial Defence, and right up until August 1914 Seely played an increasing part in the preparations for what was becoming an inevitable conflict. So much so that he was at one stage chairing five different committees, duties that continued uninterrupted even after his controversial resignation from the Cabinet in March 1914.

One of those sub-committees was to found the Royal Flying Corps. To say that flying was in its infancy is something of an understatement. Orville Wright's epoch-making debut flight at Kitty Hawk beach, North Carolina, had been in December 1903, had lasted just less than a minute and covered not more than 260 metres. By October 1908 Orville's brother Wilbur had graduated to winning $100,000 dollars from a French patent firm for becoming the first person to fly a passenger for a full hour. It was only the next July that Louis Blériot took off from Sangatte near Calais and thirty-seven minutes later bumped down on the grassy slopes above Dover to land £1,000 (no mean sum in 1909) from the *Daily Mail* for the first cross-Channel flight.

In these circumstances there are no prizes for guessing what Seely would do. On the sort of windy day that puts lifeboats on alert, he got himself down to meet the famous pilot Graham White. At first the conditions were so bad that even the intrepid 'bird man' would not risk a take-off. But eventually a familiar theme emerged – 'I induced him to taxi his machine to the far side of the ground and make a short flight against the wind.' It was, *The Times* declared, the first time any Minister had taken to the air. Seely was on the wing.

But first he was to suffer an experience that would confirm his distaste of the party side of politics. The electors of Abercromby were to kick him out. That's rather a harsh way of putting it for a man who had won a former Tory seat by just 199 votes during the Liberal landslide of 1906. But politics is a harsh game and, as passions raged across the country in the 'Peers v People' debate, Seely, with his own constituency reduced from 7,418 to 6,926, was always facing an uphill struggle as Asquith called an election for January 1910.

His friends rallied round. Both Churchill and Lloyd George came to speak on his behalf and the pro-Liberal *Liverpool Daily Post* was positively euphoric in its endorsement, calling Seely, 'the most distinguished of the nine members for the city. A brilliant young statesman whose connection with Liverpool will give the second city of the Empire her rightful share in the councils of the nations.'

Even allowing for a heavy touch of fawning, the picture it goes on to paint of Seely, the MP, suggests that his four years representing Abercromby had included quite a lot of more basic service than fetching the Queen's diamonds from the Tower of London.

> He has made himself immensely popular with his constituents and has done extremely useful service to his country. The elements of his popularity are his breezy geniality and good humour, his frankness, fairness and straightforwardness, his attention to the needs of his division and his sense of responsibility to those whom he represents. His annual addresses to the electors have been models and his readiness to answer questions and to discuss knotty points without equivocation have made for him a host of admirers and friends.

There was no lack of effort. He banged the drum calling the Lords' budget veto 'gross, un-English, un-businesslike and unfair'. He stood by Lloyd George's idea of land tax, claiming that as it had already existed for some thirty years in assorted parts of the Empire, the only marvel was that it had not been imposed before. He tried to avoid being impaled on Liverpool's religious double whammy of disgruntled Roman Catholics who disliked the Liberals' education policies and stubborn Protestants who would have nothing to do with Home Rule, and had F.E. Smith next door cunningly declaring, 'Liverpool stands by Belfast.'

Seely's opponent, Colonel Chaloner, was not afraid to play the religious card and when the votes were finally counted he had won the seat back by 526 votes, the selfsame six per cent swing that, going the other way in 1906, had got the Liberals returned. Halfway up the ladder, Seely was suddenly whizzing down the snake. 'I am so sorry', wrote the great T.P. O'Connor from the neighbouring Scotland Road constituency, whose Irish Nationalists had won a record forty-five seats. 'It made me so miserable that I forgot all about our success. I have the consolation of knowing that it wasn't

our people that failed us. But never mind, some other and better
constituency will soon want you.'

Such hopes seemed scant consolation to the crestfallen MP. But
this was 1910. Privileged connections had a habit of sliding you to
the front of the queue. T.P. O'Connor's prophecy would take only
a month to be realized.

III. A HIGH ROAD TO HELL

20

An Able Operator

Seely had been in Parliament nearly ten years. He had friends, energy and reputation. He was worth standing aside for. Stand aside please, Sir Walter Foster, Honourable Member for the Ilkeston Division of Derbyshire since 1900.

Sir Walter didn't seem to mind. Sitting in the Upper House as Lord Ilkeston would be quite pleasant, but the splendidly named *Ilkeston Pioneer and Erewash Valley Gazette* was not so impressed. 'He is in a hurry', it said of the newly elevated peer, 'to pitchfork into the position he has precipitately vacated, a capitalist in every sense of the word.'

Yet the Harrow- and Cambridge-educated 'capitalist' in question was standing for this mining seat as a local boy and a friend of the people. His father served a neighbouring constituency, he himself had been born in a Derbyshire parish, his family had a good reputation for providing improvements for the miners in their employ, and what's more he was a good friend of future Labour leader Ramsay MacDonald. Jack Seely's handsome majority was to be protected by a Lib–Lab pact.

It may seem incongruous today for a coal owner's son to be something of the workers' champion, especially with a recent bitter strike in the Northumberland and Durham coalfields. But that's how it worked at the time. Seely kept in correspondence with Ramsay MacDonald: 'You and I are old friends and understand one another.' He called himself an 'advanced Liberal' and espoused the rights of trade unionists and the abolition not just of the Lords but of the whole hereditary principle vehemently enough to force

Asquith to publicly deny this was stated Government policy. He even fended off Mrs Pankhurst when she came up to play the suffragette card.

By polling day on 7 March 1910 Seely still had 3,333 votes of Sir Walter's old 4,200 majority (on a turnout of 87.7 per cent) and the formerly carping *Ilkeston Pioneer* was warming to the 'undeniably attractive personality of Colonel Seely'. By the time Asquith took the 'People v Peers' crisis to the country a second time in November, the old charm had got to work. The Liberal majority was back up to 4,400.

Yet there was something more than a mere 'sweetheart deal' in 'pitchforking' Seely back into Westminster. Ten years into Parliament he was becoming a more than useful performer for Asquith and his Government. His South African achievements nullified Conservative attacks on that flank, and his military service and efforts on the Committee for Imperial Defence gave the more pacifist-inclined Liberals a counterweight to Tory criticism. He was keen and able. But he was going into the line of fire.

These were turbulent times. The Kaiser may have ridden alongside his cousin, the new King George V, at Edward VII's funeral in May of 1910, but the scale of Germany's troop and battleship numbers was already so vast that few people doubted a conflagration was inevitable. When Seely met the German ambassador, who rejoiced in the name Baron Marshal von Bieberstein, and asked why their two countries could not stay friends as they were, he was told firmly, 'Our people cannot accept your status quo.' When the English minister replied, 'They had better do so, it is the only way', his Germanic Excellency clicked his heels and said coldly, 'May I introduce you to my daughter.'

The threats at home were even more open. The suffragettes were increasing in both numbers and in the directness of their actions. The House of Lords' continuing refusal to pass Lloyd George's 'People's Budget' was causing a major constitutional crisis. The series of strikes and lock-outs in the mines, docks and cotton mills climaxed with the cavalry being called in to restore order in Wales's Rhondda coalfield in November 1910. And that same month Sir Edward Carson took over as leader of the Irish Unionist MPs to oppose the Liberals' Home Rule Bill with the famous refrain, 'Ulster will fight. And Ulster will be right.' Since the Liberals could not pass the House of Lords bill without the support of the Irish Nationalists, and that support came only on the guarantee of Irish Home Rule, politics promised no easy ride.

But Seely loved it. And he was good enough at it to be asked by Asquith first to speak for the Government in the Parliament Bill debate in February 1911 and then to switch jobs to become understudy to Secretary of State Haldane at the War Office, with the prospect of the full Cabinet role when his boss moved on as predicted to become Lord Chancellor.

Churchill was in Cabinet already and as Home Secretary had already been quite literally in the line of fire during the fabled Sidney Street Siege, when three holed-up anarchists had killed three police before getting themselves burnt to death. During the summer Churchill had been taking an increasingly tough line as strikes spread from ports to railways and to all forms of transport. In August 1911 there were 200,000 strikers and 50,000 troops on the streets of London and a railway strike had been called nationwide. It was time for Seely to set a record.

It was the record for getting a bill through both Houses of Parliament in a single day. Prompted by the Director of Military Operations, Sir Henry Wilson, and the Chief of the Imperial General Staff, Sir John French, Seely produced a rigid strengthening of the Official Secrets Act which even he admitted gave 'extremely drastic powers to the executive'. For a Liberal party it was a deeply illiberal bill. But 18 August was quite a day. The troops were on the streets, *The Times* editorial was saying that 'War has been declared by the Union railwaymen against the public', and with a heatwave sizzling and the summer recess starting, there were hardly one hundred MPs in the chamber.

Labour stalwarts like Ramsay MacDonald, George Lansbury and Philip Snowden forswore any raging denunciation and with Seely calling on personal friendships with Conservatives like F.E. Smith and George Wyndham, and Irish Nationalists like Redmond and O'Connor, the expected guns of debate were generously lowered. Indeed, Seely never even spoke to the bill, just moved it, and the few who rose to demur were hauled down by their colleagues. It may have been illiberal but, in the words of the future Cabinet Secretary Maurice Hankey, 'It was a masterpiece of parliamentary strategy.'

Hankey becomes an important witness as Seely enters into this high-profile and up till now widely deprecated part of his career. First Sea Lord Sir John Fisher described Hankey as, 'Napoleonic in his ideas and Cromwellian in his thoroughness'. Churchill said simply, 'He knew everything, feared no one, and said nothing.' From 1911 to 1914 Hankey worked constantly alongside Seely as the Committee for Imperial Defence prepared for war. His high opinion of Seely never faltered.

Not that the future 'Galloper Jack' was without his moments. In March 1912 he was able to announce to the Commons the King's approval of the newly instituted Royal Flying Corps, having already introduced it with a political frankness inconceivable today. 'We have worked very hard to make a good scheme', he told the House, 'but nobody is more conscious than I am as Chairman of the Committee that we must have made a great many mistakes and there must be a great many omissions from the very nature of the case, owing to the novelty of the science we have to study.'

The first mistake had come some four months earlier when he had somehow alienated a delegation of aeroplane manufacturers and so become to C. G. Grey, the editor of the *Aeroplane*, 'the personification of government wrong headedness'. When in March 1913 he claimed there were 101 flightworthy aircraft, he was shot down by an Opposition investigation revealing there were barely half that number. The *Aeroplane* thundered, 'Colonel Seely has betrayed his trust.'

An inventory of just 150 active planes by the outbreak of war does not sound a huge achievement, but 1914 was only three years after Seely had flown at Hendon, only eleven after Orville Wright himself had made that first skittering flight to herald the era of powered flight. You have also to remember that Seely was trying to procure finance from a Liberal administration in competition with his other more obvious commitments at the War Office, not to mention the dominant and funds-hungry figure of Churchill at the Admiralty.

All the way to August 1914, Seely and Churchill were on the horns of the Liberal dilemma. As the threat from Germany grew ever larger, everyone could see that the forces needed strengthening. Yet the Liberals could not sanction the taxes to pay for such strengthening when the limited tariffs necessary for Lloyd George's People's Budget had caused such a furore across the nation.

If it was hard enough getting finance for the basic needs of the army and navy, what chance for a fledgling flying corps? And what chance for Seely when he discovered that his friend in charge of the better-endowed Senior Service was actually building a flying corps of his own? Churchill's explanation tells us all we need to know:

> The War Office claimed on behalf of the Royal Flying Corps complete and sole responsibility for the aerial defence of Great Britain. But owing to the difficulties of getting money, they were unable to make any provision for this responsibility, every aeroplane they had being earmarked for the Expeditionary Force. Seeing this and finding myself able to procure funds by various shifts and devices, I began in 1912 and 1913 to form under the Royal Naval Air Service flights of aeroplanes as well as of seaplanes for the aerial protection of our naval harbours, oil tanks and vulnerable points, and also for a general strengthening of our exiguous and inadequate aviation.

Seely must have shaken his head at his brilliant friend's 'various shifts and devices'. But a start had been made not just on the aeroplanes and the pilots but on a whole wide range of services in a brand-new medium. 'I can testify', said Hankey, 'to the splendid work he [Seely] did in developing the new arm and in making a start with all kinds of technical devices including anti-aircraft guns and searchlights.'

But for all its later significance the work of the Air Committee was still only a small part of the huge task facing the country in general and Seely in particular. War with Germany, the war to end all wars, was becoming not just likely but inevitable. As political posts go, nothing could be starker in its title than the Secretary of State for War. It was to that position that Jack Seely was officially gazetted on 12 June 1912.

It was to make him and break him.

21

The War Office

On the face of it, Seely was a popular appointment. It was not just Churchill who had lobbied Asquith on his behalf, but Richard Haldane, the departing War Secretary, who now sat on the Woolsack as Lord Chancellor.

'I feel you will put great life into Army affairs,' wrote Haldane to his successor, 'more in some ways than I was able to do. I feel too, that continuity of appointment will remain unbroken.' It was an impressive endorsement from the brilliant Scottish philosopher and statesman amongst whose claims to fame was that his family had been Masters of Gleneagles since the thirteenth century. And it was echoed by Hugh Lacy in *Punch*, who said that Seely 'has been one of the most conspicuous successes of a singularly gifted ministry'.

Even *The Times*, not exactly a Liberal organ, was complimentary, saying that Seely 'had already played a distinguished part in respect to War Office organization especially in the matter of the Royal Flying Corps'. At this high point of his political life it seemed as if he took up the seals of office uniquely equipped to make a huge success of his tenure as Secretary of State for War.

He had a long-term and energetic interest in the army and had actually done distinguished service in the field. He had Churchill, the first Lord of the Admiralty, as his personal friend and political supporter. He had an affable, if at times flamboyant, style, which liked to reach out across party lines. He had six children and a splendidly supportive wife who gave him a direct family connection with Northern Ireland. It was Jack Seely's disaster that every one of these apparent assets turned out to create special problems that combined to bring about his ultimate downfall.

His army service, territorial not regular, gave the first and most serious of all. It can be best illustrated by two opposing reactions to his impending appointment. St Loe Strachey, editor of the *Spectator*, wrote glowingly, 'I am quite sure that it will be a great advantage to the army to have a man at its head who knows and understands the British soldier.' Contrast that with the military reaction of Sir Henry Wilson, the giraffe-tall and lizard-faced Director of Military Operations and Seely's future nemesis in 1914. Before the appointment Wilson wrote in his diary, 'I suppose we shall get Jack Seely. Ye gods!' Today the army nickname for the Territorials is 'STABS', standing for 'Stupid TA Bastards'. Nothing changes.

A madly enthusiastic yeomanry colonel was exactly what Wilson and the other generals did not want. For a start, they were convinced that conscription was the answer. This was against long-standing Liberal policy, and something which Seely had publicly held out against, ever since he attended that inaugural meeting of Lord Roberts's National Service League at Apsley House back in 1902. What's more, he did it with a degree of first-person, 'my-men-who-beat-the-Boers-were-all-volunteers' self-glorification which made the career soldiers grind their teeth in fury.

As far as Wilson was concerned, the place for the Secretary of State for War was in the office getting money from the Government to pay for the plans which the professionals would draw up. And to get his own way Wilson was prepared to leak information to the press and to the Opposition in a manner that, come the Ulster crisis in 1914, became little short of treasonable.

If Seely wanted to know what lay ahead he only had to heed *The Times* of 17 June. The 'military correspondent' was a Colonel Charles à Court Repington, who had been a fellow officer of Wilson's in the 4th Dragoon Guards and was the first outlet for any Wilson leak. Repington's words, under the headline 'British Military Policy, Colonel Seely's task', are a perfect reflection of Wilson's attitude towards his new political master and a scarcely coded statement of his mistrust.

The need of the Army on the civil side is for a capable and conscientious administrator of the Caldwell and Haldane type, who does not take office with the intention of making a splash in the world, or of prancing and perorating in the House of Commons but is prepared to spend long hours in his office, to live laborious days and to remember that the first duty of an administrator is to administer. No one pays much attention to speeches in Parliament these days and the reputation of a minister is made or marred in his own office.

Just in case his readers (or Seely) had not got the message, Repington drew to a rousing conclusion: 'The more we think of the duties of the British Army and of the extremely complex problems which its service in peace and war entails, the more we realise the frightful danger of a charlatan at the War Office and the better we see how little scope there is for gush and glitter and how very slight is the opportunity for fresh developments after all the practical needs of the time have been met.'

Seely had been suspicious of the 'old fashioned military mind' ever since his first yeomanry manoeuvres back in the 1890s, so you can see how he was likely to view such warnings. After all, Seely was a man who had raged at official incompetence whilst suffering on the veld and had cut his Hughligan teeth attacking Brodrick's army reforms. He was a long-standing devotee of yeomanry service, had been part of the committee which oversaw the official creation of the Territorial Army in 1907, and was so overtly proud of his honorary rank as commander of the Hampshire Carabineers, that Asquith forever nicknamed him 'the Arch Colonel'.

In Wilson's and the generals' eyes, the Arch Colonel's military interest was that of the meddling amateur. Imagine their contempt at the elegant morning-suited figure riding around with the King at the big army manoeuvres near Cambridge in September 1912. Especially when he had to steer the monarch away from a fist fight between the South African and Canadian government representatives and when his horse then bit King George's foot.

The official army mind was so set on regular rather than

territorial troops that when the war finally came Kitchener used his famous recruiting poster to raise 'New Armies' rather than using the Territorials as his base. Wilson was so set against the Territorials that he toured the country lecturing about their incompetence and the need for conscription. And as late as November 1913 there is almost a sense of glee in his diary note about his political chief's rebuke: 'Seely sent for me and tried to check me for my lecture yesterday, but I wasn't for it.'

It's hard to imagine a worse base on which to build a policy. That is until all the other problems which arose out of Seely's apparent assets are considered. For instance, Churchill's support may have been helpful in getting him into the War Office and Winston actually said so at a Chequers dinner attended by Seely as late as 1941, but it came at a price. The clue is in the pay-off to his letter of congratulation. 'My dear Jack,' wrote Winston, 'if I may use such a familiar address to a Secretary of State, accept my most sincere and warm congratulations. We must keep in closest touch.'

They were indeed great friends and kindred spirits, memorably described sitting side by side at the Speaker's Dinner as, 'Mars and Neptune, with 13 medals on their manly breasts, both from Harrow School and both ex-Tories as chirpy as two boys from a tuck shop'. But any study of Churchill will tell you that the great man could never resist influencing, if not completely taking over, any operation within his reach.

My mother had a splendid memory of Churchill coming down to stay at Brooke and taking a gaggle of Seely children down to the sea to build sandcastles on the beach. Being Churchill, the sandcastles could not just be a couple of simple, moated efforts with a few upturned buckets of sand as towers. No, they had to be a series of full-scale edifices as part of a war game fully involving each of the children. My mother would have been ten years old at the time. 'I remember how important he made it all seem,' she told me. 'He was a bit frightening, but very inspirational.'

Seely was never frightened of Churchill but he was certainly inspired by him, some people felt to a fault. He shared the same views on all the major issues of the day and now that he was at the

War Office, and Churchill at the Admiralty, their duties were literally interlinked. So much so that in 1913 Churchill instituted a monthly Admiralty–War Office conference called the 'High Level Bridge', involving himself, Seely, the Chief of Imperial General Staff, the First Sea Lord, the two Permanent Secretaries, and Hankey as overall secretary.

It did much good work in the grind towards war, but from Churchill's letters to Seely at Nuffield College it's obvious how fiercely protective the great man was of the navy's Senior Service status, its responsibility for the defence of the shores, and the pressure, as with the Naval Flying Corps, he would put on any funds that could be got from the Government.

They were both part of a Liberal administration which was instinctively against heavy expenditure on armaments. Seely was about as military as Liberals came, but even he was prepared to publicly challenge demands for greater spending on the army as well as the fleet, 'when all the time funds were urgently needed to carry forward the great work of social reform'.

Seely was no charlatan, being industrious and inventive enough to oversee a whole range of developments for rail and shipping and food in anticipation of the outbreak of war. On the shipping front he even reverted to his Boer War embarkation tactic of going straight to the top. The Admiralty could not carry the burden of troop transport, so Seely called in the chairmen of four of the main shipping lines and appealed to them to solve it. Desperation stakes it may have been, but it worked, and years later F.E. Smith, who had of course been an Opposition MP, claimed that Seely's achievement in organizing the shipping arrangements for the British Expeditionary Force in August 1914 was one of the War Office's greatest accomplishments.

For it had only been in 1911 that a newly installed Henry Wilson had been raging: 'At present absolutely nothing exists, which is scandalous.' Whilst no doubt a lot more could have been done if more funds had been available, the facts are that after Seely's two years at the War Office and on the Defence Committee Britain was in a far better state of readiness than it had been. Within five days of war being declared on 4 August 1914, the first troops, artillery, horses and supplies were landed in France and by 14 August five British divisions were stationed at Amiens under Sir John French. 'Probably Paris would have fallen', concluded F.E., 'if the shipping arrangements had been less intelligently conceived and prepared.'

But that was said in hindsight. During Seely's time at centre stage he was often on the defensive from Conservative and military-establishment attacks. And the impression was sometimes given that he was dancing to Churchill's tune. It's an impression best recorded by a sketch writer from the *Blackburn Gazette* under the headline, 'Our Smiling War Secretary, the Pavlova of Politics'. It credits Seely with charm and style and oratory. 'He is a delightful man, but as a statesman he is light-weight. He is the butterfly of the government. If he had not tacked his fate to the chariot of Mr Churchill, he would never have reached the high position he now holds.'

Delightful undeniably, lightweight maybe, soon to be ruined certainly; but whilst I must not do too much special pleading, it is worth recalling how each apparent asset had become part of the mix that was to bring him down: his military experience and yeomanry title proved to be a drawback rather than an advantage in dealing with Wilson and the generals, who despised 'amateur soldiers' and who were soon in open argument about conscription, Government funding and the looming crisis in Ulster; his Churchill connection brought a dependence which inspired allegations of puppetry but also gave the navy precedence in funding; his cross-party instincts built expectations which could not be fulfilled and led to impressions of weakness; and, finally, his wife's central role in his psyche was to be cruelly snatched away just as the Home Rule drama took us closer to army rebellion than at any time since the Glorious Revolution of 1688 against James II.

Ahead lay the most miserable as well as the most publicly challenging time of his life.

22

Alas, Poor Nim

At this stage, in the spring of 1912, it is easier to find out about the famous contacts than it is about the family. Most of the public moves of Seely, Churchill, Wilson and the rest are on the record and countless diligent historians have expressed their own perspective on events. But this grandson just wants to meet his grandfather – and grandmother.

It is possible to know Seely, the flamboyant man at the despatch box and the industrious minister at the War Office, and to know that he was a clubbable man from the days of the Hughligans to the 1911 formation of the cross-party 'Other Club' by Winston and F.E. Smith. It is even possible to have a fascinating glimpse of the philosophical debates that he and George Wyndham would have with Ramsay MacDonald, who 'gave us his books on Socialism and we would endeavour to argue him out of it'. But what about the family?

It was certainly big enough. Frank, the quiet one, was fourteen and 'doing well' at Harrow, John, the future architect, was twelve and already making model houses at Hawtreys. For the boys, even for seven-year-old Patrick, the way would be already set. But for girls in these embalmed units of high Edwardian society, the future was much more confined. Their best hope was to catch and marry someone rich enough to allow them to perpetuate the whole thing over again. So for thirteen-year-old Emmy, born with a squint and having to wear heavy glasses, life looked destined for the shadows.

Privileged shadows, of course. My mother, born in 1902, told of the carriage rides in London, of the beach parties at Brooke, of the

great fêtes they would have on the lawn, of music and games in the
house. Sepia pictures show the flag-decked marquees, horse-drawn
lawnmowers, and her alert, long-pigtailed face holding little Kitty
(born in 1907) by the hand. Harry Smith had taken over as butler
and now married Rose the cook. It was a household of service
reigned over by the proudest of public servants. Jack Seely was
certainly a hero in his own home. But that did not make a shrinking
violet of his wife.

Nim Seely was an archetypal Edwardian mother – proud of her
own family (her father Sir Harry Crichton was the son of the Earl of
Erne, a former colonel of the Hampshire Yeomanry, and the squire
of Netley Abbey overlooking Southampton Water) and proud of
her husband. But above all Nim Seely was proud of the family she
was rearing and wanted to increase it.

Although she already had six children she wanted even more.
Early in 1912, now in her forty-second year, she was going to mud
baths in Germany in the hope of conceiving again. A century on,
you wonder whether this was masochism or a cry for help. But cast
the mind back and it all becomes a little more understandable. Nim
was no scrubber of dishes. With all the servants and with Jack so
busy at the ministry, the nursery for her was a place where the more
would be the merrier.

Both parents show some signs of strain. In early 1913 Nim
turned down an invitation to chair a committee for helping service-
men's families: 'Mrs Seely regretted she could not help but is at
present weighed down by her vast family.' And at the same time
Seely's aviation critic C. G. Grey was writing, 'Those of us who are
in touch with service matters hear that the pressure of work in the
offices of the Secretary of State for War has been so great that
Colonel Seely is breaking down under a task which is too big for
him.'

Whether Grey was right or wrong in that judgement, in March
1913 he was correct in saying that Britain's War Minister would be
under unprecedented strain. For all the well-documented hassles
of preparing the army and navy for what appeared inevitable
conflict with Germany were now being compounded by the ever

growing crisis over the committed Liberal policy of Home Rule for Ireland.

There may be problems over Northern Ireland nowadays, but back then their scale was apocalyptic. By September 1912 470,000 had signed up to a 'Solemn Covenant' to defeat Home Rule. The Tory leader Bonar Law had said, 'there were no steps they would not support' in opposition to the bill and Sir Edward Carson had left a huge rally in Belfast promising to return and 'if it be to fight I shall not shrink'.

The Ulster Volunteer Force was being formed and drilling openly under its commander, General Sir Thomas Richardson. The Home Rule Bill duly passed through the Commons, only to be rejected by the Lords in January 1913. What was being promised in Ulster was nothing less than open rebellion. British troops would need calling in to guarantee law and order. But whose side would the troops be on? Most of their officers were Protestant Anglo-Irish. Sir Henry Wilson himself came from Limerick and was constantly 'leaking' to Bonar Law. Right at the heart of the War Office was an intent to overthrow the stated will of Government.

At a time when the country desperately needed to build the morale and efficiency of the army leaders in face of the German threat, it's hard to imagine a worse situation than that of a Liberal Secretary of State for War. Except that for Seely it was worse. Home Rule was merely the biggest of the political problems. The continuing high-octane industrial unrest had included a miners' strike, which had drastically reduced his majority at Ilkeston, and the suffragette movement had now taken an extremely ugly turn.

In February Lloyd George's house had been blown up in a bomb attack for which Emmeline Pankhurst was sent to jail. In June Emily Davison won posthumous immortality by getting killed bringing down the King's horse in the Derby. Ministers were under threat. Seely was overworked. And Nim was pregnant. To borrow a phrase from Sir Henry Wilson – 'Ye gods!'

A 'safety first' man would have taken time out at home. But that was not Seely's way. The baby was due in August 1913. Nim was delighted. Another face in the nursery, another prize amongst their brood. And Jack, impossible workload or not, blithely continued on his way, happy in the belief that Nim, his greatest supporter through war and peace, was always there to come home to.

It was too good to last. Sometimes, as with many memoirs, Seely's writings get bogged down in detail and self-justification, not to say self-glorification. But the calamity that befell him in the summer of 1913 is worth taking straight to understand the circumstances and hear his authentic voice. A man who had loved – and now lost:

> One evening in July 1913, I walked home from the House of Commons with my old friend T.P. O'Connor. He said: 'My dear Jack, you appear to me to be the happiest man alive. How do you manage it?' The recollections of this moment are amongst the most vivid of my life. I replied: 'I think because from my earliest years I have made a conscious effort to face everything, or anything, without fear or anxiety. For instance if you came to me and said: "I am sorry to tell you that your fortune is dissipated, your career is ruined and that to-morrow morning you will go to prison," I have steeled myself to reply, "Is there anything I can do about it in the next two hours?" and if you replied, "No, nothing whatever, the thing is done," then I hope I should reply, "Very well, let's forget about it and go to dinner."'
>
> He knew me very well and I remember him saying: 'Do you make no reservation of any sort or kind about anything?' I said: 'Yes, to tell you the truth, I do not know what I should do if anything happened to my wife. I have not found a way to face that out.'
>
> A month later my wife died quite suddenly and unexpectedly when my youngest daughter was born. Black darkness fell upon me. My friends showed me kindness and consideration which I can never repay: Mr Asquith and his wife, McKenna and his wife, Winston, F.E. Smith, Jack Pease, French, Ian Hamilton, Ramsay MacDonald (who had suffered a similar fate). But for them I know I should have gone mad. As it was, in the shadows, I resumed my work.

The blithe spirit was doused. The household took a shattering blow from which arguably the younger children never fully recovered. My mother remembered the aching agony of it all, and recalled her father, normally the very epitome of self-confidence, sitting on the end of her bed, saying again and again, 'What are we going to do?'

Little Louisa somehow survived not just birth but a desperately asthmatic childhood to live into her eighties as a remarkable woman and a much-loved mother of three. Aunt Florrie, Jack's oldest and unmarried sister, was summoned to cope with the rest of the children. Nim's body was taken from London where she died to be buried under a white marble cross on the steeply sloping side of the churchyard at Brooke.

Seely went back to work as an escape. But it was to prove a flight from one hell to another.

23

Mutiny

Sympathy, exasperation and wonder are all evoked by exhuming Seely's role in the so-called Curragh Mutiny, which eventually led to his resignation on 30 March 1914 for having added two concessionary paragraphs to a Government document designed to get the potentially rebellious generals back in the fold.

My sympathy is not just for my newly bereaved grandfather but for his difficult position in the utterly impossible political circle that Seely and Churchill were being asked to square in their linked positions of War Secretary and First Lord of the Admiralty. If Ulster's opposition to Irish Home Rule took the violent and unlawful turn that was being openly threatened, the armed forces would have to restore order. But many of those based at the key Curragh camp in County Kildare were adamant that they would rather resign than march or sail to the North. It could be mutiny on the Curragh.

The bones of the story are well known and looking back there is a ghastly inevitability about it all. By December 1913 there was an official ban on importing arms to Ulster and, with Cabinet approval, Seely had drawn up a document for the army chiefs trying (clearly not successfully enough) to spell out the difference between reasonable and unreasonable force, offensive and defensive action. 'What has now to be faced', the 16 December memorandum reads, 'is the possibility of action being required by Her Majesty's troops in supporting the Civil Power, in protecting life and property if the police are unable to hold their own.'

In January, Tory leader Andrew Bonar Law said, 'We have

given a pledge that if Ulster resists we will support her', and concluded, 'we are drifting inexorably to civil war'. Nothing through
February would have altered that view as the Ulster Volunteer
Force drilled openly. These were passionate middle-class Ulster-
men, in tweed caps and knickerbockers, not the balaclavaed thugs
that characterize Northern Ireland paramilitaries today. By 14
March the Home Rule Bill had been to the Commons again and in
Belfast Brigadier General Gleichen was reporting a Unionist force
complete with machine guns and some 80,000 rifles ready to take
the field and to storm arms depots and sabotage communications
around the province.

On the same day in Bradford, Winston Churchill set out the
Government's position in a now famous speech denounced by the
Conservative press of the time as a provocation to civil war but
which even by his own unique standards was an astonishing tour de
force and indication of the perilous time ahead :

> If Ulster seeks peace and fair play, she knows where to find it. If
> Ulstermen extend the hand of friendship, it will be clasped by
> Liberals and by their Nationalist countrymen, in all good faith
> and all good will; but if there is no wish for peace; if every effort
> to meet their views is only to be used as a means of breaking
> down Home Rule, and of barring the way to the rest of Ireland; if
> the Government and Parliament of this great country and greater
> Empire are to be exposed to menace and brutality; if all the loose,
> wanton and reckless chatter we have been forced to listen to
> these many months is in the end to disclose a sinister and
> revolutionary purpose; then I can only say to you: 'Let us go
> forward and put these matters to the proof!'

The die was cast. The situation was worsening everywhere
one looked. In the South of Ireland the Nationalists, much to
John Redmond's dismay, were arming themselves as the Irish
Volunteers and they too were planning to storm the British depots
to supply themselves for impending conflict. Sir Arthur Paget, the
general in charge, replied to Seely's directive to reinforce the garrisons in the North by stating that he had not carried out the full

order because 'such move of troops would create intense excitement in Ulster and possibly precipitate a crisis'.

Tuesday 17 March was St Patrick's Day, there were shamrocks
aplenty in the House of Commons, and the *Daily Mirror* had a photo
of the ex-Commander-in-Chief, Lord Roberts VC, receiving his
shamrock at Wellington Barracks, a silver-haired symbol that the
army and the Irish crisis were now inextricably linked. The next
day, Wednesday 18th, Paget came to London for a briefing from
Seely, Sir John French, the CIGS and Sir John Ewart, the adjutant
general. The fat would soon be in the fire.

For while, in the course of the War Office meeting, Paget was
once again assured that there was no question of an attack on
Ulster, he was instructed that troops would need to be moved to
ensure law and order. This was provocative enough. 'It appears', Sir
Henry Wilson wrote in his diary, 'that they are contemplating
scattering troops all over Ulster as though it were the Pontypool
Coal strike.' As Wilson was actually Director of Military Operations
it was hardly a supportive comment.

To try to soothe Paget's fears, the first, well-meaning but
incendiary concession was made. It was agreed that officers resident
in or specially connected with Ulster could be excused operations
but any others who refused would be dismissed from the service.
Back with his generals in Ireland, Paget's message somehow
became distilled into a test of who would or would not march on
Ulster to put the opposition down by force. To Brigadier General
Gough and the men of the 3rd Cavalry Brigade, that Friday, 20
March, the much fomented fear of an 'Ulster pogrom' was made
flesh, with all its fanciful attendant terrors of Seely and Churchill
setting both the army and the navy upon protesters in the North.

This was despite Paget taking a heroically self-sacrificing stance,
as depicted in Churchill's own detailed memorandum on the crisis.
'Sir Arthur Paget', wrote the First Lord, 'went so far as to say that,
not only would he never give the orders for troops to fire until they
had first been attacked and suffered loss, but that he intended
himself to walk out in front and be shot down by the Orangemen
before any firing in reply would be ordered of the troops.'

The reassurance did not work. Paget sent a cable which read, 'Regret to report Brigadier [Gough] and 57 officers, 3rd Cavalry Brigade prefer to accept dismissal if ordered north.' Seely and his allies were facing melt-down, with mutiny on people's lips and Irish railways also threatening to refuse to move any troops. It was not a place for faint hearts. The First Lord was ready to act.

On Thursday 19 May Churchill ordered the 3rd Battle Squadron to Lamlash, on the Scottish coast seventy miles from Belfast, and had five destroyers on standby at Irish ports ready to carry troops. 'My dear Jack,' he wrote to Seely in that compulsive, take-control way of his, 'I think you ought to make demands for railway transport to the company at the proper moment this afternoon. Their refusal will raise questions which can be awkward. Don't use the cruisers except as a second alternative. The question of taking over the line will have to be faced pretty soon.'

Seely and Churchill were now locked together as at no other time. Seely would have the sharpest of the calls ahead but there is no disguising the massive influence of the young genius to whom his wagon was hitched. Nor mistaking Churchill's readiness to carry out the final promise of that memorable Bradford speech just two Saturdays before.

'Winston talked very big about bringing the officers over in a battleship to be tried by court martial', wrote Sir John Ewart on Friday 20th when the news of Gough's resignation came through. 'I however urged that we should wait to hear what the senior officers concerned had to say. I felt at a great loss to understand why the trouble had occurred in the 3rd Cavalry Brigade, as we had ordered no officer or man at all to move in connection with our pre-cautionary measures.'

The Curragh 'rebels' had been relieved of their posts and were due at the War Office on Monday but Churchill could not wait. On Saturday morning, 20 March, he was round to call on Seely at Chester Square before the latter, his back no doubt duly stiffened, went to Buckingham Palace to see the King. While Seely was briefing the sovereign, Churchill was with Asquith at No. 10 to be followed by the King's Private Secretary Lord

Stamfordham, no doubt alarmed by what his master had heard.

The King then summoned Lord Roberts to the palace, Seely went to see Asquith and finally the 45-year-old Secretary of State and the 70-year-old ex-Commander-in-Chief met up at the War Office. There are no full minutes of these meetings but evidently an impasse had been reached.

The role of the monarch was hugely greater than it is today. Indeed the need for Seely to respond to a royal summons was to be one of the causes of the impending disaster. As it was, Sunday 22 March started with an assistant royal secretary seeing Ewart and Seely's Private Secretary George Nicholson (who attended all the meetings). Ewart then saw Gough, who had got over from Dublin, and Seely went for a second time to the palace. From there, he and Churchill went to see Asquith and the Prime Minister was then visited for ninety minutes by the Archbishop of Canterbury before spending a full hour with the King. The palace visits closed with Sir John French telling George V that he, as CIGS, would also have to resign if Gough was not reinstated.

By Monday 23 March there could be no doubt in anyone's mind that the nation was in the midst of a first-category crisis. Feelings were running high, none higher than those between the generals and their Secretary of State, who in their eyes had turned out to be just the jumped-up amateur soldier they had predicted. In his lifetime, Seely drew many accolades for geniality, but none on this Monday. However they explained it, Gough and his officers were defying orders. And Seely saw himself as the Government's instrument of command.

'Colonel Seely's manner expressed extreme hauteur', wrote Hubert Gough of his reception at the War Office.

> He was most stiff to Sir John French and Ewart and honoured me with a glare. He very haughtily pointed to various chairs and directed us to be seated in those he named. As soon as we were seated Colonel Seely, in a very truculent manner, turned his eyes on me and attempted to brow-beat me and to stare me out of countenance. I was not going to allow this and he eventually

dropped his eyes. His manner then altered. From excessive truculence he went to that of superior wisdom.

The atmosphere could be cut with a knife, but there was business to be done. Gough's refusal was all about offensive action on the North, something which should never have been an issue. With John French playing the conciliator it was eventually agreed that Gough could have some written reassurances stating that he and his men would not be used in any attack on Ulster. A statement was duly drafted but this is where the cock-up rather than conspiracy theory of history takes over. For once Seely had gone with the document to Asquith at No. 10, he could not wait for any amendments that the PM or the Cabinet wanted, but had to hustle off to the palace for yet another audience with the King.

No doubt he was by now back in optimistic mode, but when he returned to Downing Street he had a problem. Asquith had made the document more general, deleting any specific references to Irish Home Rule. Seely did not believe he could get the generals back on the boat without some allusion to Ulster, so, with Lord Morley, the distinguished Lord President of the Council, beside him, he added two paragraphs to spell out what he understood to be Cabinet policy. 'Had I been present at the [Cabinet] discussion,' he said, regretting his absence at the palace, 'none of this misunderstanding would have happened.'

But it did, and it is worth quoting exactly from the documents to show on what nuances great issues can divide.

Following the Asquith amendments the statement read:

> You are authorised by the Army Council to inform the officers of the 3rd Cavalry Division that the Army Council are satisfied that the incident which has arisen in regard to their resignations has been due to a misunderstanding.
>
> It is the duty of all soldiers to obey lawful commands given to them through the proper channels by the Army Council, either for the protection of public property and the support of the civil power in the event of disturbances, or for the protection of the life and property of the inhabitants.

This is the only point it was intended to be put to the officers in the questions of the General Officer Commanding and the Army Council have been glad to learn from you that there never had been and never will be in the Brigade any question of disobeying such lawful orders.

In normal circumstances everyone would have known what that second paragraph meant, but these were not normal times. This was the brink of chaos, with cries of 'the Army v the People' in the streets. To get them back to barracks Seely would have to spell it out. On the table at No. 10, with the Lord President in attendance, and at the end of three days of the most intense consultation with the Prime Minister and other senior colleagues, he wrote down what he understood to be the Government view.

> Her Majesty's Government must retain their right to use all the forces of the Crown in Ireland or elsewhere, to maintain law and order and to support the civil power in the ordinary execution of its duty.
>
> But they have no intention whatever of taking advantage of this right to crush political opposition to the policy or principles of the Home Rule Bill.

These additions may not seem much more than a statement of the obvious and anyway, it had used the key word, 'political' as opposed to 'military' opposition. Any apparent concession could be rescinded if the opposition did indeed take on a 'military' aspect.

But Gough had got the changed assurances in writing. What's more, when they were presented to him by French he added a rider: 'Does this mean that we will not march on the North?' To which the Field Marshal, who knew that in any forthcoming operations the role of the cavalry was to go south and west from the Curragh to protect barracks in Limerick and Tipperary wrote, 'I so read it.' Gough was later to be reconciled to Seely on the Western Front but at this time he was very lit up on behalf of the army and of his friends in the North and was being goaded by his brother Johnny, also a general, and by Wilson himself. He returned to Ireland a conquering hero and put a copy of the document in locked-up trust for his daughter. He was fêted as a soldier who had faced down the powers at Westminster and who had got a pledge against the much rumoured Churchill–Seely Ulster pogrom.

Next day someone, probably Wilson, leaked the document to the press. For Seely, the ordure was about to hit the fan.

24

Nemesis

The Opposition were soon baying for blood. The leaked documents seemed to show a Government Minister colluding with the CIGS to buy off the generals without Cabinet agreement. They had Seely bang to rights. Now they were after bigger game.

Whether or not Wilson was actually the source of the leak to the press, the Director of Military Operations was delighted to see the story hit the papers. The army now had a written guarantee that they would not enforce the Home Rule Bill. The Liberals and the despised Seely had egg, or worse, all over their faces.

Asquith, now accused of allowing unauthorized written guarantees to be given to generals, would have to distance himself and the rest of the Cabinet. But how much harm had been done by Seely's additional paragraphs? It was all very well for the Opposition to jeer, for *The Times* to snort pompously, 'It is an act of unpardonable bad faith for the Government to disown their bond', and to say that Seely, French and Churchill, 'are responsible for an episode without parallel in the history of the Army'. But the fact is that Seely got the soldiers back on the train.

Ewart, who had been in more meetings with Gough and company than anyone, had no doubt as he recorded in his diary on Tuesday 24th: 'Bethune', he said, in reference to the Director of the General Territorial Force,

> warned us that the Territorials were ready to resign in large number; Haig said there would be a sympathetic move in Aldershot; half the officers in the War Office could not be trusted.

What we did, we did to prevent something worse happening, though it was a blow to discipline. French said 'I would have signed anything yesterday to get those fellows back on duty,' and he was right. We might have had something like a general mutiny.

Asquith and Churchill and everyone knew this. That is why there had been such an intense round of shuttle consultation all weekend. That is why it was not until the next Monday, 30 March, that they finally accepted the resignations of Seely, French and Ewart. But the Government needed to get itself off the hook. There was terrible trouble looming in the mines, railways and building trades – by early June two million workers would be on strike. The suffragettes had taken to slashing masterpieces and attacking churches. By July the Kiel Canal would be open, giving the German fleet access to the Baltic. The British Government needed a mutinous army and navy like a hole in the head. Seely had got them back into barracks, but now the press was presenting his additions to the document as proof that the Government had reneged on its Home Rule commitment. He would have to go.

It would be neither easy nor quick. The generals got on the train on Monday evening, 23 March; Asquith did not disown the amendments until Wednesday 25th when he also refused to accept Seely's resignation and so drew the brilliant quip from Bonar Law that 'It was the first time someone had been thrown to the wolves with the wolves then not allowed to eat him.' Next day French and Ewart also had their resignations refused. Then followed more frantic shuttling of all the usual suspects between Downing Street, the War Office, Chester Square and Buckingham Palace. But, despite acres of critical newsprint and fiery condemnations from Carson and his supporters in the press, the resignations of Seely and the others were not actually accepted until the next Monday, 30 March.

Asquith christened the disowned amendments the 'peccant paragraphs', one of the few public uses of the Latin verb *pecco* (to sin) other than Sir Charles Napier's one-word telegram when he had captured the Indian province of Sind in 1857 – 'Peccavi' (I have sinned). Such sophistication was a typically Asquithian move to distance himself from a mess of whose making he could hardly be called completely clean.

For of course Asquith's, and particularly Churchill's, finger-prints were all over the situation. 'Winston is completely running the show,' Lord Esher had written in his diary on Sunday 22 March, 'marvellous that his colleagues allow him so much rope.' There is no direct evidence of this, and by the time Churchill was defending the Government position during Seely's 'resignation' debate on Monday 30 March he was saying that the now former Minister, 'on his own responsibility and after the document had left the hands of the Prime Minister, added the last two paragraphs himself'. Such a brazen attitude did indeed get the Government off the hook, but its relationship to the truth looks to be somewhat tenuous.

For a start, Morley was present during the whole 'peccant paragraph' saga. George Nicholson was adamant about this. He may have been Seely's Private Secretary but the detailed account he wrote of proceedings is a cool, detached document which also claims that 'no one in the Cabinet ever dissented from the sense of the two paragraphs'. And it was the Morley point on which F.E. Smith fastened during the 30 March debate.

F.E. was a lifelong friend of both Seely and Churchill, with whom he had been in private contact over Ulster. F.E. would have known the score. His duty in debate was to discomfit the Govern-ment and to do so he fastened on the claim that the Cabinet's attitude to Gough's request had not been passed to Seely. 'No one will ever believe it', he said. 'Lord Morley never left that Cabinet meeting. He took part in all the discussions.' Politics can be a murky game. Maybe Seely wasn't quite murky enough.

The Curragh incident was indeed marked by both exasperation and wonder. The exasperation comes first from the intransigence on the Unionist side (they had already been offered the Six County exclusion which continues to this day) and the unscrupulously destructive politicking of Sir Henry Wilson and his military allies; second, from the inability, as we have seen, of the Government in general and Seely in particular to get the army to accept the difference between helping with 'the support of the civil power' and the scare-mongering about an Ulster pogrom. The wonder stems from the way the country was pulled back from the very brink of public revolt without a shot fired, soldier sacked or a single extra Cabinet resignation by the simple expedient of tossing them Seely's flushed and hook-nosed head.

A year later Asquith wrote to his young 'confidante' Venetia Stanley, 'For three weeks at least no one thought or talked of anything else. Now it is all as dead and securely buried as Queen Anne.' For the rest of the century most of the blame for what Asquith was then able to dismiss as the 'Arch Colonel Fiasco' was squarely laid at Seely's door. Military memoirs and Liberal critics liked to characterize him as either weak or stupid, or more usually as both. He was an over-the-top, not to say boastful figure. He was thick as thieves with Churchill who faced down the Ulster-pogrom and 'Belfast Butcher' abuse and got through without a scratch. Seely was fair game and into the lexicon went, 'if he had more brains he would be half-witted' and 'Churchill's credulous dupe'. All good, contemptuous, fall-guy stuff, only partly rectified by Ian Beckett's scholarly and exhaustive compilation of official papers in *The Army and the Curragh Incident 1914* in 1986. Then Miss Cooper came along.

Cathleen Cooper was head of the history department at Havant Sixth-Form College from 1973 to 1989. She is a silver-haired spinster passionate about birdwatching and the Western Front Association. In her early fifties she retired to write a 90,000-word thesis for her doctorate which was accepted by Southampton University in 2001. The thesis had been inspired by a visit to the trenches when she had noted a memorial funded by subscription from her native Isle of Wight. She found that the man responsible was a General Seely of Brooke. She read about him and felt him wronged. In 1989 she set to work.

Her study, 'Jack Seely, Soldier and Statesman', is much more than a mere labour of love. For a start it is a truly magnificent monument to industry. A glance at the twelve pages of bibliography and sources at the back is an awesome tribute to Miss

Cooper's relentless quest. From library to archive office she has left
no page unturned, no claim unchecked. She has been through
twenty-nine individual sets of private papers, eleven different
archives, twelve articles and essays, fourteen books of printed
references, twenty-one newspaper and magazine articles, forty
autobiographies and memoirs, forty-six biographies and no less
than 130 other books and dissertations.

But she has written no hagiography, she makes no sensational
claims, she gets into no vendettas. She simply plugs away to dig out
all the available facts (and sadly parts of both Asquith's and Seely's
archives are missing) and in particular the interpretation of facts,
and holds them up to quiet scrutiny.

I, for one, have long felt crushed by George Dangerfield's
elegantly brutal judgement that Seely, 'besides being possessed of a
kind heart and pliable disposition, was remarkable, even among
Secretaries of State of War, for an extreme ineptitude for the office
he held'. Cath Cooper works her way quietly through her sources
and then tut-tuts that so many other people have perpetuated
extreme ineptitude as a catchphrase. 'They just repeat the same
judgment, even use the same "inept" word,' she scolds in just the
way she would have rebuked a pupil for copying someone else's
essay. 'They don't go and look at original sources.'

My own sympathy does have a bit of bias. According to my
mother my poor old grandfather was not just grieving for his wife
but had the most terrible chain-smoker's cough. Once a week the
ever-present Harry Smith used to go to the corner of Chester
Square to get him an extra strong cough mixture. It was 'laudanum'
which would have been heavily morphine-based and hardly conducive to sharp judgement. But before Miss Cooper's opus came on
the scene during the writing of this book, I had been prepared to
accept much of the old 'ineptitude' line for Seely's performance and
at best take his own verdict: 'Harm was done, but disaster was
averted.' After reading Cooper combined with Beckett's compilation of official papers, I am happy to settle for something rather
better. Indeed, you don't have to be a Seely blood relative to find
her conclusion persuasive.

In view of the extremely volatile position at home and the looming German crisis abroad, 'Seely,' she suggests, 'was forced to act very quickly to get the generals back to duty. He had thrown a lifeline to them and in so doing had prevented what Ewart and Sir Edward Grey had seen as a potentially revolutionary situation resulting. Given the spreading dissatisfaction among both the officers and other ranks in the Army and also in the Royal Navy, such prompt action could be seen as urgently necessary rather than inept.' It would be absurd to blame him, as some have suggested, for practically everything.

But at the time it was necessary to blame someone. Who better than the politician whom, even more than Churchill, the professional soldiers had come to hate. Jack Seely's was a very good head to roll.

25

From the Wastes of the Infinite

Seely never squealed but he was shattered to the very core.

His private life had been devastated by Nim's death eight months earlier and now his public role was in ruins too. *The Times* wished him well: 'As a minister he has been easy to work with, loyal to his colleagues and a real friend to the army', but most of the others depicted him as either villain or fool. The cough was bad. He came back to Chester Square and sat at the end of his eleven-year-old daughter Irene's bed and said bitterly, 'Oh, how I wish your mother was here.'

It was the most unhappy time of his entire career. 'Seely goes about like a disembodied spirit,' Churchill wrote three weeks after the resignation, 'trying to return from the wastes of the infinite to the cosy world of man. He is terribly hard hit and losing poise. The world is pitiless to grief and failure.' On 30 April Seely complained privately that he had been made a scapegoat by the Government. Talking to Lord Riddell he claimed that 'John Morley [The Lord President of the Council] says that I have been treated in an infamous fashion and that I should state my case to the public, but I don't mean to.'

Churchill himself had characteristically fought his way out of the corner but what he went through from both sides only highlights the predicament Seely and French had been in a month earlier. Undaunted by abuse – 'a Lilliput Napoleon of unsound mind whose one absorbing thought was personal vindictiveness towards Ulster' was one of the more graphic descriptions – Winston carried the battle on behalf of the Government. By 29 April he was able to write revealingly to his wife: 'I have just come back from the Pogrom debate. You must read all about it. We smashed the "plot" altogether, but as you will see, I yesterday at the end of my speech greatly daring and on my own account threw a sentence across the floor of the House of Commons to Carson which has revolutionised the situation, and we are all back again in full conciliation. It is the biggest risk I have taken.'

The reaction in some quarters to any suggestion of conciliation shows just what Seely had been up against and just how long-standing are the antipathies that still bedevil Anglo-Irish affairs today. 'It is absolutely vital', Liberal MP Robert Harcourt wrote to Churchill, 'that you should realise the extent of the fury – for no milder terms will fit the facts – which has been aroused in the Irish party and among large numbers of our Liberal colleagues by the offer to Carson with which you concluded your speech. Devlin is beside himself with rage and is openly telling everyone that you have betrayed the Irish cause. Radicals, and among them the most active and talented debaters in the party, are comparing your action with Seely's surrender to Gough.'

So there it is. Jack Seely, the ultimate cross-party figure, an army reformer, a war hero himself, married to a granddaughter of an Anglo-Irish Earl, a friend of Redmond and T.P. O'Connor, was broken on the wheel of Ulster like so many Ministers before and since. Normal human nature must have tempted him to lash back at critics, or to complain about colleagues who seemed to have left him out to dry. But whatever Seely's faults, public carping was never amongst them and to draw a line under the great disaster of his political career he is entitled to his own conclusion.

His view is that the whole episode was an illustration of the problems when the passion of party politics climbs past boiling point. He wrote,

Suppose that the officers and men of the Army had been able to attend the Cabinet meetings of February and March, 1914. No crisis could possibly have arisen. They would have heard a group of intelligent men discussing with honesty, and not without

competence, the best way to supply the solvent which had
brought peace to South Africa to the case of Ireland. They would
have heard each one of them say that under no circumstances
ought we to attack and overwhelm Protestant Ulster however
misguided their views might be. They would have observed that
all these men obviously cared much more for England and the
Empire than they did for anything else, and incidentally that they
were all Protestants. But since that could not happen – and never
will – the Army was left to read passionate speeches and wild
newspaper articles.

But the 'disembodied spirit' had always been made of resilient stuff
and did not take that long to return from Churchill's 'wastes of the
infinite'. For a start, and most significantly, Asquith kept Seely on
the Committee of Imperial Defence, where he continued to ener-
getically chair committees to do with railways, food, transport,
supplies and the Royal Flying Corps.

The popular conception remains that the start of the war was a
shambles. That the British army was in a chronic state of unpre-
paredness, that the whole embarkation process was a hopeless
muddle. Of course there were mistakes, certainly the army was still
underfunded, the Liberal view being that defence was the most
important factor, and defence rested upon the navy being up to
strength. By the outbreak of war the army was still very short of Lee
Enfield rifles and much else. But the fact that within ten days of war
being declared Sir John French had five divisions at Amiens ready
to march was a visible and not inconsiderable achievement of
organization.

Any credit, in the past, has been attributed to either Haldane,
Asquith or Kitchener, neatly leaving out the figure in between. But
Colonel Maurice Hankey, seconded from the Royal Marines to be
the secretarial linchpin of the Defence Committee, a man in Lord
Fisher's immortal phrase 'with brains bulging out of his forehead'
was in a better position to judge than anyone. And he concluded
'that no one except Haldane and Asquith did more to help Britain's
preparations for war than General Seely'.

Even the famous Kitchener poster had a Seely imprimatur. For it was inspired by Hedley Le Bas, printing magnate and golfing friend, who back in 1913 had suggested to Seely that the War Office get its public relations act together to stem the fall in recruitment. The 'Your Country Needs You' slogan was Le Bas's idea. To think that if Seely had weathered the Curragh crisis, it could have been him with the pointing finger. Would it have had the same impact without the Kitchener moustache?

In August 1914 Seely had been through another of those adventures of his that made it a miracle that he was there at all. For one morning he had been down to Farnborough to be given a demonstration flight in a new 'inherently stable' plane piloted by an intrepid 'bird man' who rejoiced in the name of Busk.

To apply the phrase 'inherently stable' to any of those early biplane contraptions was a bit optimistic to say the least, but up into the heavens Busk and Seely went, the goggled ex-Minister in front, the gallant pilot behind. 'Our aeroplane was flying at about 65 miles an hour', says Seely as if this was an impressive rate of knots. 'I felt a tap on my shoulder and saw my valiant friend Busk holding both hands up.' If it were proof of 'inherent stability', it was not to last.

'All at once', continues Seely,

> while I was intently surveying the country in front of me, a great splash of fluid struck me in the face, just as though a man had thrown a pint of water out of a jug straight at me. Before I had time to think, the propeller had stopped and we were nose-diving to the ground. Within a few seconds we had attained an incredible speed. My most vivid recollections are clutching the sides of the cockpit to avoid falling forward, the violent uprush of air, and the almost unbelievable shriek of the wind tearing through the struts and the wires of the aeroplane.

It sounds like a good moment to say one's prayers but something told Seely that,

> Busk was still in command of our frail craft. I tried to turn my head to look at him but the violence of the wind made me bend

my head down again. For a few seconds more I saw the earth rushing up to meet us; then one had the sensation of terrific strain as we flattened out. There were loud clacks and twangs, a tremendous bump, and I found myself still in the aeroplane half upside down. Without much difficulty I clambered out, followed by Busk who was behind me. As he climbed out, the aeroplane, which had been standing on its head, rolled over on its side.

We lay down on the heather and spoke not a word for, I suppose, two or three minutes. Then Busk said with a happy smile on his pale face:

'Well I can't explain that.'

'What?' I asked.

He said: 'Why we did not catch fire.'

I replied: 'I suppose it was petrol that flew into my face?'

'Yes,' he said; 'I saw it fly and switched off on the instant. Even so, there is such a mass of hot metal round the engine that a big splash of petrol must mean ignition. I thought there was just a chance, though a remote one, that we might reach the ground before we were frizzed up.'

26

A Weapon Called Warrior

The great engines of war cranked up their armies, but Seely had a secret weapon. Warrior would be on the boat.

To say that Warrior was his horse is not enough. In the next four years Warrior became the symbol as well as the instrument of Jack Seely's indomitability. Through mud and bullet, bomb and trek, summer and winter, Warrior miraculously survived, head erect and ears pricked, ready, quite literally, to gallop where the deadliest danger lay. Seely rode him at the Marne, at Ypres, at the Somme, at Cambrai, all but lost him in the mud at Passchendaele, and it was on Warrior's back that he faced the supreme moment of his life on Easter Saturday 1918 when leading his Canadian Cavalry in the dramatic attack on Moreuil Wood.

Relating to a general, albeit one as open and charismatic as Seely was to prove, would always be difficult for troops further down the food chain. But Warrior wore no uniform, gave no orders, had no staff car to whisk him away to meetings. Warrior was in there with them. A bigger, braver target than any of them; a gentle-eyed presence whose neck you could slap with a tactile affection that war was starving out of you. Readers can be rightly sceptical about any claims a grandson may make about his grandfather. But whatever view one takes of Seely, one should never detract from the true phenomenon that was Warrior. He was one of the greatest horses in history.

He was the third and finest of the chargers with which Seely bonded in the manner that the desert chief had spelt out to him under the Somali stars in 1895. Seely was brave and able but not an exceptionally gifted rider. With all three horses, circumstances and temperament enabled the relationship to develop into the closeness normally associated with man and dog. With Maharajah it was the utter interdependence of those months living and indeed sleeping together on the veld. With Warrior's mother Cinderella, whom Seely bought in 1902, it was partly her own devoted nature. With Warrior himself, it was part genetic, part outstanding good early education and part Seely's own experience of the earlier pair.

The purchase of Cinderella was something straight out of the more extravagant pages of the Seely canon. On an August morning on Salisbury Plain in 1902, Seely atop a hill on Hampshire Yeomanry manoeuvres saw a lovely, long-tailed black thoroughbred gallop effortlessly by below him and immediately decided that this was the new horse he had been looking for. And for which, needless to say, his father had promised to pay.

He immediately spurred Maharajah in pursuit, cut off his quarry, and then and there agreed to buy her for seventy pounds. The owner, who had bought her only six months earlier for sixty pounds, was even happier half an hour and a whisky and soda later back in the yeomanry tent when Seely wrote him a cheque for eighty pounds. That was on condition that the little mare, just 15.1 hands and a thoroughbred from County Leitrim, should immediately join the Hampshire horse lines and her owner should get another ride home.

Eighty pounds then could buy you a small car now, but after an early scare it proved to be money wonderfully well spent, particularly in regard to her temperament: 'She would let my children climb up over her head', wrote Seely, 'and slide down her tail. Even more remarkable, swarm up her tail and slide down over her head.' She became so attached to her owner that she would jump out of her field to come and greet him. When he became a Minister he took her to London and rode her in Hyde Park before going to work at the Colonial Office.

The early scare had come from Maharajah on that very first morning among the horse lines on Salisbury Plain, the old white horse now tethered next to the gleaming new black. No amount of sugar lumps and 'meet your new friend' pats could prevent a first surge of jealousy towards this panther-coated little madam who seemed about to supplant him in his master's affections. When Seely's back was turned, Maharajah snapped his halter rope and with a wild squeal, sank his teeth into the mare's shoulder.

It was to be their only tiff. Soon they became such inseparable friends that when Seely rode one horse the other would follow. And when on an icy morning four years later Maharajah slipped up and broke his neck in the field, Cinderella was so inconsolable that she would not eat. Eventually 'Young Jim' Jolliffe, Seely's principal 'master of the horse' advised nature's best consolation: Cinderella was put in foal.

Sadly this too ended in disaster when the fine-looking foal died suddenly at just a few months old. But the second attempt at motherhood was a happily uncomplicated success. The sire was a handsome chestnut called Straybit who was based at the Jolliffes' thatched-barn farm at Yafford, just five miles east of Brooke. He was on a ministry lease scheme and in December 1909 was sold to go to Austria where he fathered many horses who would take the field against his British-born son. But before that he had scored a notable double. He had won the Lightweight Race at the Isle of Wight point-to-point. And he had fathered Warrior.

So in the spring of 1908 a telegram was despatched to the Colonial Office which the great but somewhat austere Civil Service Secretary opened with fears that his Minister's well known fearlessness had spilled over into bedrooms not his own. 'Fine child for Cinderella', read the cable, 'born at Yafford this morning. Both doing well – Jim.' What was a non-horseman like R. V. Vernon supposed to think?

It says much about Seely, and about the more equestrian climate of the times, that throughout this most intensely pressured period of his political life he was in constant touch with his horses and in particular with Warrior's development. They were not just an interest, they were a passion, and in the aching agony after Nim's death in 1913, educating Warrior was just the therapy needed to keep him the right side of sanity.

Warrior was kept in a south-facing field called Sidling Paul, which looks across the road at Brooke Church on its steep little mound with the sloping grassy graveyard where that August the wreaths still lay clustered around Nim's grave. It was in Sidling Paul Seely had first saddled and ridden Warrior and got bucked clean off for his pains. It was from there that he later rode quietly down through the village, past the Seely Reading Room, past the rectory and the forge, to introduce the young three-year-old to the sea. It took time, and a couple of soakings, but eventually Warrior would remain as calm among the waves as he would become steady against German shelling in years to come.

Jim Jolliffe had done Warrior's early schooling and done it well. He felt he was fast enough to be a racehorse, but with war looming Seely thought that military training was necessary. In January 1914 he was duly despatched to Burley-on-the-Hill, just west of Oakham in Rutland, where Seely's friend and Churchill's cousin Freddie Guest had a high-class establishment run by the distinguished Life Guards riding master, Major Douglas Hall.

Freddie Guest was an able and well-connected man who was to became Secretary of State for Air in 1920, who started the war as ADC to Sir John French, and who in August 1908 had Churchill and F.E. Smith amongst his guests when the house burnt down. Churchill immediately donned a fireman's helmet and was even seen on the roof with a hose directing operations. F.E. Smith had been ill, so confined himself to inspecting the wine which had been rescued from the cellar and laid out on the lawn. 'There,' said the great advocate, 'I thought the port was not what he said it was.'

One summer morning in 1914, F.E. was back at Burley, not to check on the port, but to accompany Seely as he watched Warrior go through his paces. Jim Jolliffe's early training had now been superbly supplemented on what had grown to be a deep-girthed, smallish (15.3 hands) dark brown gelding with a small but open and intelligent head with a white star on the forehead.

Only months before, Seely and Smith had been on opposite sides as the former's political career was broken on the Ulster crisis. But the bonds of friendship amongst this inner Churchillian group went way beyond party divides or swings of fortune. Before the year was out F.E. himself would be riding Warrior in France while Seely was away. He would have liked what he saw that morning at Burley-on-the-Hill.

'His training as a cavalry charger', ran Douglas Hall's Warrior citation, 'embraced the facing of grotesque sights and rifle-fire. He also went through the intricate figures of the musical ride, the rider whistling a popular tune. Had Warrior received circus training he would certainly have become a star performer, so great was his courage and placid intelligence.'

But Warrior was only six. As July ran into August and the inevitable declaration of war, Seely had to decide whether so young a horse should be asked to face the furies. He was uncharacteristically uncertain when Freddie Guest met him in the House of Commons at the beginning of the month. But Guest reassured him in words that conjure up the gung-ho opening enthusiasm for what was to prove such a horrific ordeal for so many.

> Well, we decided weeks ago that we would throw everything into this war, in addition to our obvious duty as officers in the Reserve to go there ourselves. Our motor cars are going, anything else that can be useful, and as many of those who have been with us in any capacity as are fit and ready to come, our grooms, our chauffeurs: you told me all your children too as they get old enough. Surely it would be a shame to leave Warrior behind ? He would hate it, and besides, Hall tells me that he has a wonderful constitution. He has never been sick or sorry all the time he has been with us.

Warrior would be tacked up, so would be Seely. If things had gone differently four months before he would still have been in the Cabinet room, trying to implement the plans he and Churchill had spent so long preparing for this hour. But while he remained the MP for Ilkeston throughout the war, it was action he now sought. And to get it he would need to call up favours due. Even if, for many in the military, Seely on their strength was something they would like to avoid at almost any cost.

But he started, and succeeded, at the top. He got himself appointed as Special Envoy to Sir John French, who had bobbed back up after his Curragh crisis resignation to become Commander-in-Chief of the British Expeditionary Force. Other generals might not fancy Seely but French did. Back in June 1912 it had been on Seely's recommendation that the little general had been raised to the rank of field marshal. It had prompted him to write very personally to Nim about her husband.

'I have been deeply touched by this evidence of friendship and trust. Thank God our relations have been ever most cordial, and I shall never cease to be grateful to him, not only for this act of friendship, but for the pleasure he has caused me to feel in the work I have to do under him.'

The roles might now be reversed but from that letter you can see that French was not going to desert his friend in his hour of need. Besides, Seely's boundless energy, his knowledge of all the original planning arrangements, his rhino-hided ability to mix and converse with both French and English, made him the ultimate galloper, scooping up and spreading news hither and thence. There was admiration as well as amusement amongst his friends as they now nicknamed him 'Galloper Jack'.

War was declared on 3 August. Kitchener took over at the War Office on 5 August and one of the countless tasks he did on that first day was to gazette 'Seely Lt Col and Hon Col (Hon Capt in Army) Rt Hon J.E.B., D.S.O., T.D. Hamps Yeo' as Special Service Officer in Belgium to the Commander-in-Chief. He would be on his way, but he would leave as a much wiser, more reflective soul than the young dasher who had hijacked his uncle's ship and dyed Maharajah brown before embarking for Africa fourteen years before.

Thanks to Lord Riddell's diary we have a perfect cameo of the way we were and there is a vivid picture of Seely's departure:

Monday, August 10th, 1914. In the evening I dined with Jack Seely and his son at the Reform Club – a farewell dinner. He thinks we have a hard job before us, and that the mortality will be terrible. As we walked back to Queen's Gate through the park, we sat on the bridge which crosses the ornamental waters. In the distance we could see the Foreign Office with the aerial gun on the roof. Seely said: 'I shall often think of this moment as I lie out in the field looking at the moon and stars as one does when one is campaigning.' Turning to his son, he said: 'You will have to be father to the family while I am away. If I don't come back you will have to look after them. I shall rely on you.' The boy said: 'I shall do my best.'

I went back to his home to shake hands with his valet – a very nice man who is accompanying him. They went through the South African war together.

Next morning Smith and Seely and the chauffeur Corporal Anthony travelled down to Southampton docks where Warrior and his groom Corporal Jack Thompson were waiting to take the boat to Le Havre. By a miracle, all five of them came safely home to celebrate Christmas at Brooke in 1918.

27

'Bravo, Mon Colonel' – 'Voilà, Madame'

Seely got a wound on the very first day.

The disembarkation had gone smoothly enough, perhaps something to do with the Le Havre docks being cleared and the traffic control appearing to be operated by local boy scouts and scout masters. Warrior and Corporal Thompson were despatched on to Sir John French's HQ at Le Cateau, some 100 miles to the east of Le Havre. Seely, Smith and Corporal Anthony, the driver, not to mention Freddie Guest in his open top Rolls, were due to motor in the morning. Dinner was booked with the well-informed General Grierson at eight. Time for a swim.

The greatest conflagration in history was about to start. The man who knew as much about its ghastly potential as anyone would be driving towards the enemy in the morning. But Seely always loved to mix action with reflection. His roots would always remain near the sea. It was high summer and hot. All he needed was a towel and that strange black one-piece thing called in those days a 'bathing costume'.

The old French gentleman on the beach was happy to provide. In view of Seely's leanness it must have been a baggy fit, but it gave the full prudish cover up required in that era. The sea that August evening gave its full plunging release, he swam up and down, floated on his back, looked at the cliffs beyond the town and thought of his children doing the same in the waves of Compton Bay. It was too good to last. On his way out he stepped on a piece of broken glass and with blood gushing had to tourniquet his foot with the towel. It was all too much for the patriotic old Frenchman:

'He ran down to me, and putting one hand on his heart, and holding the other outstretched said: 'Bravo, mon Colonel. Vous avez déjà versé votre sang anglais pour la France.'

Next morning Seely set off for headquarters at Le Cateau. Cured by General Grierson's port, if not cheered by his prediction that, far from some quick march to Berlin, the situation was likely soon to depend on whether the French could prevent the Front collapsing all the way to Paris. He arrived in rude health to meet a sense of still optimistic expectancy, but that night the poor old general took a sweltering hot train east and died of a heart attack on the way.

With Sir John French still delayed in London, someone like Seely was not going to hang about playing cards. Especially not when the HQ staff included his friend Hugh Grosvenor, the Duke of Westminster, married to the sister of Churchill's young stepfather, George Cornwallis-West. The duke was known to all as 'Bend Or', a tag deriving, one hopes, from the name of his grandfather's Derby winner in 1892. Bend Or had not come to war unequipped. He had reached HQ 'complete with two Rolls-Royce cars, and two admirable chauffeurs'. He and Seely would only need one.

On the way to Le Cateau, Seely had stopped outside Amiens to talk to General Robb, who repeated Grierson's gloomy prediction of the night before. He did not think the French lines would hold. He too thought saving Paris was going to be the most immediate issue. The trouble was that no one really knew how far the Germans had already come. The French said they would never cross the Meuse. How long would that last? It was clearly a question that needed answering. In the absence of a C-in-C, Seely and Westminster might as well find out:

Early next morning we started for the Meuse; Bend Or driving, I by his side, and the chauffeur with a carbine sitting behind, nearly blown to bits by the speed at which we travelled. It was an extraordinary journey. All the villages were 'En Fête'. The approach to each one reminded me of entering a town where

there was a flag day in progress. As we slowed down to the
entrance of each village the whole population turned out and
lined the road, waving little Union Jacks and tricolour flags, the
Union Jack predominating, and crying out in chorus 'Vive les
Anglais,' with occasional shouts of 'A Berlin! A bas les Boches!'
Women and children of all ages and old men were all that were
left. Mobilization had been so complete that hardly an able-
bodied man was to be seen. At last we approached the Meuse,
and I noted that, in the village which we passed some four miles
from Pont Ivoir, our first destination, the cheering was less loud
and few flags were to be seen.

They were about to reach the reality which Seely knew was bound
to come. But, being Seely, it would have its comic as well as its
deadly side. In Pont Ivoir they thought they would just rock up to
the colonel in charge to find out the state of play. They climbed out
of the Rolls, marched through the wicket gate and up towards what
presumably was the colonel's door.

'Suddenly from behind a bush jumped out an officer who placed
his revolver within 6 inches of my head, saying "Rendez-vous".
From behind the same bush another officer and an orderly appeared
who volubly said something. I caught the word "espion". They also
had revolvers, and the officer presented his at Bend Or's head.'

Seely launched into a long spiel about being a special envoy from
John French and a personal friend of everyone from King George to
Marshal Foch. But the French colonel's finger still looked very itchy
and unconvinced on the trigger until Bend Or broke the spell.

'It seems rather rough luck,' he said as only a proper duke could,
'for these people to shoot us just when we have come such a long
way to cheer them up. Couldn't you ask the colonel to give us a
drink instead?'

Revolvers were eventually lowered, much verification was
done by telephone and eventually the Frenchman reverted to type.
A bottle of Bordeaux and four glasses were brought in and he said,
'Whether you are spies or not – but I think you are – I cannot allow
two thirsty men to leave my headquarters without a drink.'

The style if not the substance of this encounter had clearly got back to John French when they reported to him next morning. He was, to use that most wonderful of military phrases, 'in a towering rage'. He had not read their report but he had received the protests from French HQ about two unauthorized officers wandering around their lines. It was exactly what the Alliance did not want. He would see them later but the correct procedure would be for both of them to be sent home at once.

It was a nasty moment. Six months earlier, Sir John French had been accepting Seely as his political master as Secretary of State for War, now he was treating him as just another insubordinate junior officer. To make matters worse, the man in charge at this Le Cateau HQ was none other than Henry Wilson, the arch-snake in the grass during that crisis over Ulster. It says a lot for all three men that by evening French had calmed down and was entirely reconciled with Seely, whilst Wilson was happy to deploy all his old adversary's energy as the situation began to crumble to the north and east.

There were other trips in the Westminster Rolls, most notably a late-night one with an urgent message to the old fortress at Maubeuge, where the wife of the commander for a long time refused to go and wake her husband: 'He has a bad cough, he needs his sleep.' But just about the most alarming journey was when French's HQ had been moved back to Saint-Quentin and the redoubtable Sergeant Anthony was at the wheel. Anthony always had a rifle in the car; in 1920 he saved French from an IRA assassination attempt in Phoenix Park. His cheery advice to Seely was, 'Well sir, I will kill one German before I am shot. And if every other Englishman did the same, we shan't do so badly in this war.'

It was raining and getting dark when Seely and Anthony got back to Saint-Quentin. The place was empty but the road was blocked by a flock of sheep. As Seely got past them, the shepherd said despondently, 'Nous sommes trop tard, tous les deux.' Optimistic as ever, Seely did not get his meaning until he marched into the town hall and discovered he had just walked past a German sentry. He raced back to the car, Anthony roared away from the shots and they got safe out of Saint-Quentin, although, typically, not until they had checked that John French had indeed left his HQ and retrieved the gold pencil he had left behind.

As the situation deteriorated through August, the close shaves accumulated. Very soon it was Warrior who was under the severest threat. After watching the French engineers fail to destroy the Oise bridge at Compiègne, Seely set off back to Paris with Smith sitting with the luggage in the back saying gloomily, 'Looks like they have got us this time, sir.' They were still within earshot of gunfire when they came on a broken-down HQ lorry full of secret papers. Its bonnet was open and looking inside along with the driver was Corporal Thompson his arm hooked through Warrior's bridle, the young horse's ears pricked at the rifle shots in the distance.

There was, in the truest use of that most classic phrase, no time to lose.

> It was midday and there was a bright sun. I said to Thompson: 'you see the sun?' He answered 'Yes, sir.' I said: 'Mount Warrior and gallop as hard as you can straight for the sun for half an hour, then, and not until then, inquire for the British General Headquarters.' He disappeared in a cloud of dust. We piled all the confidential boxes into Freddie Guest's car and mine. The Germans got nothing of any value, but everything else, except Warrior in that little outfit fell into the hands of the enemy.

Warrior was saved but it looked as if France was falling. The Cabinet were evacuating for Bordeaux and Seely was sent to seek out and support General Galliéni, who had been appointed governor of Paris. Seely's trip, and the language used to describe it, were once again a beguiling mixture of history and farce:

> There was no one on the streets. When I say no one I mean, literally, not a single human being or vehicle. I went to the British Embassy in the Faubourg St Honoré, but failed to make anyone hear; thence to the Ritz Hotel, where I was determined to have a bath and a shave before interviewing the Governor of Paris, but the Ritz too was shut and locked. Fortunately I bethought me of

going to the Hotel Lotti in the Rue Castiglione where, after much banging on the door with a heavy spanner, I induced someone to open it about two inches. It was Monsieur Lotti himself who let me in and provided me with the bath of which I stood so much in need. He told me that the Government had left by special train the night before, that it was universally believed that the Germans would march in at 10 o'clock that morning and that when I banged at the door he had assumed that it was the beginning of the German occupation. He told me where to find General Galliéni, and after a never-to-be-forgotten meal of chicken and eggs, I betook myself there.

Galliéni was a veteran of the 1870 campaign who told Seely about his never-say-die plans to use squads of old men and boys to fight off the advancing Germans and then to gather other French troops for a counter-attack on the Marne. But even the unquenchable optimist in his visitor must have wondered if the old war dog was not just growling to keep his spirits up. If they wanted it, Paris was the Germans' for the taking. So much for all those brave words and telegrams of the War Office days.

Yet as Seely drove away he was reminded that no position is completely hopeless if shafts of humour can still beam in:

The streets were absolutely empty, but in the Place Vendôme I saw an old woman walking across the middle of it. Standing at the foot of the famous statue was an aged gendarme. Just then I heard the hum of an aeroplane and looking up, saw a German Taube like a peregrine falcon moving across the sky at an immense height, I suppose not less than eight thousand feet. The French lady threw up her hands and shouting, 'C'est un Boche, sauvez-moi' rushed toward the gendarme and threw herself into his arms. He put his left arm round her, and with his right pulled out an old pistol from a black holster. Then, saying, 'Calmez-vous Madame,' he fired four shots at the distant Taube. I suppose the effective range of his pistol was about fifty feet, and the aeroplane was no less than eight thousand. Of course the unconscious aeroplane pilot continued on his way and soon vanished from view. 'Voilà, Madame,' said the gendarme, 'je l'ai chassé,' and kissed her on both cheeks.

Seely could smile. But he knew that soon there would be precious little to smile about.

28

Antwerp and the First Lord

Being alive was becoming a matter of celebration, desperation and frustration. Celebration came early. In September there was a French counter-attack which Seely loved to describe as 'the crowning mercy of the Marne'. He was back on Warrior, riding towards the early-morning sun. To have a young thoroughbred moving easily beneath you will lift the most jaded spirit. Seely felt so good that he wrote in his diary, 'the best day of my life'.

The mood swing from an army about to lose the long-awaited conflict within five weeks of the start, to one back on the attack, was overwhelming. But Seely had bitter personal problems of his own. Louisa, the youngest and sickliest of his seven motherless children, was just one year old in August. He himself was a glorified runner for people of whom he had been in supreme strategic charge only six months earlier. And the bullets were flying.

At a place called La Ferté-sous-Jouarre, some thirty miles east of Paris, the Germans were dug in on the opposite bank of the Marne and the fighting nearly did for both Seely and his horse.

Once they had reached the town, Warrior and a group of horses were tethered in a bunch whilst Seely and the others tried to work out a way to dislodge the Germans. It nearly happened the other way round. A shell came over and landed slap amongst the horses, killing some and wounding most as was the woeful pattern for the whole campaign. Warrior escaped without a scratch.

So too did Seely from a subsequent incident which, even if his account is divided by half, still seems death-defyingly unbelievable. La Ferté-sous-Jouarre was a typical small town on the Marne with one principal main street running down to the river. As Seely came down it a machine gun opened up and he dived into a side street where he discovered a sergeant and eight men who had just had the same experience.

The next safe siding was only about eighty yards further down. Should they try to rush there singly or together? Seely had this doomed theory that there would be some sort of safety in numbers. So on the blast of the sergeant's whistle the luckless little legion legged it down the road. Luckless – for all bar one. And there are no prizes for guessing who was the one.

'Rifle and machine gun fire was intense, and came from some concealed point less than a hundred and fifty yards away. When I got to the side road, in safety but with a bullet through my hat and another through my stick, I looked round for the rest. Every one of them was lying dead in the roadway.'

A few days later a letter came through in a familiar hand. 'I hope', it said somewhat belatedly, 'you will not expose yourself unnecessarily to danger.' It was from Churchill. The sentiments expressed therein take us straight back to the feeling of optimism which in hindsight seems untenable, but which came from just about the best-informed mind of the time.

> Here the feeling is absolutely united and running breast high for a prolonged and ruthless struggle. There will, I think, be no difficulty in putting a million men in the field in the spring of 1915. But we must keep the necessary minimum of officers to train them.
>
> I rejoice more than I can say at the splendid deeds of the army and the military repute which our country has by a few weeks of their achievements altogether revived.
>
> The Navy has been thrilled by all their prowess and valour. We sit still on the cold-blooded game and can, I think, keep it up indefinitely.
>
> Doom has fallen on Prussian military arrogance. Time and determination are all that is needed.
>
> Yours ever,
> W.

Twenty-five years later the Western world would begin to rally to that same voice uttering phrases like those last two rolling sentences. By then Churchill would be in his mid sixties. How much more electrifying must he have been close up in 1914, just forty years old and bursting with vigour, brilliance and self-belief? Seely was soon to be in a position to tell.

On 25 September he was up in Dunkirk to report for John French. To his delight there was present not only Churchill, checking on his naval forces, but F.E. Smith keen to talk about a 'special mission'. It was an odd place for an Other Club reunion, but the three friends would quickly be putting the world and the future of the war to rights. Their immediate future and everyone else's was in the balance. Within a week all of Belgium was under threat; by Saturday 3 October Antwerp was in crisis, with only the 3,000 Marines and 4,000 naval volunteers of the Naval Brigade to stiffen the exhausted local defence. But they had Churchill himself in charge, and by typical coincidence Seely was there to join him:

'From the moment I arrived it was apparent that the whole business was in Winston's hands. He dominated the whole place, the King, ministers, soldiers, sailors. So great was his influence that I am convinced that with 20,000 British troops he could have held Antwerp against almost any onslaught.'

So deeply was Winston involved that he even telegraphed Asquith asking to be relieved of the Admiralty and be given official command of the troops. It was not granted, but for four days he was a classically inspirational figure, holding meetings, summoning reinforcements (the Naval Brigade that arrived included the poet Rupert Brooke), and driving to the trenches to see for himself the situation at the Front. He loved being in the thick of the action. So too did the old friend in the car beside him.

There is a picture of Seely and Churchill on one of these trips. Seely very functional in his khaki uniform, Churchill a touch more extravagant in a dark blue overcoat with a white silk scarf around his neck beneath a naval cap. The pair of them were to get physical evidence of just how tough things were.

'A car came from the direction of the front lines and drew up,'

the then eighteen-year-old seaman John Mitchell later reported, 'an
open tourer. Its windscreen was all smashed and the Marine who
was driving had a bandage round his head. Churchill was in the car
together with Colonel Seely.'

Mitchell told how he had not been able to sleep for three days
and could not that Tuesday night. Not surprising when you hear
the much harsher testimony of Able Seaman Jack Bentham for that
same Tuesday evening:

'Had to dig trenches and earthworks until dusk and were not
allowed to sleep or talk. Severe frost and shivered all night as half
of us had oilskins which were no protection. We cursed a car
containing Churchill who came out to see what was going on and
we were glad when he departed.'

That night Churchill left for London and the admiration of his
desk-bound colleagues. Seely went back to get two hours' sleep,
albeit in a four-poster bed with the gallant Smith sleeping outside
the door for protection. Over the next two days he had the
frustration of no longer being involved in any of the old Cabinet-
room strategy, but as he physically shepherded the last troops to the
bridge over the Scheldt, he was in desperation up to his neck.

'As a result of the bombardment, fires were burning in many
parts of the city, and viewed from the trenches a great pall of black
smoke hung over the city, pierced in places by yellow sheets of
flame. One extraordinary lucky thing for me was that in all these
trips through the burning town I never punctured a tyre, and
though often held up by shell-holes, broken electric light standards,
fallen houses and wires, always managed to get through.'

That morning he was the principal link back to London,
telegraphing Kitchener and Asquith, passing on the King's message
of support to the local commander, General Paris. He was hopeful
they could hold out another couple of days but that afternoon Paris
decided to withdraw, leaving no option but for the British to follow.
Come eight o'clock everything was ready. It was going to be hairy.

The men had no warning but they behaved with extraordinary
coolness and courage. There was the great host in front of them,

whose presence was only shown by an occasional rifle shot and by the unending stream of shells whistling over their heads. Behind them the blazing city through which they had to retire, covered by the dense pall of black smoke; beyond that again the broad ribbon of the Scheldt, brilliantly lighted up by immense flames from the huge stores of oil which had been set on fire. However they [the troops] all moved quietly and silently away, while I stayed behind with an officer and 100 men, who kept up an intermittent rifle fire. The officer then withdrew all of them except four men, who kept on shooting, finally I put these four in the car and drove away.

Seely may have officially been a mere yeomanry colonel acting as a galloper for HQ but he was also the man who had been court-martialled and later given the DSO for refusing to leave his men to Boer attack. When things got rough you could not change his nature. He would be the last man.

Through the dark and deserted streets of Antwerp marched the weary troops. It was 10 p.m. by the time they reached the bridge over the Scheldt. With miraculously few casualties they were eventually almost all over. Seely's closing comment is not without its usual touch of immodesty. But there is no doubting its accuracy:

'After reporting to General Paris I drove back across the bridge of boats to see if there were any stragglers still coming down the road which led to it. I found two exhausted men who had been left behind and brought them back. We were the last to cross the bridge.'

On the Saturday before, Asquith had written a bit caustically, 'The Arch Colonel has turned up at Antwerp full of fight and hope.' A week later he was telling Miss Stanley that 'the Arch Colonel, characteristically was the last to leave'. The Prime Minister was actually being affectionate. But snide remarks are easier said from the safety of the office. The Arch Colonel was in Belgium. Where he was going both the desperation and the frustration would only increase.

29

Front Line

Antwerp was hardly even the beginning. Like Shakespeare's soldier, Seely already had the 'bubble reputation', and he would remain addicted to the 'cannon's mouth'. And to helping those in there beside him. Sir John French's HQ was temporarily way back by the mouth of the Somme at Abbeville. Down there the old white-moustachioed supremo was using Warrior as his hack. Seely reported the delayed collapse of Antwerp and the three of them came back up to the Belgium border. The first battle of Ypres began. The prospects were bad and the weather terrible. For Seely the experience was seminal.

> One evening I went up to our front line. It was bitterly cold and sleet was falling. I failed to find the battalion headquarters whither I had been sent, and going forward, found myself in a veritable hail of bullets. So I toppled into a little trench, where there was a corporal and two men; four other men lying dead, having been killed by shell fire which had been very severe and most accurate. 'Here they come!' said the corporal, and sure enough, a hundred yards away was a great number of advancing Germans.
>
> The sleet had turned to snow, but they were so near that one could distinguish them quite clearly. I see those grey figures now, trudging along towards us through the snow, some with their heads bent down, others with their left arms shielding their heads, marching on but for some curious reason hardly one of them lifting his head to look death in the face. I snatched

one of our dead men's rifles, and the four of us shot as fast and as straight as we could. Though there were but four of us the Germans had no chance at all. The nearest man who escaped death or mortal wounds did not get within thirty yards of us.

The forebodings he had experienced during those German manoeuvres six years earlier were now made flesh in the most ghastly fashion. War was indeed a bad, bad business and this one was rapidly becoming the most terrible ever fought. A few days after that snowstorm slaughter, Seely and an intelligence officer called Greenwood were leaving Dixmude.

> Very big shells were raining on the doomed town, and by the time we got there every house was in flames. The streets were quite deserted and bullets were singing along them. The heat from the burning houses on each side was so great that we had to run down the middle of the street. Dead bodies were lying around in great numbers, and to add to the horror of the scene, quantities of pigs, mad with fright, were galloping about making the weirdest of noises. Greenwood shot several with his revolver to put them out of their misery.

It was no place for a pacifist and when Ramsay MacDonald, Britain's most famous anti-war campaigner, came over to visit Dunkirk hospital he was, mistakenly, arrested and locked up. Seely was despatched to release him. Quite soon Ramsay would wish he hadn't.

They met in Poperinghe, near Ypres, where Ramsay had been taken in the back of a Red Cross motor ambulance. Seely put him in the back seat of his car and drove up through the Menin Gate and then took the road north running along the west side of the Yser Canal towards the future Prime Minister's intended destination at Dixmude. Ramsay had asked to go to the front line. Seely had explained that as a non-combatant this was forbidden. As they neared the village of Liserne, rules faded and reality intervened.

Their car was suddenly raked by machine-gun and rifle fire. The bonnet, windscreen and mudguards were all hit, but somehow the occupants got to a bank where they could throw themselves out and shelter in the mud. Hardly had they registered that the French front line was just the other side of the canal and the German trenches barely three hundred yards beyond it, when a massive artillery barrage started up from behind them. Whistles blew, machine guns rattled and the French leapt from their trenches in full assault.

In a trice Seely was legging it across the bridge with MacDonald in tow for the two of them to jump into the French trench in solidarity. Quite what the luckless platoon thought of the future premier and former war minister dropping by at this juncture might be gathered from the odd cry of 'espions' that went up. But Seely produced his credentials, passed on British good wishes and then evacuated their hapless guest to make a delayed and mud-caked inspection of Dixmude hospital up the road.

The frustrations of being something between a King's messenger and a khaki, as opposed to blue-chip, tourist guide, were partly offset by the quality of his visitors and the actual fact of being at the Front, at that time the only acceptable location for a man of honour. The Duke of Marlborough, like Freddie Guest a Churchill cousin, had a soaking and dangerous trek over a bullet-spattered causeway to deliver a message to the beleaguered Belgian village of Ghent. And an entry in Seely's diary for 19 November 1914 reads, 'awakened by my future King'. It was the Prince of Wales asking to borrow a sword to wear at Lord Roberts's funeral.

But the most significant and most treasured confederate to come out that autumn was F.E. Smith, who was attached to the Indian Corps based, and suffering horribly, in the front line further south near Béthune. F.E. had begun the war as the head of the Press Bureau (in essence the 'chief censor'), a job arranged for him by Seely from the Committee of Imperial Defence. At that Seely farewell dinner referred to by Lord Riddell, F.E. had promised his friend that after getting the bureau into action he would make his way to the Front for 'any task, however menial'.

The 'sword of sacrifice' still reigned supreme, but both Smith and Seely were a bit more than their apparent minor roles might suggest. F.E. with his intimate links to Churchill back in England, and Seely with his attachment to French had already met for a secret exchange on a destroyer near Calais and on a cruiser off Dunkirk. As October became November and rain turned Flanders into mud. F.E. had installed himself in a rectory, at Hinges, not far from Béthune. He had brought three of his best hunters with him, and for a while even took on a now shell-steady Warrior when Seely was away. Fortunately for the future, Warrior was off sick when Seely came to call.

In a few brief weeks F.E. had seen the hopelessness of it all. 'Oh! My dear!' he had written to his wife, 'the suffering of the refugees; it is beyond tears. Everything in the world gone.' And in bitter irony after his previous job he complained of 'the swagger and ignorant optimism of the British Press', explaining that, despite reports otherwise, 'the Indian troops are not doing very well (rather the contrary) and we are very anxious about them.'

When Seely arrived at the rectory, F.E. still had enough of his sense of humour to make his friend avert eyes from the entrance of the curé's 'shy but stunningly beautiful daughter', only to discover the server was actually the father's elderly and toothless sister. But when they rode out towards the front line the mood changed quickly. They had barely gone 300 yards when a shot rang out and the horse F.E. was riding crashed down. He took the spare horse from the orderly but before they had gone much further the great lawyer took a package from his pocket and asked Seely to post it if anything happened. Letters to loved ones had been written. F.E. thought that Seely looked like a legend made to last.

Once they reached the trenches they dismounted and walked the front line. The conditions for the Indians were quite deplorable. Where trenches could be dug they filled with water, the parapets they built for defences were often not thick enough, and the climate, with ice and snow to bite before the end of November, was utterly unbearable for troops newly shipped in from the sub-continent.

And to think that a comparable division of territorials had been shipped off from England to Palestine. Seely's suspicion about the army establishment's prejudice against territorials which had been such a feature of his time at the War Office now had the most dismal of proofs. Imagine how he would have railed about 'the closed military mind' as he and his brilliant friend made this inspection of misery.

To F.E. he would have expounded his theories on periscopes (he was there to see how the latest version was working for the Indians), on searchlights, plane-tangling kites, telephones, hand grenades and the many other things that his fevered mind had dealt with in the Committee of Imperial Defence and felt ought to be implemented now. It may have been an Other Club meeting with a difference but Seely was not a man without opinions, nor an ex-minister without friends. F.E., for all his gallantry, was wasted at the front and within six months was not just in London but in government. For Seely this was natural habitat. Yet for senior soldiers he was still a territorial, a politician, and an over-the-top ex-war minister to boot. 'I longed for a command', he later wrote, 'however small.'

It was a plaintive note from someone so well connected. And a yearning which he was entitled to feel able to fulfil. Especially after he himself had been on the receiving end of a plan straight out of 'The Passchendaele Book of Military Madness':

'Very heavy rain had fallen and our trenches were half full of water', he wrote. It had been near Lille one evening before Christmas.

> The attack was timed for dusk and the signal was to be the bursting of the few heavy shells available – an elementary kind of barrage. We heard our shells humming over our heads, and as they burst we jumped over the parapet. We were about six yards apart, and with difficulty ploughed our way through the deep mud. When we got about half way to the German front line, over a very slight incline, a bouquet of Verey lights went up, and very heavy machine-gun fire opened from a concealed German redoubt about fifty yards to my right.

At that moment both my legs were stuck in the mud up to the knees. The machine-gun fire was deadly; a man about six to my right fell riddled with bullets, then the next, then the next, and the next – I could hear the bullets thudding into their bodies – then it was my turn. I was sure that my time had come at last and waited for the thud that had killed my comrades. But the bullets went humming by about two yards to my right: I could see the flash of the machine gun quite clearly. Then it dawned on me that the gun was in an embrasure, and the gunner could not traverse it far enough to reach me. I lay on my back for a moment and slowly wriggled my legs out of the mud. I looked to the right and left, and saw that the attack had failed.

Seely's memoirs, for all their heroics, are astonishingly, at times irritatingly, free of censure. So for him there is real bitterness in his three-sentence critique:

'I wondered then and I wonder now, what real purpose was served by sending the infantry over the top in that muddy area. The slow moving infantryman has a poor chance in any case against concealed machine-gun and rifle fire; his only chance is a short rush at the double. But if you slow him down to two miles an hour by sending him through deep mud, his fate is sealed.'

If Seely were finally to be given a command he would be no caricature general. It was getting any post at all that remained a problem. Visiting endless HQs and trench systems and writing reports for French may have been useful, but it was hardly the man-to-man commitment his temperament and his South African experience had readied him for. Racing Warrior against aircraft on take-off may have been an amusing rest-day diversion, but it was not the reason he had brought Cinderella's son to the front.

Christmas 1914, 'a miserable business,' came complete with its armistice, which in Seely's diary was neither as jolly nor as extensive as later legend would have it:

'It lasted about three hours, during which time both sides fraternised. Some of our men went into their trenches, which were wetter than ours. The occasion was taken to bury the dead, service read by German officers in German and English. Invited to football match between Saxons and English on New Year's Day.'

Both sides prayed to the same god. What madness these war games were. How futile the New Year's armistice must have seemed:

'Walked across the road within 50 yards of the German trench. One German stood up to look. A voice from the Hampshire trench, 'It's all right sir, they won't shoot.' Wished everyone in trenches a Happy New Year from C in C. Both sides busy improving their positions at night. Much rain.'

Back home Churchill, F.E. and other friends championed his cause but Asquith wrung his hands with characteristic urbanity. 'I don't know what can be done for him,' he wrote to the ever attentive Venetia, 'unless some fattish Colonial Governorship crops up.'

It was a cheap shot, but to be fair Asquith had weightier problems on his mind. It was left to Seely's greatest ally to come up with an idea. And even then there was probably an element of getting Jack off his back. After their experiences together in Antwerp Seely thought he might try to badger Churchill into putting him in charge of the Naval Division. By mid January Winston was writing to finally block the plan: 'It is much better for you to serve under the War Office than under me, for then your employment will be free from all suggestion of personal or political favour.'

But, incredibly inventive and supportive friend that he was, Churchill did not leave it there:

> I spoke to Kitchener about you. Without finally committing himself he said that there were left here two regular Canadian cavalry regiments which, with a yeomanry regiment added, would make a good cavalry brigade – out of the general line and very suitable for you.
>
> I strongly recommend this. I gathered that the date of the actual formation of the brigade would depend rather on when you wanted to take it up. But I advise your coming over and getting into the saddle here as soon as possible and then leading

your own men out in the regular way. This will be best for your interests and the right thing for the service.

Kitchener is very well disposed towards you.

Yours always.

W.

The Canadian cavalry: to the outsider they looked a displaced, half-trained, makeshift bunch of ranchers, clerks, cowboys, ex-pats, mounties and Red Indians, whose connection with Seely was about as distant as you could get. But they were made for each other.

IV. LIFE EVER ON THE LINE

30

The Canadians and the Comeback

It was not going to be easy. The British army disapproved of the appointment and the Canadian Government didn't want an Englishman to command their men, least of all an English politician. But putting Seely in charge of the Canadian cavalry brigade had a double attraction for Kitchener as War Minister. At a stroke it removed the trickiest of wild cards from the British army as well as cutting the separatist ambitions of the Canadian elite. Seely was much too energetic, much too influential to continue as Galloper Jack. But Sam Hughes, the forceful Canadian Minister for Defence had overweening plans for a Dominion force in its own right. Seely had been the War Minister who split up the fisticuffs between Hughes and the South African General Beyers at those Cambridgeshire manoeuvres in 1912. He would clip 'Big Sam's' wings. He and Warrior, and Thompson, Smith and Anthony, had better get on the boat.

First stop was Brooke. Seely to see his children; Smith his wife, Rose; Warrior his mother Cinderella. All were there except John and Frank who were away at Harrow. 'Baby Lou' was now eighteen months old and despite her periodic asthma attacks was defying the first gloomy medical forecasts. She had no idea who this thin, tired, ruddy-faced man in uniform was, but nine-year-old Patrick and seven-year-old Kitty knew well enough. For Irene and Emily there was a mixture of desperate delight at their father's return and sorrow at the news that he was off in just days to the War Office and from there to his new command, which was to take him to the Front.

Just as less-privileged families were, they came to realize that this war was much more than an adventure for 'King and Country'. With their mother dead the children would have clung to their father, he to them. But in this era the call to arms was overwhelming, its acceptance unhesitating. 'I longed, like everybody did,' he wrote, 'to take my place in the line.' Seely caught the ferry and the train to see Kitchener in London.

As Churchill had told him the new 'Canadian Cavalry Brigade' was to link two Canadian cavalry regiments with their horse artillery and add a yeomanry regiment of British-based colonials called 2nd King Edward's Horse. The two Canadian regiments were Lord Strathcona's Horse, taking men from the west, and the Royal Canadian Dragoons, who drew their strength from the east. Since October they and the 1st Canadian Infantry Division had been encamped at Pond Farm Camp on Salisbury Plain. It all sounded impressive enough but Seely was soon to find out different.

For a start, the conditions were truly appalling. It had been the wettest winter on record. Seely was appointed on 1 February 1915 and didn't waste time:

'I went to Salisbury and started off in a motor car to a place called The Bustard. It could not be reached by car, as the mud was too deep; however I borrowed a horse and managed to ride there. Then I was given the general direction of the Royal Canadian Dragoons and set to work to ride to them. After a time the horse could go no further, being up to its knees and hocks in mud. So I dismounted and walked the rest of the way. Even in Flanders I had not seen such a sea of mud.'

A year earlier he had been shuttling between Whitehall, Westminster and Buckingham Palace dealing with the whole army. Now he was sloshing from camp to village in command of less than 2,000 men and horses. For him this was no humiliation. It was exactly the challenge he wanted. And straightaway he began to put his past to good effect.

'Colonel Seely is much in evidence these days', wrote one of the Canadians, 'and there can be no doubt that the cavalry will fare well as regards men and equipment. One can hardly be War Minister without knowing which ropes to pull.'

Or which men to appoint. Jury, the brigade major, and Docherty, the staff captain, later proved themselves in higher rank whilst the man he brought as ADC was 25-year-old Lieutenant Sir Archibald Sinclair of the Life Guards, future leader of the Liberal Party, owner of 100,000 acres in the north of Scotland but so utterly charming and dependable that he was called 'Archie' by officers and privates alike. He and Seely may have seemed like the greatest anachronisms the Canadians had ever met. But they delivered.

Within days Seely had got the remaining troops out of muddy tents to village billets on the north part of the Plain. Within a week he and the brigade were reviewed by the King as part of the main Canadian division prepared to embark for France. Within a very short time he put to shame the carping reservations expressed publicly in the British Parliament and privately by the Canadian Prime Minister, Sir Robert Borden. As testified by this story from 25-year-old Lieutenant Luke Williams of Strathcona's Horse.

> Field Punishment No1 used to include being strapped to the wheel of a wagon for varying periods of time. This was discontinued in the Canadian Cavalry Brigade on the express orders of General Seely. He happened to come by one day and saw Private Shand strapped to the wagon wheel paying the penalty of his crime. The General ordered him to be released and then insisted on being strapped to the wheel in Shand's place. After spending a few minutes of being strapped to the wheel he asked to be released. Then he said 'there will be no more of that in this Brigade while I am in command of it.' From that day on there was no more No1 Field Punishment. In place of it the men had to do periods of pack drill in full marching order.

Williams had come into the cavalry because he had spent his early years with horses when his father kept a hardware store in a small town in the west. Many of his fellow soldiers, some of them of part or of full Native American blood, had had similar experiences. The Canadians had brought 1,800 horses over with them with their first draft. It was into this environment that Seely rode on Warrior. The horse, even more than the man, was an instant hit:

'This handsome, gay, bay thoroughbred with the white star on his forehead was my passport wherever I went. As time went on, especially in France where we soon returned, the men got to love him more and more. As I rode along, whether it were in rest billets, in reserve, approaching the line, or in the midst of battle, men would say not "Here comes the General", but "Here's old Warrior."'

Soon the Canadians were wanted at the Front, but they were wanted on their feet. It was not exactly what the officers and men had been training for. As that soggy winter had turned to a more promising spring they had been moved to Maresfield Park in Sussex where the lodging for both men and horses was a great improvement. Once there, the troop exercises had included plenty of sword-drawn scurries aping the Charge of the Light Brigade. In three years' time, the resemblance would be all too real.

For at the end of April a new form of torture had hit the Canadian Infantry Division already at Ypres: gas. At Easter 1918 Seely would take a crippling dose. For now he was summoned by Kitchener to the War Office to ask his brigade to go as infantry reinforcements to the Front. These were still the days of unswerving, undamaged patriotism. The cavalry volunteered one hundred per cent.

On 5 May 1915 Seely himself led Warrior off the boat at Boulogne and as the Canadians marched past, still ludicrously kitted out in riding breeches and spurs, they did so as a unit already filled with corporate pride. Within hours that pride was under threat. Other generals did not fancy someone as well connected as the former War Minister having a force of his own. The brigade would be split into mere drafts for other regiments. But Seely had been assured by French himself that this would not happen. It was time to act.

'To rest camp', reads his diary note. 'Great concern at order to break up Brigade. Issued necessary orders. Then 200 mile journey with Archie [Sinclair – his ADC] to put things right. CIGS's letter worked a charm. Orders issued by QMG reconstructing the Brigade at 10–15.'

A brigadier general may be quite low down the hierarchy of military top brass, but Seely was not someone to push around. The British were finding it now, just as Sam Hughes, the Canadian Defence Minister, had discovered a month before. 'Big Sam' had insisted that the cavalry carried the Ross rifle. From Boer War days rifles were a Seely speciality. He switched the whole brigade to Lee Enfields. 'Big Sam' fumed. But very soon reports came through of the Ross rifle's unreliability in action. Seely was right.

At Festubert, where they were headed south of Ypres, he was dead lucky, too. From 24 May to the 27th they were in the front line which, when first seen by moonlight, must remain a perfect vision of hell. An RCD veteran recorded his impressions:

> Everywhere were men stretched out, apparently asleep, but we soon found that they were dead. Hundreds of them, lying in all sorts of postures and conditions, and judging by the stench many had been there for a long time in the sun. The trench was about 3 feet deep and wound across a swamp and every step squelched as one stepped on one of the bodies that floored the trench. The walls were part sand bags and part more bodies. We could hear cries of the wounded outside the trench and in the bright moonlight we could see the churned up land on either side with a maze of trenches running in all directions.

What a place for a baptism. Somehow, with virtually no trench-warfare training they got through three impossible days with virtually no ground gained and 'only' 199 casualties. According to Seely it could have been many, many more.

> Towards the close of the fierce fighting at Festubert and Givenchy we were ordered to support an attack timed to take place at the moment of explosion of a mine. I stood on the fire-step and watched the leading battalion go over at the instant when the mine went off with a loud roar. The mine did not explode in the right place; as a consequence the enemy machine-guns had not been silenced, and practically every officer and man of this gallant battalion was killed or wounded. I actually had one

foot on the parapet ready to jump over when an officer came pushing his way along the crowded trench and handed me a message. I read: 'Attack postponed.' It was a wonderful escape for us all.

It was also a sealing of the bond between him and the men he had been controversially 'parachuted in' to command. Whatever they had thought of him before, they knew now what he was made of. And that now applied from the privates to the generals who only three weeks earlier had tried to prise Seely and his Canadians apart.

Private V. O. Smith, no relation to Harry, kept a diary. His entry for 28 May takes us there direct:

> Bathing parade to some margarine factory in Béthune. Believe me it was good, as I can still feel the itchie-coos. General parade of the Brigade and an address by General Alderson. He congratulated us on our good work in the trenches – said that he hoped we would get our horses before long. When references were made to our casualties which were 114 out of 490, we all took our hats off.
>
> When he mentioned General Seely as a leader all the boys cheered, as according to General Alderson we were fortunate in having a leader who went into the trenches with us.

It is time to dig out that Churchill post-Curragh crisis summary of thirteen months earlier: 'Seely goes about like a disembodied spirit seeking to return from the wastes of the infinite to the cosy world of man. He is terribly hard hit and losing poise.' Festubert and its corpse-strewn trenches was much more 'wastes of the infinite' than 'cosy world of man'. But the comeback was complete.

31

Horseless in the Trenches

Seely and his horseless cavalry were up there south of Ypres right through to January 1916 – in the trenches summer, autumn, winter – at Festubert, Kemmel and Messines. What a way for horsemen to go to war. Yet in a peculiar way they made the best of it. The notion of all ranks being in it together was right at the core of Seely's Liberal instincts and his lifeboat experience. The war, like the storm at sea, was an inevitability. When it came you had to face it with a deep breath and a trusting heart. 'Odd as it may seem,' he wrote, 'we were all very happy during these times. We grieved at the loss of comrades, but we all knew that it was no good going on grieving.'

For the crumping shell or the whining bullet was as likely to get General Seely as anyone else, in fact it had a lot more chance with the general. 'He was always poking around in the Front Line', said Luke Williams. 'How he was never killed or at least seriously wounded will always be a mystery.' And that in an even more astonishing sense applied to Warrior too. For the attrition in horses was truly horrible. Four million of them perished on the Western Front, plenty out of sheer bogged-down exhaustion, but the great majority from the rifle, machine-gun and shell fire for which their too visible bulk made them such easy targets. That summer it was shells that almost did for Warrior.

The first cut the horse beside him clean in half. The second set fire to the farm building where he was stabled while his owner was still asleep. Seely wrote:

I jumped up in pyjamas and with bare feet ran across the yard to
Warrior's stable. I would not dare to recount this episode but that
there are many eye witnesses living who would confirm it. I
could hear Warrior beating against the door with his forefeet. I
threw it open and out he bounded. I ran after him to catch his
headstall, and before I had gone two yards a shell burst right
inside his stable, and knocked the whole place to smithereens. It
was a miraculously lucky escape.

After this crisis Warrior instinctively took on a habit inherited from
his mother Cinderella and also shown by the white pony Maharajah
in South Africa. He walked to heel.

It was during this period that Warrior took to following me about
like a dog, without a saddle or bridle, when I was riding a pony I
had called Patrick. Part of the force was in the Front Line, and
another part in the immediate reserve about two miles behind,
and I made it a rule to ride around and see those in reserve each
day, before or after going into the Front Line.

One day Warrior broke out of his stable when I was starting
off and followed me. The men wanted to catch him, but I
dissuaded them. For weeks therefore, and indeed all through that
summer, Warrior would follow me, whether I was mounted or
on foot, wherever I went.

Fashionable men from the Dominions sought commissions in
English regiments of the line. These Canadians were a less pre-
tentious but much more solid lot. That May two sergeants came
into the team: Charles Connolly, a tough, brush-moustachioed
Irishman originally from County Carlow, and Gordon Flowerdew,
the ninth son of a Norfolk farmer, whose ranching days in British
Columbia had included hunting down a pair of armed bandits long
before the sheriff's posse got under way. They had immortality
ahead of them.

To men like Connolly and Flowerdew, their commanding
officer and his young, fair-haired, elegantly aristocratic ADC, with
their upper-class English accents, not to mention the classy young

thoroughbred at heel, must have seemed almost beyond the music hall.

'His voice was something once heard never forgotten', wrote Luke Williams, the young Strathcona whose diary is a unique record of the time.

> On one occasion he was up visiting the front line trenches as he was in the habit of doing. His aide-de-camp Captain Sir Archibald Sinclair had gotten a bay or so behind or ahead of him in the course of the tour and General Seely was calling out 'Ahchie, Ahchie, wheah aah you?' One of the men in the adjoining bay who had never met the General said, 'Who the —— is Ahchie?'
>
> General Seely heard him and called out, 'Not you my man, not you.'
>
> On another occasion he called down into a dugout, 'Hello down theah, who is down theah, and what are you doing down theah?' A robust Canadian voice called back 'Who the —— wants to know, and what do you want to know for?' General Seely, not a bit disconcerted called back, 'Because I happen to be youah Brigadeah, my man.'

Then there were the friends who dropped by. Prime Minister Asquith, the Commander-in-Chief Sir John French, Bend Or Westminster, this time not in his Rolls but in a high-powered armoured car which duly got plastered with shrapnel. 'His Grace', as ever, survived. But all this colourful eccentricity would have swiftly become an irritation if it had not been matched by energy and imagination in their cause. For instance, when the Canadians suffered heavy casualties from shelling at one stage in the summer, Seely got Staff Captain Docherty with two officers and a hundred men to construct an elaborate set of dummy trenches. 'Imagine my delight when next morning I stood in the front line and saw the whole of the enemy shells dropping on the dummy trenches, dug outs and strong points.'

In a drive which reduced casualties to less than half the previous rate, he had dug deeper and better camouflaged communication trenches. He got periscopes, gumboots, water pumps, and thicker telephone wire to try to make trench life safer and more bearable. He told Churchill that he had spent £600 of his own money getting extra equipment and made the War Office refund him. In the same letter he says his troops are 'real good stout-hearted men who are nearly as fond of me as I am of them'. It was the truth.

Even at the Front soldiers needed their diversions. Especially where life was so precarious that there might not be the chance to take the pleasures again. Private Cork's diary talks of swimming, baseball and poker games when back in the reserve trenches. Back on 29 May, only three days after the worst horrors of Festubert, he made an entry which is quite graphically concise:

'Al Burden and I went to Béthune. Met two friends (girls, 'nuff sed). I couldn't speak French.'

Seely may have been a loving father but he was also an energetic widower. Whether Archie Sinclair or anyone else laid on a real-life Mademoiselle from Armentières for Seely's delight is not known. But there is an intriguing link to the remarkable American actress and theatre manager Maxine Elliott, who had installed herself and friends in a large barge on the Seine whence she gave succour to both the needy and the mighty.

Maxine was already in her late forties and described at the time as someone 'who must have been very beautiful'. She was a remarkable woman who had come to London to offer her fame and wealth and energy as a sort of greasepaint Florence Nightingale, and in fifteen months her barge had dealt with over 300,000 Belgian refugees. Churchill met her that autumn and started a (platonic) friendship which lasted through to the 1930s when he used to visit her Riviera villa to paint.

Quite how platonic Seely's relationship was is unproven but his letter to Archie Sinclair when the ADC was on leave and visiting Churchill (they had first met playing polo) in London that September is suggestive:

'The principal thing I have to tell you is that Miss Maxine Elliot is not on her barge but believed to be in London, will you go and see her and give her my-well-whatever is the respectful and admiring message.'

But one liaison was utterly proven. Not for Seely but for Warrior's ageing mother, Cinderella. That August the General had been home to visit the remaining Canadian cavalry and all the brigade's horses in Sussex and so took the ferry across the Solent to see the children at Brooke. Very soon he asked about Cinderella.

> 'Cinderella has had a baby and we have christened him Isaac.'
>
>   'Why Isaac?'
>
>   'Well, we thought she must be almost as old as Sarah was in the Bible! Come and see him.'

Isaac really should have been called Esau because, like Esau in the Book of Genesis, he was 'an hairy man'. His father had been a precocious young carthorse foal whose family were reared to pull the lifeboats and who himself had got into the field to give the old lady pleasure. Isaac had a sweet and elegant head of which his half-brother would have been proud. But in the leg department, the carthorse 'hairy heels' added a clownishly awkward comic touch. Still, Cinderella was very proud.

It was a happy diversion. Other sights, other thoughts, were bound to make him sad. Nim's gravestone was white marble. Seely would have walked up to it from the house and then climbed the steep path to the church door from where he could look back towards the sea. For the children, for the country, for his men, he wanted life and victory. But every month the chances increased that he would soon join Nim on another shore.

32

Winston's Woe

Outwardly Seely was all ebullience beneath that red-ribboned general's cap. But there was loneliness there. August 1915 had baseball games, sports days and a review from 'Big Sam' Hughes where the Germans did everyone a favour by sending over a shell just as he began a long oration to the assembled troops. But it was coming up to a full year of war, eighteen months' exile from the centre of Government, exactly two years since Nim had died. His letter to Archie Sinclair in London with its teasing reference to Maxine Elliot also finished by saying, 'I miss you dreadfully.'

Not everything missed. Private V. O. Smith had been made a Lance Corporal and was looking into joining the Royal Flying Corps. On the evening of 17 September he took a party to the front line up the communication trench grandiosely called Seely Avenue. In the line he was detailed as the NCO in charge of trench guard. At about 8 p.m., a German machine gun gave one of its killingly casual sweeps across the position.

> I was hit, the bullet entering just below the left eye and coming out on the right side of my nose. It was a strange sensation. At first I thought it felt more like being hit by a sledgehammer. The boys insisted on carrying me into the dugout nearby. Isaac Pritchard and Walter Land carried me in. Percy Baker bandaged up my face and in a few minutes I was on my way to the First Aid Post. Captain Forin, our medical officer, was very nice to me and said he guessed I was good for 'Blighty.'

Someone a touch more famous was keen to come in the opposite direction. A week after Corporal Smith's bullet, Seely got a letter from the Duchy of Lancaster. It was to there that Churchill had been shuttled following the failure of the campaign at Gallipoli. The man of action was longing to escape. It was to his front line friend that he would write:

> It is odious to me to remain here watching sloth and folly with full knowledge and no occupation.
>
> I was deeply touched by the very great kindness of your letter. I hope you will not go beyond the line of duty sportingly conceived in going into danger. Do not seek peril beyond what is necessary to discharge your full task, and do not get Archie into trouble.
>
> God bless you and guard you both is the hope and prayer of your faithful friend.
>
> W.

His kindred spirit was getting frustrated too. 'We first took over the defence of Kemmel', wrote Seely, 'and later of a difficult part of the line in front of Dickebush, at the south of the Ypres Salient. The autumn rains had come, and many of the communication trenches were full of water. We managed to drain them and reconstruct a good deal of the trench system, but it was a miserable place to hold. I thought then, and I think now, that the whole proceedings on the Western Front in this matter of closely contiguous trenches was extremely foolish.'

Seely was no Churchill, either with the pen or in office, but he was still a proper player. He remained MP for Ilkeston throughout the war, although the January 1916 conscription debate was his only Westminster appearance at this time. The Front was his real constituency and he was a passionate, humane and hugely informed participant, sharing with Churchill ideas of using tanks and smoke and planes to avoid deadlock, and his greatest redeeming feature was that he was always determined to experience things for himself. He, more than anyone, was entitled to say that:

the tragic mistake that was made throughout the war on the Western Front was throwing men's lives away by sending them over the top.

We never could see the purpose of advancing by slow degrees, the most we could hope to do, the most that was ever intended by infantry attack, was the gaining of two or three miles of ground. We all used to say to each other: 'It is four hundred miles to Berlin; at this rate the war can't be over for a hundred years.' But the voice of the front line was only faintly heard at general headquarters. Daily personal contact alone can cure these melancholy errors.

In his own case that contact was as instinctive as it was duty led. From an early life he had pursued the maxim that fear was a failing over which you should struggle daily to overcome. He was never completely free of it, but he had come to realize the strength that could be drawn from the battle with oneself. With bullies, boats and Boers he had felt the clammy hand of danger trying to stuff fear down his throat. He had noticed that by refusing to flinch he could encourage others to do the same. There was nowhere more terrifying than the Front.

So there was calculation behind the apparent vanity of forswearing the front-line tin helmet for the unabashed unprotectedness of the general's military cap with its red silk band and its 'Lock's of St James' origins marked inside. For troops in the place of most danger it was a physical statement that 'the greatest fear is fear itself'. For the Canadians, it told them that they had a commander who cared.

'On the first day that we were up digging', writes Luke Williams, 'General Seely came up to see what work we were doing, and although we were getting some pretty heavy shelling he didn't seem to mind it.' Williams was then a young lieutenant in charge of fifty men. For most of them, life back in Canada had not been without its share of jagged edges. But this was something else. Here a lieutenant needed support.

'As for myself,' he continues revealingly, 'I was more afraid that the men might know that I was afraid than I was afraid of the shelling in itself. The day that General Seely came up to see us at work, he walked back with me on the way back to camp and I have to confess that I didn't feel so nervous when the General was with me.'

Visitors to the Canadians during that summer of 1915 brought glimpses of the future and the past. There was George Nicholson, who as private secretary had for seven years been Seely's closest private aide. 'He had joined the Royal Flying Corps in the founding of which he had played a great part, and had become a first class flyer. He flew constantly over the German lines, and had a series of miraculous escapes. At intervals he would flop down somewhere near by and come to see us. He was much loved in the Flying Corps.'

There was John Redmond, the Irish Nationalist leader, finding it increasingly impossible to square the circle between his own loyalty to the Empire and the gathering tide for complete independence which was to burst so bloodily in Dublin's Easter Rising the following spring:

> He came to see me one winter's night at my headquarters, about half a mile behind our front line trench. His brother Willie was serving in the trenches not far away. Redmond had much to tell me about his aspirations and his difficulties on the day when war was declared. He had announced in the House of Commons at a dramatic moment his whole hearted support, and, he believed that of his fellow countrymen in the great conflict of liberty. But he had a series of rebuffs and disillusions not so much from his own countrymen as from the authorities at home.

But the most difficult visitor needed a 'Foghorn' to shut him up. Corporal 'Foghorn' Macdonald to be exact, so dubbed because of the penetration of his voice, an instrument he had honed during long days underground in his years as a mining expert in Canada. Naturally Seely put him in charge of mining operations they were holding on the Front by the Messines ridge that winter, and 'Foghorn' was in the room when General Sir Arthur Currie came round and began to wrangle with Seely about the actual construction of his whole defensive system.

General Currie was a big, self-assured man. For a while the corporal kept out of the argument. Then Currie added: 'There is another thing. I am very dissatisfied with where you put your mine, Seely. I don't believe it has been started in the right spot, and I am sure you won't get the water out; you will drown your own men without doing any harm to the enemy.'

The conversation had been repeatedly interrupted by shells falling outside. But the next interruption came from in the room.

'Look here, old man Currie,' said 'Foghorn', 'you don't know the first thing about mines. I have forgotten more about them than you will ever know. You must say what you like about the rest, but don't you try coming it over me about the mine just because you are stud duck in this puddle.'

Currie had the good grace to laugh at the correction, and he and Seely developed a working relationship typical of the slightly maverick improvisation that the men and the circumstances came to need. But other 'stud ducks' were soon to assert themselves in what had been Seely's dream scenario for the bigger local 'puddle'. Churchill came to the Front with the promise of, like Seely, commanding a whole brigade, only to find that when the CIGS Sir John French was withdrawn in December, so was the promise.

It had all started so well:

My dear Jack

I cross tomorrow to join my regiment near St Omer. I have no plans except to remain with them. It will give me real pleasure if you and Archie can come and see me there, and though it is hardly for a general to visit a major, I dare say you may be able to contrive an occasion.

I am extremely pleased with the way my own affairs have gone; but miserable about the situation in the near East. However, it is a relief to let it all slide off one's mind, and I shall be so glad to be back again with the army.

Write and let me know.

Yours ever,

W.

On his first night over, 18 November, Churchill dined with French and John Redmond at GHQ: 'a fine chateau, with hot baths, beds, champagne and all the conveniences'. Next day the commander of the Guards Division was summoned and a crash 'refresher course' was arranged for Churchill with the Grenadiers. The 'old firm' were back at work.

True, the Grenadier colonel first greeted Churchill with the icy announcement, 'I think I ought to tell you that we were not at all consulted in the matter of your coming to join us.' But the greatest ever Englishman was not going to be cowed for long. Within four days he was writing to his mother, 'I am vy happy here & have made good friends with everybody now. I always get on with soldiers, & these are the finest.' His postscript, close to his forty-first birthday, is typical of the mood: 'Do you know I am quite young again.'

On 2 December he drove over to Kemmel and had lunch with Seely and Archie Sinclair and walked all around their line. Ideas were bursting from him; about tanks, wire-cutters, smokescreens, everything. He was due to see French about the brigade in a week's time. It was arranged that Archie would join him. This was how friends changed the world. On 9 December the news came through. He was to become a brigadier general in command of the 56th Brigade of the 19th Division. One or two cautious souls, including both his wife and Henry Wilson, advised against jumping so high so soon. But Churchill was ecstatic. All the more brutal that the good news lasted just seven days.

Pressure had been building to replace French with Haig. On 14 December the little field marshal was summoned to London. On 16 December Churchill got a call from French to say that it was bad news on two counts: Haig was taking over, and Asquith had personally vetoed Churchill's appointment. It was the blackest of moments for Winston. The letter he wrote to Clemmie that night was so dark and depressed that next day he asked her to destroy it. Back in France, his friends too were shattered.

'I saw Churchill just after he had received this intimation', wrote Seely. 'In forty years of close friendship I have never seen him so disappointed and hurt. Indeed he had every reason.' Seely was biased but his conclusion does make you wonder at the might-have-been. 'I said at the time that if Napoleon had had the opportunity he would, without doubt, have promoted him to command an army straight off on the chance that the qualities that had made for his meteoric rise in peace might be of equal value in war.'

As it was, Churchill swallowed his pride, accepted the post of lieutenant colonel in charge of a battalion of the Royal Scots Fusiliers, took Archie Sinclair as his second-in-command, and for the next two months set all his unique energy and inspiration to a soldier's life in the trenches. A general's role might have held him, but confined to a battalion the call of politics would prove too strong.

It had not worked out the way they had wanted it, but at least he and Seely and Sinclair were all in France together. On 17 January 1916 Churchill wrote to his wife telling of the sports and concert he had organized the day before. 'Jack Seely presented the prizes for the sports and called for three cheers for me, and an extra one for you. The night went on carousing with Jack Seely at the piano.'

The conditions were miserable, but at this crucial stage in their nation's history, Churchill and Seely were sharing the misery. For them the front line seemed the honourable place to be. 'Since you have become a soldier,' Clementine Churchill had written to her husband, 'I look upon civilians with pity and indulgence. The wives of men over military age may be lucky but I am sorry for them being married to feeble and incompetent old men.'

In hindsight this widely-shared sense of the purity of military crusade has a dreadful doomed ring to it for families all across the nation. My mother remembers groups of girls gaily walking the streets of London with white feathers in their hands. They were looking for young men in civilian clothes to whom they would sing, 'We don't want to lose you, but we think you ought to go.'

Over in France, Smith brought a letter to Seely's table. It was from the sixth form of Harrow School. It had been bound to happen, but the scene was now to be set.

Dear Daddy,

I hope you will not mind, but I thought I should not remain at home while other people are being shot, so I arranged to go to Sandhurst and have passed all the examinations. I think it will be all right about my age.

Perhaps I might join you as a Canadian.

Your loving son,

Frank.

For a devoted father there would be pride in the simple heroism of the sentiment. But there was no escaping the fear. He would reap what he had sown.

33

Still No 'G' in 'Gap'

He did what all fathers would like to do. He put the boy under his wing. He contacted Sir Herbert Creedy back at the War Office. He was Permanent Under-Secretary of State as he had been under Seely. He was a small, fastidious man and urbane to his fingertips: 'I have seen, as others have seen, Creedy anxious, but neither I nor anyone else has seen him ruffled.' Creedy duly fixed it for Frank, twenty years old in June, to join his father as an ADC.

Frank was quiet and fair, the sepia pictures of him in the scrapbook suggest a typical First World War 'lamb to the slaughter'. But he had survived to prefect level in the *Tom Brown's Schooldays* environment of Harrow. Although devoid of swagger, he had Seely's essential openness. And he brought with him his own four-legged passport, a small, handsome black Arab called Akbar, with a comical white splash across his forehead. For the Canadians, 'Here's Akbar' would be his hello.

His father, of course, was a 'fixer' not far short of the 'Sir Herbert' class. Seely had never swerved in his support for Sir John French, and one letter was particularly appreciated. 'I have to expect abuse from many quarters,' French wrote to him, 'but if it has the result of drawing a letter like this from a man like you I welcome it.' Haig was a different, cooler creature. He didn't seem to be the man to be borrowing Warrior for a hack or sending Seely on a special intelligence mission. But at the end of January 1916 that is exactly what happened.

Being Seely, it was a mission with a certain style. It involved checking out documents in the British Embassy in Paris, interviewing the leading French generals Galliéni, de Castelnau and Franchet d'Esperey, and touring the French front line to write a memorandum for the chiefs. But it also meant staying at the Ritz, sleeping between sheets, being dined by the mighty, even going to the theatre. Life expectancy might be short, but life was still for the living.

With his energy and the cosmopolitan contacts, Seely was of course the perfect man for this job. But in strict military terms he was a junior general whose main priority was to get his makeshift bunch of Canadians reunited with their horses for the first time in ten months. The likelihood was that in strict parade ground terms those troops would look 'an absolute shower'. The strict military minds had been gunning for Seely ever since he had started agitating about army reforms in 1902. In their eyes he would always be a 'politician' and they still blamed him squarely for the 'Curragh crisis' of 1914. They thought they would have him before the year was out.

Seely himself sailed blithely on to then make the most inspired of all his appointments. He had returned to England to supervise the equipping of the Manitoba-raised Fort Garry Horse to take over from the 2nd King Edward Horse as the third regiment of his cavalry brigade. But when he came back to France he had a real live prince among his men: 33-year-old Prince Antoine d'Orléans-Bragance. Antoine was an 'Orléans' because he was the great-grandson of France's last reigning monarch, Louis-Philippe, a 'Braganza' because his maternal grandfather was the last emperor of Brazil.

Forget about the breeding, Antoine was an exceptional per-former, and that's not just in the boudoir. He could speak five languages, had got a first in history at the Sorbonne, he was a fine horseman who had done five years in the Austrian cavalry, he was bright, tough and infinitely well connected. He was about five foot nine inches with something of an anteater nose accentuated by a lantern jaw and slightly hooded eyes that missed nothing. He was everything that a staff officer should be.

But he could not fight for his country. Louis-Philippe had been deposed in 1848 and died two years later in his house by the Thames in Surrey. And such were the arcane French fears of some old loyalists rallying to the ancient cause that Antoine and his brother, Louis, as princes of the Orléans–Bourbon 'sang royale' were not allowed to serve in the French army. This was not lifted even when Austria became at war with France, so it was to the British army the young Bourbons came. And it was to Seely, whom Antoine had first met during those mad early days at the Le Cateau HQ, that the prince made appeal.

Accepting Antoine's offer was such a 'no-brainer' that it was as if Seely had engineered it in the first place. The central reserve training ground for the Canadian cavalry (and indeed many other detachments) was the flat countryside running to the coast west of Abbeville between the Somme and Bresle estuaries and ported by Saint-Valéry to the north and Le Tréport to the south. It was an area of fenced fields and small villages, ideal for billeting men and horses. At low tide a huge expanse of sand opened up between Ault and Cayeux, perfect for drilling large groups of horses in all weather. But best of all it had one dominant building, the palace-sized, eighteenth-century chateau at Eu, just up the river from Le Tréport. This was Antoine's family home.

Not surprising perhaps that Seely's HQ down here was not some ruined, lice-ridden farmhouse but another chateau Antoine knew just west of Eu, belonging to the Marquis d'Hardivilliers, whose title, according to Seely at least, came from Henry IV, who at the successful conclusion of the Battle of Arcq called his gallant knight Villiers before him and uttered the immortal line, 'You shall be called "Hardy Villiers".'

Conditions for the troops were also a considerable improvement on the front line, as they were billeted up in little villages like Béthencourt, Martaigneville and the unpronounceable, chateau-adorned Yzengremer. Their beds were comfortable, their hosts, women and children who spent their days filing brass, welcoming. And of course at last they had some horses. Not very good ones to start with, a loaned batch from the Indian cavalry. 'We found them mean little beggars', says Luke Williams, 'that would as soon take a nip at you as look at you. Every one of them would kick the stars out of the skylight at the slightest opportunity.'

But soon their own horses came over from England, and after roll-call in the village street the troops would repair to 'morning stables' to look after their charges before beginning the long task of getting some organization into their training. Just how far short they were of the famous 'strict military' drill standard is obvious from Williams's account of the practices on the beach:

'On these parades we new recruits often took the place of the centre guide for the very simple reason that we had more recent cavalry training. Our N.C.O.s in the regiment and for that matter the officers too, had been doing trench duty for the best part of a year, so we were understandably rusty on cavalry drill.'

Seely's staff might have been pretty 'posh' on the personal side, but the officer corps around him was developing its own meritocratic esprit. Among the Strathconas, Sergeants Connolly and Flowerdew were to be commissioned, Captain Donald Macdonald had returned after being wounded (and winning the MC) on that first bloody outing at Festubert. And in charge of the Fort Garrys were the Winnipeg paint magnate Bob Patterson (who had raised much of the strength single handed) and his splendid second-in-command Colonel Stevenson, a forestry officer from Manitoba whose special skill was shooting pike in the Somme with his revolver.

It was to the Somme that they were headed. Through the spring the cavalry training intensified. General Gough, along with Wilson, Seely's nemesis during the Curragh crisis, came down to inspect the troops paraded by the Minister who two years earlier had sacked him. The two men had been partly reconciled when serving alongside each other at Festubert, but there was still a bit of tension as the Canadians tried to look like 'parade ground' cavalry. Gough could see their limitations, but they would have to do.

Their job, in hindsight, seems one of the most ludicrous in history. We all know what happened on the first day at the Somme. How on that 1 July morning, thousands upon thousands of Englishmen were machine-gunned into eternity. Not many of us remember that they were just going to be the warm-up act. They were going to open up the line and then the cavalry would thunder through and complete the rout. They would, in the then honoured phrase, 'Gallop through the "G" in "Gap"'.

Seely did not believe in it either.

'On the preceding evening I flew in a reconnaissance aeroplane all over the front to be attacked and some way over the enemy territory beyond. My orders for the next day were to gallop right through Cambrai, encircle it, and cut the railway lines to the east. Other brigades were to be to my right and left. I tried to make myself believe that the operation was possible, though my reason told me it was not.'

There was of course no gap to gallop through. Seely and Antoine waited just behind the front line, while up ahead of them an unthinkable slaughter was being wreaked. Right up until Easter 1918 Seely and his Canadians had their tough times 'but', he wrote, thinking back to that deceptively pretty summer morning in 1916, 'the fortunate thing was that although we had of course, severe casualties, we were never mown down. It takes a regiment, battalion, brigade or division a long time to recover from that experience.'

There were equine casualties that morning but, amazing as ever, Warrior was not among them. When Seely and Prince Antoine finally galloped up the valley to briefly cross the front line, there were some optimistic cheers from the soldiers they passed. But there were also bullets that hit both their horses. Antoine's was killed, Seely's eventually recovered from a leg wound. But he had been on a chestnut called Bazentin. Warrior had finished his morning. Lucky once again.

Two weeks later Warrior was lame in the morning so Seely took Bazentin in his place: 'A chance shell hit him and killed him. I had three ribs broken myself, although I did not know it, but my first thought was: "What luck it was not Warrior."'

A week after that death was even closer. Seely and Warrior were shacked up in separate parts of a ruined farm at Bray-sur-Somme. At midnight Smith came rushing in to say, 'There's something wrong with Warrior.' The horse, with something stuck in his gut, was literally going berserk.

> I ran out to the remnant of the stable where Warrior was living. It was pitch dark, but Thompson was there with a lantern. Anyone who has never seen a powerful thoroughbred suffering agonies of internal cramp can have no conception of the terrible sight. The energy of those wonderful muscles, which enable him to gallop at 30 miles an hour and jump 6 feet in the air, is used in the most fantastic and fearful contortions in the endeavour to dislodge the cause of the pain. Warrior was leaping about in this battered loose-box like a mad thing, hurling himself in the air, falling on his back, jumping up again, lashing out with his hind legs, the wind whistling as it does when one hits a really long drive with a golf club, and striking with his forefeet at the wooden walls.'

These situations are usually as fatal as they are distressing but by some miracle the paroxysms that Warrior was going through shifted the obstruction in his gut and he finally slumped almost lifeless but free of spasms to the floor. Many many horses and people were not so lucky. Seely's spring had been ruined by the news from England that George Nicholson had been killed when his plane had flown in fog into the chalky face of the Portadown Hills inland from Portsmouth on a training flight.

Although ten years younger, George had been his closest and most devoted ally through all the fever of the Curragh crisis. Any study of Nicholson's memorandum on those events demonstrates his intellect as well as dispelling the long-accepted wisdom that Seely had acted without thought or consultation. Seely had seen quite a bit of George up in Belgium. As he, a widower, wrote an anguished letter of sympathy to Nicholson's widow Evelyn, he was not to know that it would spark a (mostly postal) romance that would link their futures.

Meanwhile all was frustration and gloom; cavalry with nowhere to go, therefore soldiers with no one to fight. Back in England the feelings were darkening too. On 13 July Seely got a package in that familiar Churchillian hand. It contained a set of articles Winston had written, parts of which echoed exactly what Seely thought in tones that no one could ever match:

'The chaos of the first explosions has given place to the slow fire of trench warfare: the wild turbulence of the incalculable, the sense of terrible adventure has passed. A sombre mood prevails in Britain. The faculty of wonder has been dulled; emotion and enthusiasm have given place to endurance; excitement is bankrupt, death is familiar, and sorrow numb. The world is in twilight; and from beyond dim flickering horizons come tirelessly the thudding guns.'

The accompanying letter shared the same mood:

> My Dear Jack,
> Archie has had a good rest but has now succeeded in getting ordered to France as a squadron commander in the 2nd Life Guards. I am vy fond of him & shall always remember yr kindness in letting me have him when I was at the war.
> Let me know if there is any way in which I can serve you. It is vy painful to me to be impotent & inactive at this time: but perhaps a little later on I may find a chance to be useful . . .
> This is a morose letter – but do not let it depress you.
> Your devoted friend
> W.

Seely's almost incurable sunny-ness was one of his great attributes – especially when France was a place where the lights kept getting turned out. But he had his own depressions looming – especially in August when there would be the ultimate in bittersweet anniversaries: his wife's death and his daughter's birthday.

So much of his reportage is couched in the often cosy and prejudiced view of hindsight. Not so this letter written to the about to be three-year-old Louisa on 4 August 1916. It comes directly from the heart.

> My Baby Lou
> Many happy returns of your birthday – how I wish I could be with you, and give you a great big hug, and then take you for a swim

in the sea. We must do all that next year. Think of your being three years old! And ever so big and strong they tell me. I don't suppose you can ever be quite as good and kind and gentle and brave as your Mummy, because nobody could be, but I expect you will be nearly.

Anyway I love you my Lou and long for the day when I will see you again. I am very well and so is Frank. Give my love to all the others and to Aunt Florrie and Nannie too.

God bless you.

Your loving <u>Daddy</u>

I am sending you a tiny wee present.

At last Seely got across to Brooke. He reached the house on a Saturday afternoon. The children were growing fast. 'Baby Lou' was quite able to walk but he scooped her high in his arms. He heard Emmy's plans to work in the hospital, Irene had laid out maps of the Front on the drawing-room table. John was drilling with the cadets at Harrow and wanted to follow Frank to the Front next year. Patrick and Kitty both had Union Jacks they waved at the car. At last, as fathers do, he went with them to visit the animals. 'Let's go and see Cinderella,' he said. But there was sadness there too.

For a few months earlier Isaac, Cinderella's wonderful, gangly, hairy-heeled colt, had broken his neck jumping out of the paddock and left his old Sarah of a mother without much to live for. When Seely reached her, the old mare looked ancient, dip-backed and sad. She had nickered through her nostrils when she first saw him. Now she nuzzled the sugar in his hand, pushed her black ears into his side for him to rub. She was dead next morning. There were no horses available to drag the corpse away so she lay flat and old and dead by the church path as they walked up to the service that Sunday. When Seely got back to the house, there was a telegram recalling him to France immediately. He missed Cinderella's burial next day. It hardly augured well for what lay ahead across the Channel. Before the year was out the war, the winter and the more blimpish warlords would do their worst.

34

Beating off the Blimps

Leave-taking became more difficult every time. Smith and Corporal Anthony in the car. The children on the steps. The last kisses, the forced jollity: 'I'll give your love to Frank and we will be back soon.' The small children clinging. Emily and Irene, tall and damp-eyed; at eighteen and fourteen they knew they should be brave but knew too that this time might be the last time.

Then into the open back of the Bentley, the cheery backward wave as the gravel drive takes them past the great full-leafed shade of the Garibaldi Oak. One last enduring image of that classic children-and-aunts-and-servants farewell line-up on the Brooke House steps. Then the car would dip out through the lodge gates and turn left up the hill. Within a quarter mile the road flattens briefly and there on the right is the steep grassy slope of the graveyard, with the church set on the knoll above it, where only three hours earlier he and the children would have stood after the service and looked out to the sea. Where they had told the villagers how well Frank was doing, how Warrior and Akbar were stars, how there had to be a 'breakthrough' soon.

But Seely knew better. He did not need the memory of Cinderella's corpse or even the white marble cross of Nim's tombstone right there to remind him of his own mortality. The road steepened quickly, the car had to work. Brooke Hill was crested and then in the distance the long, wave-ruffled sleeve of the Solent came in sight. There was peace here. But the war remained. He was merely leaving one family for another.

Over in France there was some temporary relief. Towards the

end of August the brigade was taken out of the line and went back
to those winter villages in Antoine land, north of Eu, and better still
to the beach. At low tide the whole 500-strong collection of men
and horses would parade down through the wide main street at
Ault, would pass the large station yard where the cattle were
gathered on market days, and then would file out on to the sand
with the villagers all agog. They had plenty to watch.

For the sands were used for bathing as well as parading. The
men would strip off and ride their horses into the sea until their
horses were swimming, when they would slip off the horse's back
and paddle round holding on to the tail. It was quite a spectacle if
you hadn't seen much naked white Canadian flesh. It was a long
time before the days of the full-frontal centrefold.

One day the whole village got a close-up glimpse. While the
main group of cavalry were drilling half a mile from the slipway, an
individual trooper and his horse were happily having a 'skinny dip'
together further up the beach. As he played in the surf he had not
reckoned with the power of the bugle. The horses, like the men,
were taught to recognize the calls. Now from the receding distance
the bugle could clearly be heard calling 'home'. For the horses this
also meant lunch.

He didn't need saddle and bridle, and he certainly wasn't
waiting for the trooper to get dressed. Off he set at a gathering
gallop with a naked male Godiva bumping uncomfortably on his
withers. Along the sands, up left through the slipway, cantering on
up through the midday throng in the market square. 'Mon dieu,
quelle horreur, quel physique.' At Ault, they talk of it still.

At the end of the month there was a sports day and the great
hulk of Sergeant Major 'Big Nick' Nicol helped the Strathcona team
to win the tug of war. Warrior took part in the showjumping, but it
had poured with rain and the ground was muddy and unforgiving.
Major Jack Critchley and his grand, raking, black horse won it. In
those conditions it was some achievement to jump five foot nine
inches.

But the big jump for these cavalrymen was to gallop through
the 'G' in 'Gap'. That is what all their training, all those practice

charges with swords drawn, even that tent-pegging which Luke
Williams's team had won on sports day, had readied them for. That
was the dream they sustained during those long bogged-down,
horseless days in the trenches.

Come September and they were up near Bray-sur-Somme
again. They could hear the shelling, could see the familiar double
line of observation balloons, watch the groaning journeys of the
trucks. They dug a line of trenches. More optimistically they built a
cavalry trail up towards Montauban, filling in the shell holes,
flattening the old trench lines, clearing the barbed wire, ready at last
to gallop through that 'Gap'.

On 15 September 1916 dawn broke with a huge opening
barrage. They stuffed grass in their ears to ease the hammering in
the head. At 6 a.m. they trotted up to the Montauban ridge. They
saw the first tanks caterpillar forward, the fulfilment of a Churchill
vision. They then saw many tanks get stuck. They watched streams
of wounded and prisoners filing back and fresh troops going up.
There would be no 'G'. There was no 'Gap'.

At the end of the month the rains came. They moved back to
some villages around Le Mesge, on the south bank of the Somme,
some ten miles west of Amiens, the men billeted in farms and
cottages, the horses in makeshift shelters open to the weather. They
spent six weeks there. It was not a place to look spick and span. 'Le
Mesge, we remembered', wrote Luke Williams, 'chiefly as a period
of mud-schemes-mud, exercise rides, mud, drills and more mud.'

They were beginning to look the worse for wear. 'Our horse
lines were in terrible shape and in the last couple of weeks of our
stay it was impossible to get the horses' legs dry at all.' It was not the
place to parade one's troops to an officious visiting general.
Especially not one like Sir Archibald Home of the Cavalry Corps
who like many of his fellow regulars could not say the word Seely
without adding, 'bloody politician', and usually quite a bit worse.

One can almost hear the splutters in his diary of Sunday 29
October:

'Yesterday went down to inspect part of the Canadian Cavalry
Brigade under Seely. The whole thing is a failure, the material is

excellent but with such a Brigadier the thing is impossible. We asked him to review the operations and he made a speech which was useless from a military point of view. He ought to go back to politics, that is his proper sphere. Honest downrightness is what is wanted with soldiers, not fine phrasing and verbiage.'

Three days later the brigade, which consisted of nearly a thousand men and horses, moved further west to their old haunts up north of Eu. The officers got put up in the chateau again, the troops in cottage billets, the horses in barns and sheds but many of them with head cover only. They had only been there a day when the old splutterer was back.

'The weather still very bad', wrote Sir Archie, who for reasons unknown was called 'Sally' by his friends. 'Yesterday went down and saw the Canadian Brigade on the march commanded by Seely. I have never seen such a show. It was very bad.'

For the military establishment, here was the chance to settle old scores. General Kavanagh got in on the act. Home had told him the tale so off he went to the coast to see just what that 'damned politician' and his undisciplined band of ranchers and Red Indians was up to (in the summer the Germans had circulated a rumour that the Canadian cavalry were scalping their prisoners). The sight was a bonanza for a blimp.

'The Brigade at this time', wrote Luke Williams, 'was a sorry looking spectacle after our six weeks of mud. General Kavanagh, the Cavalry Corps commander, was not at all pleased with the appearance of the Brigade on the line of march. He called for a parade of all officers of the Brigade at Tully a few days later and told us several things which were anything but complimentary. We felt like finding a nice hole somewhere and crawling into it.'

Sally was delighted. 'It was a good straight talk of a soldier and must have been very different from the political jargon of Seely', wrote Home. 'I think it will do a lot of good.' It would be even better if they could get rid of Seely altogether. Kavanagh had the bit between his teeth. He went over to England and complained to both the King and to Sir William Robertson, the CIGS, that Seely was incompetent and should have been sent home. He had already moaned to Haig. He was pushing the knife in as deep as it would go. But neither the King nor the CIGS would have it. Haig finally pacified Kavanagh by giving Seely an official warning. Seely's men managed to clean most of the mud of the Somme from their outfits and by 6 December Home was back and had to grant a degree of grudging acceptance:

'Went down and inspected Fort Garry Horse in marching order. They are Canadians and belong to Seely's Brigade. It was a good turn out and a great improvement.'

The blimps had been beaten back. 'Events proved', Luke Williams said much later, 'either that we had profited from what we had been told, or that perhaps were not so hopeless as he made us out to be.' Seely was even more maddeningly generous calling Kavanagh 'a fine soldier, a loyal and great hearted man' and confining his criticism to him being a 'bit of a martinet'. It would be fourteen months before a one-eyed, bohemian-clothed artist called Alfred Munnings would wander up the line and put Kavanagh straight.

The truth is that Seely cared about his men. He did not believe in wearing them down with boring routine. What's more, the brigade was split: half were up in the front line digging trenches, and the rest were with the horses by the coast. The weather that winter was once again becoming an enemy worse than all the rest.

It was the hardest time I ever had. I spent four days each week with my men on the Somme front, and two days supervising the rest of them eighty miles to the rear. The remaining 24 hours were occupied going there and back again. It was a very cold winter. A bitter frost came and froze the churned up mud which covered the stricken fields into a hard crust with a quagmire beneath. Long before this, the roads had become impassable for wheeled vehicles, ammunition being brought up to the forward guns on horses and mules in panniers. These horses would at intervals break through the crust and many of them could not be extricated.

At Christmas time we were engaged in building a new front

line. We could get along finely for a time until the enemy would decide to stop the work. Then would come bombardment, and a certain number of people would be hit. Directly it was over we would start building the trench and twisting the wire again. Thus I spent my third Christmas in the front line.

Where would they be, and who would be there – for the next one?

35

The Band of Brothers

Like Eliot's Magi, 'a cold coming they had of it' that Christmas of 1916. But for Seely's Canadians this winter was to bring no revelation – except perhaps of the absolute need to bond together when stuck in such a muddy, and often very snowy, corner of hell on earth. The brigade may not have had the Three Kings but in Antoine they had their very own prince, and by this stage they were being strengthened by some very considerable players.

The two Nordheimer cousins, Victor and Roy, had joined the RCD (Royal Canadian Dragoons). They had both been born in Germany and the older one, Roy, had to lie about his age (he was forty-two) to enlist as a private, even though back in Ottawa he was actually a major in the reserve. Both of them got commissions in a couple of months.

So too did a contrasting pair in the Fort Garry Horse. Harcus 'Jock' Strachan, the tough, slightly stiff, pebble-spectacled Scottish bank manager from Winnipeg, and Bill Cowen, the German-speaking adventurer who had a career as a Hollywood director ahead of him. Strachan was brave but careful, Cowen generous to a fault. On one long march in the worst of the winter, he was noted carrying not one, but two rifles of troopers whose boots were making things unbearable.

Amongst the Strathcona group so painstakingly listed in Luke Williams's book *Stand to Your Horses*, were the live-wire lieutenants, 'Barney' Torrance and 'Hammy' Harrower. The ever smiling 'Jackie' Tatlow had been with them from the previous December. The more serious Gordon Flowerdew was also now a lieutenant, his fellow sergeant 'Con' Connolly had become a captain and was adjutant for the regiment. And when it came to singing at the Eu subalterns' dinner, Welshman Andy Morgan sang the songs of his fathers joined by 'Big Nick' Nicol with that great voice which had roared the tug of war team to victory.

But two other guests at that dinner were to have central parts in the story: 'Spider' and 'Harv'. Spider was Williams's horse, Harv was the six foot two Lieutenant Frederick Maurice Watson Harvey. He was everyone's hero. For Williams, Spider was 'not merely a horse, but a real friend'. He was called Spider because of the spider's-web effect when you groomed up his bright bay coat in summer. He was long backed and a shade lumbering at the trot and canter. But he was 'a Christian', he would do anything you wanted him to do. After the subalterns' dinner, he even pulled the gang home in a cart.

Harvey should have been used to that sort of thing, he was a rugby player. A vicar's son from Athboy, County Meath, he had been a rancher in Fort Macleod, Alberta, but had returned to his homeland in 1911 to win the second of his two caps for Ireland, something both his brothers had done before him. Compared to the boys in green, this hiccuping mob in khaki being dragged out of Eu on the Spider-drawn mess cart should have been a doddle:

'Harv,' enquired Barney Torrance, having some difficulty with his words, 'would you mind very much if I was sick over the edge of the cart?' The former Irish fullback assured Lieutenant Torrance that such a procedure would indeed be in order. So Barney was.

There is a photo of the eight officers of 'C' company of the Strathconas taken at this time. They are all sober and correct, perhaps a slightly wolfish grin playing beneath big Donald Macdonald's black moustache. To his right Barney Torrance and Luke Williams stand calm and confident, to his left Gordon Flowerdew looks neat and strong, his brown boots matching the leather on his Sam Browne belt. Then the eye goes behind Macdonald to 'Hammy' Harrower, hand on hip and quizzical and 'Fred' Harvey towering over them all. They look back unflinching. Between them the eight officers won two VCs, four DSOs, four MCs, and one Croix de Guerre, a record unequalled in the war.

There would also have been frustration in their eyes. For any sort of cavalry action still seemed way over the muddy horizon for these young men and their fellows, still so enthused with the Empire spirit. Some in the brigade got themselves transferred to the Flying Corps or to the newly formed Tank Corps, young Frank Seely got back with the Hampshires at the Front. All of them went because action was what they wanted. Whatever the cost.

But in January 1917 the brigade had a transfer in the other direction. Geoffrey Brooke, a 32-year-old cavalry officer destined for the very top, came across to become brigade major. Brooke was eventually to rise to the rank of major general, having along the way also become the outstanding showjumping rider of his generation. He had an eye for a man as he did for a horse. His memoirs open the window and invite us in.

> It took a little time to get to know my new Chief. He had one rather disconcerting habit – or perhaps it would be best described as a happy boyish trait; everything he possessed was better and more worthy of affection than the possessions of anyone else. This applied to his horse, Warrior, to his wife and family, to his friends and even to such articles as his compass, his field glasses or his wrist watch. When you first encountered this serene outlook on life you were apt to resent this somewhat patronising attitude. Later when you realised that you yourself were included among his cherished affections you ceased to feel any resentment and liked him all the more for it; besides one was then young enough to feel flattered when he would remark 'of course I've got the best Brigade Major in the Army!' although you knew that even if he had convinced himself of this fact, no one else held the same opinion.

It's a vivid portrait, but what was Seely like to deal with on a professional basis? Brooke's testimony is a first-hand counterpoint to the disparagement meted out by Home and Kavanagh three months earlier:

'From a Brigade Major's point of view he was delightful to work for', was Brooke's considered testimony. 'If ever you had occasion to put up a point, he grasped it immediately, appreciated its significance, and even if it should be in opposition, accepted it then and there.'

That sounds a bit like game, set and match against the more blimpish military establishment. But fate was always a far more threatening enemy. In February Frank had three days' leave and came down to be with his father and the Canadians. The pair of them got their horses and rode round the villages, seeing the billets, the stabling and the makeshift parade grounds, above all talking to the troops with whom both of them had already shared so much. The 48-year-old general, still so lean and weather-beaten atop Warrior's proud thoroughbred strut. The twenty-year-old lieutenant, so fair and slim aboard the shorter legged, comic-eyed, black-coated Akbar. The villages ever a-clink with camp life and the winds still gusting in from the shore.

The memory has a wistful agony about it: 'My men crowded round Frank and cheered him as he rode away. Then we rode down to the sea that we both loved so well and galloped along the sand. To the rhythm of the hoof beats the dreaded words kept coming to me: "Our last ride together."'

Seely got Corporal Anthony to drive him and Frank back to the Hampshires. He was introduced to the officers and listened to the latest plans for the next push. It had been his son's wish to come, his son's wish to stay. He held his arm firmly in farewell.

It was the most privileged of leave-takings, but about it there was the dreadful democracy of death. So many fathers, so many sons.

36

A-gallop at Last

The cavalry had to keep believing. Believing that there might be a way through. And in the case of Seely and his thousand men and horses drilling on the beaches and practising sword-drawn charges, they had to believe that cavalry could yet be the weapon to break the lock. To think otherwise killed the central reason for their separate existence, the heartbeat of their special esprit de corps. At last, in March 1917, there came the call.

It was on Monday 19 March. They were to go east again to the Somme battlefield, but this time they were to take the horses with them. The main German strength was pulling back to the newly reinforced Hindenburg Line, leaving scattered but often strongly defended villages in their wake. These were just the sort of obstacle the mobility of the cavalry could outflank. 'Mobility' – now there's a word that soldiers must have thought had died from lack of use.

Cavalry were still the paratroopers of their era. The Canadian cavalry were trained to wing a thousand fully armed men half a mile across country in a couple of minutes. Each individual trooper carried everything with him. Not just his own sword and rifle and bayonet, but the horse's head collar under his bridle, his hay net on one side, his feed bag on the other. These animals were carrying up to 300 pounds. The system depended on their well-being. Yet it was they who would always present the greatest target, they whom the enemy would most easily take out.

The original horses had come with the brigade from Canada. They needed to be square and sturdy to carry the weight, survive the conditions. They were trucks compared to the sports-car sleekness of a thoroughbred like Warrior. But even though they, like their riders, had never been through a complete 'wipe-out' like the infantry had suffered in July 1916 at the Somme, the casualty rate through shelling, sickness and sheer attrition was still high. Remounts were shipped in, not just from Canada and the UK but from as far away as Argentina. And the men patting the necks of the still strong horses beneath them knew that many more would be needed if the machine guns took their toll.

On the first day, 20 March 1917, the Canadians trekked south through driving rain and snow to gather with the complete 4th Cavalry Division at Serenpont. They were about to transfer their whole four-legged, four-wheeled operation to the open country north of the battle-ravaged town of Péronne, east of Amiens. It must have been one of the longest crocodiles ever seen. A brigade on the march would stretch almost two miles, a whole division almost twelve.

The Canadian part alone would have included rickety-looking lorries carrying all the equipment to set up an HQ at no notice, as well as horse-drawn supply wagons pulling everything from squadron stores to extra riding fodder and tack. They would have a team of cyclists to send messages up and down the line, a motor-cyclist to take news further afield. There would be vets and farriers, as essential as present-day engineers and mechanics; doctors, padres and, most crucially for what lay ahead, a squadron of horse artillery under Major Bill Elkins to give the cover for any cavalry attack.

This time they wanted to give the word 'attack' validity. They talked again of 'breaking through'. It was a hard thought to hold as they slogged east over muddy, shell-pocked roads through continuing rain and snow and biting winds. By Friday evening 23 March they had somehow crossed the pontoon bridge over the Somme just west of Péronne without, unlike many other brigades, losing a wagon over the side. Saturday morning they moved up to establish an HQ in a ruined farmhouse in Moislains and bivouac around as best they could. They were tired and muddy. But they were ready. This was what they had been waiting for.

On the walls of Péronne town hall the retiring Germans had

scrawled, 'Nicht argern nur wundern' (Do not be angry, only reflect), but as Seely and his team rode through, the wilful devastation all around them had very much the opposite effect. Houses, trees, farmhouses – all were flattened. Orchards were destroyed and in some cases poisoned at the roots. The last German positions were in the villages like Havrincourt, Equancourt and Guyencourt, scattered along the ridge in the open country north and east of Moislains. As Brooke and Seely trotted and hacked the twelve miles of this Front next day they could feel real anger rising towards their enemy and satisfaction that at last the cavalry were to have their say.

The Fort Garrys were first in. On the morning of Saturday 24 March their 'C' squadron commanded by a Captain Sharpe took the village of Ytres, despite shelling from the distant German lines and a fair bit of sniping from the upstairs windows in the village. It was hardly the biggest or most costly of engagements, although three horses were killed, a Corporal Johnson was wounded and captured, and the bold Bill Cowen was quite badly hurt when his horse fell into a dugout. But it was the first village taken by Allied cavalry since October 1914.

It was a case of justification as much as celebration. The conditions might be appalling, alternate rain and snow with the horse lines quickly knee deep in mud, but this was what all that training had been for. There was more action and more cost next day, one trooper and eight horses being killed, and eight more troopers wounded. Hidden machine guns in places like Equancourt had taken their toll. The Germans would not be moved lightly, but shifted they could be. Seely, as a mere brigade commander, was supposed to move only with orders from above. But he had kept telling his men about targets. When you identify them, you go for them.

As for planning, he had more people than himself and Geoffrey Brooke reconnoitring the positions. Both Flowerdew and Harvey had been out around Equancourt during the night of Sunday 25th, not getting back till 7 a.m., whilst from early in the morning Prince Antoine was hidden in close with his sketchbook. When it came to conference time, planning for the 6 p.m. three-regiment pincer movement with Elkins's artillery support on the small but well-defended village of Equancourt was complete. It needed to be. For Seely was out on a limb:

> Geoffrey, Antoine and I established ourselves in a hollow just in front of the artillery and waited for the moment. It was an anxious time for not only was I attacking a place without orders, but I was withdrawing the whole of my troops from where I had been ordered to put them. The attack was an overwhelming success. All three regiments galloped forward to their pre-ordained positions with great speed and with surprisingly little loss. Strathcona's captured Equancourt and all the Germans who were not killed or captured fled in confusion. Never shall I forget the joyous moment when Geoffrey Brooke, Elkins and Antoine and I galloped at full speed into Equancourt. It was a tiny little affair but it was a glorious success.

In its own small way this was a microcosm of the glory, the ghastliness and the absurdity of the whole situation. That there was morale-lifting glory in it there is no doubt. 'Oh the thrill that goes with a charge', wrote one soldier, 'and what shouting by every man as he rides on.' And when Seely sent messages back to the infantry telling them that the village was clear, they set off at once and came into Equancourt still joshing (all too prematurely), 'No more bloody trenches now.'

But even though casualties were officially very light, they had their own tragedies to tell. Five horses were killed outright, six more were shot to end their suffering, six men were wounded and after showing Seely all round his part of the captured position Major Jack Critchley slumped down in a chair. 'He was hit through the chest,' said the sergeant to the general, 'but he wanted to complete the tour.' Jack Critchley, who had jumped that splendid five foot nine showjumping round the previous August, was dead within the week.

For the rest of Seely's Canadians the next twenty-four hours went from glory to farce and back again. Seely's recollections are beauties of their kind but have to be put into the context of men who have been a full week on the march in extremely 'inclement' conditions, three full days in direct and mortal combat with the enemy. But they were cavalry. At last they had been given a running chance and had cracked it. They had the bit between their teeth.

Exactly three years earlier Seely was in the deepest throes of the Curragh crisis, shuttling between Westminster, Downing Street and Buckingham Palace, meeting the King, Asquith, Churchill and Lloyd George, his name plucked and kicked all over the front pages. Now he was into the small hours, finishing an unsung but astonishing and exhausting day in an obscure village in northern France with his only wider-world contact likely to be the restrictive hand of superior military officialdom. But, as much as you can be in wartime, he was happy.

'After going round the whole line for the third time with the senior infantry officer, I rode back to my headquarters at Moislains. Thick snow was falling, and the farm house had no roof. However, I took off my clothes, put on woolly pyjamas, curled up in the flea bag and a mackintosh sheet and let the snow fall on me. Geoffrey and Antoine agreed with me that it could snow ink for all we cared.'

Seely may have thought he had earned his rest. Others didn't.

At 6.30 next morning I was awakened by Geoffrey Brooke with these words: 'Johnnie Du Cane who commands the infantry corps, is outside in a towering rage.' I could hear him roaring. I jumped up and ran out to the ruined doorway in my bare feet. There was General Du Cane, sitting on his horse as angry as could be, with a flow of language of which I had not believed him capable and which I could not but admire. He wanted to know from me where his infantry were, and why I had ordered them about as if they belonged to me, without any reference to him. I endeavoured to explain that I had sent no orders, only sug-gestions which had so appealed to his officers that they had acted on them without delay. While I was saying this I heard the sound of a motorcycle ploughing its way through the snow and mud up to the back of the farm. General Du Cane's justifiable anger was not in the least appeased by what I said. He said to me that he would see that the most severe disciplinary measures would be taken against me.

Just at that moment Geoffrey Brooke who had dressed, came up with a message which the motor-cyclist had brought. It ran as follows: 'Heartiest congratulations to you and all under your command on your most brilliant feat of arms. Commander-in-Chief.' I said to the General: 'I am extremely sorry sir, but will this make any difference?' He said nothing while you might count ten, then burst into a roar of laughter and said 'yes I freely forgive you. Perhaps you will now send an officer of your eccentric command to show me where my men really have got to.'

It was a bad morning for blimps. For Seely, better and much worse was soon to come.

37

Fred Harvey VC, Frank Seely RIP

They wanted Seely to do it again. Far from censuring their maverick commander, the top brass wanted a repeat of something they had begun to think would never happen, a successful cavalry attack. The target this time was a little hilltop hamlet called Guyencourt, just a couple of miles south-east of Equancourt but commanding the land all around it. Any advance of the infantry would have first to eliminate any garrison in Guyencourt. These Canadians looked as if they could do the trick.

Seely was never one to hold grudges. He was already reconciled with Gough, and would be a house guest of Du Cane's after the war. But at this moment he could have been excused some uncharitable thoughts about that Home–Kavanagh denigration six months earlier. By his side was the highly professional young major, Geoffrey Brooke. Now the generals were seeing the truth of Brooke's verdict on these Canadians: 'Tough, hard and resourceful, madly keen to get to grips with their opponents and to prove their superiority, and imbued with an indomitable spirit and a high degree of intelligence.'

Some of the men were hardly more than boys. Evan Price was just nineteen. He was a lieutenant in the Royal Canadian Dragoons but it was he who was first into action that rainy, snow-swept afternoon. His squadron came upon a 25-strong group of Germans whom he immediately charged, swords out and at the gallop. Three Germans were killed, nine captured, but then some heavy machine guns opened up across the hilltop. Horses don't normally argue with machine guns. Price and his team needed shelter. They found it in a quarry. Their problem then was how to get out.

The answer came in a snowstorm. For once the atrocious weather was an advantage. For many cavalry regiments, morale amongst men and animals was very low, especially for the latter, what with rain and mud, the lack of fodder and the inability to get supplies forward, not to mention the crow's-feet spikes the Germans sprinkled at river fords to puncture the hooves of horses crossing. On that Tuesday, 27 March 1917, the Canadians took the snow as a cloak.

At 5 p.m. it was snowing so hard that they delayed the opening barrage and the encircling swoop on Guyencourt until 5.15. Machine guns were the problem, but the artillery fire silenced some, the undulations in the fields around the village provided cover from others. But not from all. Lieutenant Fred Harvey was cantering through the snow at the head of his troop of Strathconas when the harsh, rattling chatter of another Maschinengewehr began its own deadly form of conversation.

The machine gun was in a trench dug into the slope thirty yards in front of the walls of the village. When the cavalry approached, some twenty Germans ran down to the trench and the machine gun opened up. Like Evan Price, who was now getting his men out of the quarry under cover of the snowstorm, Harvey did not want his whole squadron to argue with the machine gun. He galloped them across to the shelter of a ridge to his right. This was an argument he would have by himself.

Harvey was a sportsman. His first cap for Ireland had been on the receiving end of a 29–0 thrashing by the Welsh at Cardiff Arms Park in 1907. He had been the fly half behind a losing pack. He had been just eighteen and a half. His only other cap had been as a stop-gap fullback in Cork when he had temporarily returned from Canada four years later. He missed a crucial tackle, France won 25–5, critics were unkind. But here in France he was playing a different game. And against much greater odds.

He had to calculate. To work out just how quickly the machine-gunner was able to rotate the weapon across the line of fire; how long before he would need to reload. There were only forty rounds on a clip. When they were used up, Harvey would have a chance in the fading light. The watching Seely already knew that the towering 28-year-old lieutenant was a star. But what was Harvey doing galloping back towards him as the machine gun spat? He was calculating, that was what.

Then the moment came. The machine gun had stopped. Harvey whirled round and galloped hard from the cover of the hill straight at the machine gun set up at the end of the trench. There were twenty men in that trench. Even without his usual three-man crew the machine-gunner ought to be able to reload in a few seconds. There was a stretch of barbed wire thirty yards in front of the trench that should strip any horse of its ambitions. By normal standards, Harvey's odds were hopeless.

Except that he was coming at them, and coming at them hard out of the gloomy sleet. It was a hundred yards, slightly uphill, before he hit the wire but he had his Colt revolver out and was galloping in every sense like a man possessed. It would take him just ten seconds. The machine-gunner suddenly began to have an extremely intense experience of what Harvey had felt when he was that fullback under a high ball from the French XV six years before.

The gunner's fingers fumbled as this four-legged tornado came murderously on. Beside him in the trenches, the riflemen were confused, some missed, others began to shout warnings. Harvey was crashing into the wire. Then, in an extraordinary somersaulting moment, he was off his horse and over it. He was on his feet with the revolver out and coming at them. It was the last thing that machine-gunner ever saw.

The riflemen didn't feel too good either. Most of them dropped their weapons and legged it back to the village. With mighty strides Harvey got to the machine gun and with a practised hand yanked it round to hammer away at the remaining Germans in a trench on the village corner. They legged it too. The snowstorm had been struck by lightning.

It had been more than a one-man triumph. All three regiments had been used in taking the village and its sister hamlet of Saulcourt, and had been directed with a degree of forethought that was another stinging rebuke to the previous military disapproval. 'We had very few casualties', wrote Geoffrey Brooke in his textbook judgement. 'The success of this little operation was due to well-thought-out preliminary steps, use of ground, speed of movement, a plan which was simple though unexpected by the enemy, and finally, a determination to carry it through.'

But in the end it was an engagement which celebrated the unstoppable power of the fired-up human spirit. 'Harvey was a great athlete,' continues Brooke's sober verdict, 'but a tiger in action, his courage only equalled by his modesty.' Indeed Harvey himself could never be drawn to expand on his legendary feats that snowy afternoon. 'He does,' he said about Seely's description, 'to say the least, exaggerate a bit.' Among his own family there was a hush when, on a visit back to Ireland years later, a great-nephew, greatly daring, asked the old soldier how he had won his VC. Harvey looked around at the temerity of the question, and then just dismissed it. 'I lost my temper', he said.

Modesty, of course, was not Seely's second name and he was not going to have this Canadian success recorded without some honours on its flag. When the brigade got moved away from the line to Athies next day he wrote his reports and put both Harvey and Evan Price in for MCs. On reading the citation for Harvey, Haig upped the award to a DSO and at the next divisional parade that medal was pinned to his chest. But when the King read the citation he thought nothing less than the crimson ribbon of the Victoria Cross would do. The Canadian cavalry had won their first VC.

It was something to celebrate. After two full years of almost entirely trench-bound warfare, after all those months of preparation for mounted attacks that most had come to believe would never happen, the Canadians had been given a chance and had quite gloriously taken it. No matter that the line had closed over again. Seely's HQ was in the cellars of a ruined chateau near Athies. On the night of 14 April 1917 he invited all the senior officers of the regiment to feast there and toast the tall young hero in their midst.

By its nature it was to be a memorable evening. But for Seely that memory was to take the most bitter of twists:

'Antoine d'Orléans, Jack Seely's indefatigable A.D.C., somehow managed to produce unlimited champagne,' recalls Geoffrey Brooke,

> and the party went with the usual swing. Before the end of dinner a telegram was brought in to me which I opened and read without divulging the contents, thus provoking ribald jokes at my expense as to the origin and nature of the message. Later when our guests had departed, I told my general of the contents.
>
> It was from General Cavan asking me to tell Jack Seely that his oldest boy had been killed in action. He was devoted to his son and very proud of him. It was indeed a great blow but he took it as I knew he would. Even in that moment of anguish, he realised how difficult the last half hour had been for me, and said, 'Of course my dear Geoffrey, you were right to withhold this until we were alone.'

Courage may be defined as grace under pressure, but this time the grace could not hide the grief. Seely called for Warrior. He rode north through the night.

38

Frank and Thomas, All Our Sons

The battlefield of Arras is thirty miles north of Athies as the crow flies. But Seely did not get very far. After a while Brooke gathered Anthony and Thompson and the Crossley and set off in pursuit. It would be easier and quicker by motor. The car would have bumped up through the ruins of Péronne and Bapaume and the awful agony would have gone on.

Frank had paid the ultimate sacrifice. Frank 'the dreamer', Frank the schoolboy who had written, 'I hope you will not mind, but I thought I should not remain at home while other people are being shot.' Frank the ADC who had insisted on going back to his regiment in the line. Frank the firstborn; so this was what sacrifice was like.

It was April 1917. The war to end all wars had begun nearly three years ago. All that could be shown was killing and devastation and mud. Now Frank had been killed too. It should have been enough to drive a father to rage at the futility of the whole campaign. But for Seely that would break the belief that sustained him, the belief that the sacrifice was worthwhile.

Next morning I wandered about the battlefield of Arras, not caring where I went so long as I could find some trace of my boy. At last I found his Company Commander of the First Battalion of the Hampshire Regiment. They were holding on by their eyelids to an advanced trench on a forward slope. He said kind things about my son; his courage and the love his men bore to him. It was all the consolation he could give me but it was the best. He

lies buried at Haute-Avesnes between a South African and an
Irish soldier.

The little cemetery is the most poignant of spots. Haute-Avesnes is
a small village just south and above the main Saint-Pol road, some
three miles west of the ugly rebuilt city of Arras. Its main feature is
a farm on the crest of the hill. A small road leads down to the south
with an irregular orchard with a couple of cows in it on the left.
Next to them is the cemetery. It is about the size of a suburban
garden and is pristine and perfect in its guardianship; the regulation
gate with the visitors' book waiting in the metal locker set in the
wall; the white crosses, the names, English, Irish, South African,
Scottish, Welsh; even Chinese, a dozen orientally inscribed headstones up in the far corner showing that Empire labourers also paid
the highest price. The grass is cut. The walls are low. Beyond it are
just dull flat fields – and incomprehension.
　　Wilfred Owen's closing lines squeeze hard at the throat:

> My friend you would not tell with such high zest
> To children ardent for some desperate glory,
> The old Lie: Dulce et decorum est
> Pro patria mori.

But for Seely; for Harvey, Antoine, Brooke, Flowerdew, Williams,
Cowen, Smith, Anthony, Evan Price and all the rest, it was not a lie.
It was what bound them together. Grotesque as it may seem in
hindsight, Harvey had it right in seeing this as the ultimate rugby
match. Win or lose, believing was the best way to play the game.
　　It might have been thought that all this would have quite
brutalized the mind but there was sensitivity as well as humour
behind the harsh mask of war. The Canadian cavalry had a brigade
band, concert parties were a feature behind the lines and their newly
bereaved commander never stopped finding wonder in every day.
　　The galloping heroics at Equancourt and Guyencourt had
proved yet another false dawn and soon the Canadians had sent
their horses away and were back in the trenches near Le Verguier,
just north-west of Saint-Quentin. It was Seely's third spring near the

Somme. He had supped full of the horrors of war. His own son had been added to the long black lists of the fallen. Yet life was for the living. His little daughter would be four years old in August. Writing to her had become his way of giving the family wider instruction and reassurance.

May 3rd 1917

Darling Baby Lou,

How are you I wonder – very well and very gay I'll be bound. Won't it be nice when we can play again at Brooke? Well I can't come just now, but I will come along as soon as I can.

Yesterday evening I was in a big wood, most of which those stupid Germans had cut down. But they couldn't spoil the flowers, and there were ever so many cowslips, and primroses, and anemones and wild violets.

Here is one of the cowslips. It is lovely summer weather, but the trees have not come out yet; but the swallows have come and are busy building nests in the ruins; so are all the other birds – robins and blackbirds, and owls, and magpies, and jackdaws, and lots of partridges all going about in pairs.

Major Docherty came back yesterday, and told me all about you, which was very nice.

I haven't time to write to anyone else, so you must give some messages for me. Please tell Uncle Aubrey to order me eight little wrist compasses from Sifton Praed of St James's St, the same as Major Docherty bought for 15/6.

Ask Aunt Florrie to let me know what has happened about the Flying Corps. Are they coming back to the house on the hill when you go or have they decided to go somewhere else.

Ask Emmy to be sure and not get too tired when she goes to her hospital.

Ask Nanny how many times a day she beats you now! Ask Kitty if she would like to ride with me on the nicest pony ever seen after the war – ask Irene why the Muscovy ducks build their nest in a tree. Did you ever have so many messages in your life?

Bless you my Baby Lou, your loving <u>Daddy</u>

One message he had not yet shared with his family was the increasing intimacy of the letters he was now receiving from George Nicholson's widow, Evie. He had shared her grief, now she was mortified for him over Frank. It was all very well having belief but while life lasted Seely also needed a soulmate – and a mother for his little ones. It would happen sooner than he thought.

But first he and his team had to make the best of things. The feature of the new lines near Le Verguier was that no-man's-land was a full mile wide instead of the mere couple of hundred yards which had been standard for so much of the war. Trying to dominate this area became a Canadian cavalry obsession, so much so that, except for a few sentries, they slept all day so as to patrol and drive away the enemy all night. All through May they kept up the pressure, but one huge obstacle remained: on the right of their lines, half a mile into no-man's-land, was a huge crater with a small wood in the centre and a number of bushes on the slope on the far side. The bushes concealed a whole rush of German dugouts. The place was called Fisher's Crater. On the night of 26 May the Canadians were intent on making it their own.

This was making the best of it. This was not the global strategy with which Seely's previous peer group were now wrestling so unsuccessfully. This was war in microcosm, where you knew everybody by name, where every life counted because you knew yours could be next on the line. This was Antoine lying hidden all day with his sketch map and crawling back to design a replica crater to rehearse the raid.

The painter's eye was just one of the prince's many talents, but crawling out to the edge of that crater and lying up in broad daylight took nerve of right royal order. It was a nerve that held and a scheme that won. Again and again they practised the attack, which would happen in conjunction with an intense machine-gun barrage on the position. It was timed for 2.15 a.m. 'Jock' Strachan would lead a party of forty Fort Garrys, 'Jackie' Tatlow a similar one for the Strathconas. Needless to say Seely was not far away in the darkness:

I crawled to a point about 400 yards from the crater. With me was a squadron which was going to rush forward in support if the attack was not at once successful. It was anxious work waiting. At last the moment came. The signal was the bursting of the shell of a particular gun. Hardly had the vibrations of the burst died away before the air was rent with terribly angry shouts, followed by screams of surprise, fright and pain. I confess after taking part in so many desperate battles my heart stood still at those awe-inspiring and ghastly sounds of human rage and fright.

It was a brutal but successful saga. The Fort Garrys killed eight Germans with the bayonet, the Strathconas a full dozen, and some twenty prisoners were brought back through the lines. But Jackie Tatlow was not with them. Seely ran to the crater to find him. Tatlow had apparently killed three Germans in those violent opening seconds, but now he was just a smiling figure smoking a cigarette, his arms laden with enemy rifles. 'I thought I would take some souvenirs', he said.

Afterwards Seely wrote Military Cross citations for Tatlow, Strachan and Antoine but he was not around to receive the replies. Instead he was in hospital at Wimereux near Boulogne. He was lucky to be there at all. There had been another attack in no-man's-land and this time Seely had overdone his Galloper Jack bit. He and little Akbar had gone to see the patrol leave and, on the opening barrage, planned to gallop off to the temporary HQ. What happened next, even by Seely standards, was quite close to the line. I had some crashes in ten years as a steeplechase jockey, but nothing quite as dodgy as this:

> When I got to about halfway the Germans opened up with their return strafe. A shell burst about a foot in front of my pony's nose and he instantly fell over sideways like a stone with me firmly fixed to his back. I heard my collar bone crack as I hit the ground and immediately felt acute pain in my shoulder, arm and left leg. Akbar lay quite still, and I presumed he was dead. I tried to wriggle out, but the pain was so severe that I gave it up. Then above the sound of the occasional shells, I heard the rattle of our

heavy machine guns, with their limbers (carriages), galloping towards me. I was right in the centre of the track, and it was almost pitch dark. I knew that they would not see or hear me, and that they must pass right over me. I moved, the pain was so great that I almost gave up the attempt.

But the love of life was strong, and I put my right leg up against the pony's back and gave a tremendous push. The pony was only slightly wounded, and stunned; the movement woke him up, he rolled to his feet and galloped away. The machine guns were within a hundred yards and going full speed. So, in spite of the almost unbearable pain, I managed to roll over three times before they thundered past, the nearest within 6 inches of my head. I shouted as they went by, but of course they did not hear me. I lay there in the dim light, and remember thinking that at last my time had come.

Not for the great survivor it hadn't. The guardian angel this time materialized in the shape of the faithful orderly Corporal King who hunted him down, got stretcher bearers and lugged him off for the bumpiest of horse-drawn ambulance rides to the advanced dressing station. Others had not been so lucky. The patrol leader Fred Butterfield, a Saskatchewan-based lieutenant who had been pro-moted from the ranks, had a bayonet wound in his side. Lancashire born Thomas Cain was in much worse shape. He was put into the ambulance alongside Seely. It was to be his final journey.

The poor man in the opposite stretcher began to wander as we bumped and rolled along. I had seen so many men die of wounds, that I knew his end was near. First he talked about the attack in disjointed sentences; then he began to swear at his enemies of an hour ago; then his voice changed. Three times he called 'Mother.' Then he died. It is a strange and touching thing that when men die quickly after dangerous wounds, in almost every case 'Mother' is the last word that crosses their lips.

It is also touching as well as true that in the aftermath of such a reprieve, thoughts turn again to home and to the most vulnerable there. So much blood had been shed, shells had been spent, mud and other horrors endured – by Seely as well by many much less fortunate men. But a father's love can conquer all:

39 Casualty Clearing Station, France
June 21st 1917

My own Baby Lou

You should just see me now – lying in bed with two adorable kittens fast asleep against my good leg. They play with each other and with me all day, except when they get tired and then they go to sleep. They are so fond of me that they won't leave me even at night – they take them away but they always manage to get back again before long. I never invited them – they just came. The other people are quite jealous. I am not very far away from where poor Akbar fell on me during one of our little fights – but tomorrow or next day they are going to put me in a train and send me to a place near Boulogne where I shall get quite well in three weeks. It will be a hospital train all covered with red-crosses with lovely nurses flitting up and down with beef-tea – quite looking forward to it, I can't bear going away from my Brigade.

I am not really a bit ill as I can't put a crutch under my left arm I can't help my left leg – so just have to lie flat.

I am always thinking about you and all the others – you are all so good in writing to me. It is much colder so I am afraid I won't be able to swim for a bit.

The kittens have gone to sleep again so I expect I had better follow their example.

I have an awfully nice nurse who sends you her love.

Your loving <u>Daddy</u>

Ten days later Nurse Betty, 'an angel in human form', had worked her miracle. Seely had been shifted to the coast. Antoine had been a visitor, so too the Queen who had said sweet and affecting things about poor Frank. The family suddenly didn't seem so far away:

14 General Hospital,
Wimereux, France
July 3rd 1917

My own little Baby Lou,

I do like your letters so much.

Today my leg was so much better that I walked up a grass slope to the edge of the cliff and looked over the sea towards Brooke where you are. It hurt rather, but the doctor says it's good for it about once a day, and I'm sure he is right. On the top of the cliff there were sea-pinks, so I picked one for you and send it in this letter.

Do you know, my dearest, that I think it <u>just</u> possible that I might come over and see you in about a week or ten days' time, and stay for ten days at Brooke while my collar bone gets quite mended up and the leg quite strong. But I'm not at all sure so you will have to tell Aunt Florrie and Emmy and the others not to count on it. It would be very nice to see Baba Robson and her baby if she were there.

Tell Aunt Florrie I will talk like anything about governesses if I come home; also tell her it's very nice of her to write me such lovely letters about you all.

I must not write any more because it is time to go to sleep.

God bless you dear Baby Lou.

Your loving <u>Daddy</u>

The homecoming would be treasured but it would also contain a shock. For Baby Lou was not the only person Seely had been writing to from hospital. Quite early on he had made a big decision and sent a telegram. It was to Evie Nicholson. It was to become a loving and well-balanced partnership, but as proposals go it was short on supplication.

Am coming home, and we are going to get married.

At the end of the month, on 31 July at St Ethelburga's Church, Bishopsgate, they were.

39

Marriage, But No Mercy

It was raining but *The Times* reported that 'quite a crowd' had gathered outside the church. Inside Archie Sinclair had come back from commanding the Life Guards in order to be Seely's best man. Evie's father, Viscount Elibank, was so late that she had to be 'given away' by her late husband George's father, Sir Charles Nicholson. Only immediate family were present. According to my mother, some of them were in a state of shock.

There was nothing scandalous. There had never been any question of a relationship before George had been killed in 1916. But Jack was forty-nine, Evie some eighteen years younger. He had six children aged from nineteen down to four years old, not to mention three brothers, six sisters and assorted spouses. She had only six-year-old John, red-headed, wary and uneasy with it. It was a classic stepmother scenario. The arrival at Brooke was never going to be easy. It was a big house with five children, a huge retinue of servants, all presided over with charity to the point of laxity by Seely's 57-year-old spinster sister Florrie, whose next destination was to be the Church Army. Evie was a small, musical, bird-like young woman. She was in devoted awe of her new husband and determined to become a mother to his household. But she hadn't realized the half of it.

To make matters worse, Lou had a major asthma attack. 'I was so looking forward to them coming,' she remembered, 'when they arrived they brought lots of furniture with them. I rushed down but the different dust from the furniture started up my asthma. It got so bad that I had to go upstairs to recover.'

Evie may have been young enough to be a daughter rather than a mother. But she was Scottish. She brought with her a large number of petrol cans prudently filled by her late husband in expectation of fuel rationing. She brought a numerate mind which quickly realized that Seely's expenditure and his income were in vastly differing ballparks.

His income as a brigadier general was a little over £500 a year, not much more than £13,500 in today's terms, a considerable way short of the equivalent of £88,000 that he took as a junior minister in 1908–12 and the whacking £5,000 per annum (£265,000 today) he had earned as Secretary of State for War. The actual wage for a Secretary of State remained the same from 1831 to 1937, not a lot by the end date, an extremely handsome stipend in the early years.

Seely had, of course, also lost his principal sponsor when his father died in 1915 and the surprise bequest of Brooke was becoming a mixed blessing. It was a splendid place for a large family, but an extremely costly establishment to run. Old Sir Charles was a famously benevolent as well as enormously wealthy man. The man who ensured that all his tenants and dependants in the Isle of Wight and Nottinghamshire got a ton of Seely coal at Christmas liked to feel that those who worked for him were looked after.

In his declining years Sir Charles divided his time between Sherwood, Brooke and the not entirely modest London home he rented from the Government, No. 1 Carlton House Terrace. Each of these places was fully staffed up; in the case of the country estates this included whole teams of gardeners, estate carpenters, black-smiths, gamekeepers and chauffeurs as well as the butler, cook, chambermaid, footman of the indoor establishments. Overseeing the household on his behalf had been his oldest daughter, Florrie, who, in the spirit of the times, had forsaken the prospect of marriage to step in as chatelaine and hostess when her mother died in 1894.

Florrie, as her Church Army work was to confirm, was a splendidly generous and open-hearted woman. She had naturally offered to help her beleaguered brother when Nim had died in 1913, even though her father, now eighty, rather grumbled about being 'neglected'. When Jack went off to war in August 1914 she moved the whole family down to Brooke House. During term time Frank, then seventeen, and John, fifteen, went off to Harrow, poor un-mothered Patrick, nine, went to board at prep school. Seven-year-old Kitty and Baby Lou were the governance of 'Nanny' Williams in the nursery, while the older girls, Emmy, sixteen, and Irene, twelve, had 'improving' lessons from assorted governesses and music teachers. In my mother Irene's case this also involved run-ning fairly tomboy wild whilst the more decorous Emmy confessed in later life a sense of frustration that she, the responsible older daughter, was still treated by her father as a child rather than as someone who could help with his life and share some of his concerns.

So it was a huge household that Florrie had overseen, and twenty years into playing the Seely chatelaine she was not inclined to change the paternalistic indulgence that kept everyone on the payroll, however little they might do. As far as she was concerned, and of course as far as her brother Jack had been concerned, their father had been the fount of a lifestyle where the funding came without question. The problem for Evie as she tried to settle herself and her son into this huge and trouble-strewn nest in 1917 was that even a funding as massive as that of the now interred Sir Charles had begun to run out.

For a start, the income from coal was decreasing. The first entirely oil-fuelled British battleship was launched in 1914 and the frequent miners' strikes were caused by the coal owners' fears that increases in wages would make their product uncommercial. Even in those desperately primitive working conditions (women and children had been going down the mines until 1910) there was already the mix of opposing attitudes and alternative energy sources that would finally collapse the British coal industry in the 1970s.

If the original Charles 'Pigs' Seely had been about he might have thought his way around this ebbing tide. But his sons and grandsons were too commercially staid to float off any new enterprise from their original holding. There were still massive funds and the sons of the family continued to embrace a wide sense of public duty, being justices of the peace, colonels of the yeomanry, members of parliament. But the family was ever widening and the diminution of those funds was beginning to seriously limit the available support for Jack and Evie's future.

When Jack's older brothers, Charlie and Frank, had got married they had been given the massive estates of Gatcombe and Ramsdale in the Isle of Wight and Nottingham respectively and were also granted substantial shares in the family Babbington Coal Company which Frank began to manage in the later 1890s. There were also six sisters who would be given handsome allowances as long as the situation demanded. Florrie was head of her father's household, Daisy and Nancy married in Nottinghamshire, but the younger three, Lily, Mary and Sylvie, all settled in the West Wight in houses bought by their father. Maybe not full of vipers, but the Seely enclave was indeed quite a nest.

So it was to this family, these finances, those sisters-in-law, that Jack's wife faced her crash introduction. If you wanted to, you could find trouble everywhere you looked. Lou had asthma, Patrick and Kitty were in between the nursery and adulthood, Irene and Emily were consumed with hurt at their hero father's sudden marriage to this much younger woman. Evie's own son, John, was making a horrendous start, being as openly hostile to everything Seely as only a spoiled seven-year-old redhead could be. Just to round off the nightmare, John Seely was now eighteen and his gazetting with the Royal Horse Artillery in Italy made everyone hold their breath lest he follow Frank into those simple brutal initials K.I.A. (killed in action).

And that was just the children. Evie later admitted that, to begin with at least, her new sisters-in-law gave her a pretty bad time. She did, after all, come in on this receding tide. One of her husband's other nicknames was 'Spendthrift Jack', many of the family were surprised and a touch jealous when he, rather than his oldest brother Charlie, was left Brooke in their father's will.

There were clearly some storm clouds, both familial and financial, banking up on the horizon, but that August nothing could affect the sunny-ness of Jack's smile. He was home. He had a summer that might not have been, that might well not come again. He could play with the children, walk to the shore, talk to the fishermen, spend time with his daughters. And he now had a beautiful and adoring young wife to share his future and his bedroom. At least Florrie was supportive. Evie could soon play mother to the brood. Problems, what problems?

Now his other family beckoned. 'I see General Seely is engaged to be married again', a soldier in the 8th Hussars had written home. 'You know he's in our Division and the regiment was under him in the line, many like him most awfully out here. He's as brave as ten tigers.' Antoine and Patterson and Harvey were all writing more direct congratulations. But they were also asking a greater favour. Notwithstanding injury and marriage, they wanted their tiger back.

He was happy and healing slowly amongst his old and new beloved. But those letters from the Front had an addictive, haunting pull about them. Seely was not an introspective man, but he would have recognized the closing lines of Siegfried Sassoon's poem 'Sick Leave', penned at Craiglockhart Hospital at just this time:

> And while the dawn begins with slashing rain
> I think of the Battalion in the mud.
> 'When are you going out to them again?
> Are they not still your brothers through our blood?'

Seely's answer was in the affirmative. He was still not fit, the legs were wonky, he could hardly use his left arm at all, but he got himself a medical certificate and was signed through to return to France. The newly increased family at Brooke greeted the news with a mixture of fear, pride and bewilderment. But they knew that it had to be.

Antoine met him off the boat at Boulogne. He seemed delighted to see his commander and they set off south-east towards Saint-Pol. He told of the 'Great Raid' on 8 July led by Connolly and Campbell, with Atwood, Harvey, Williams, Strachan and Cowen all involved.

A raiding party some 190-strong had dragged a high-explosive Bangalore Torpedo device close up to the enemy wire, blown a big gap, destroyed German positions and killed or captured practically everyone in range. Connolly received the DSO, Campbell and Atwood the MC, Cowen and Strachan were both wounded but survived. It was a good story, yet the nearer Seely's car got to Saint-Pol, the more closed and uncommunicative Antoine became. It was as if he was hiding something. He was.

> At last we arrived in the little square. To my astonishment there were loud cheers from a crowd of men. I saw an old-fashioned char-a-banc with four horses and one of my officers on the box. I was hoisted up to the box beside him, and for three miles went through cheering crowds. The whole of my Brigade turned out, waving their hats and firing off Verey lights on each side of the road. Truth to tell, I was so exhausted from my journey and with the pain of being hoisted on to the box that I hardly knew what to do. But it really was a most affecting homecoming.

That last word is the key. It might soon become a hellhole again but for Seely and those Canadians it would remain the home they shared. And they knew that his return was the deepest of commitments. That he was willing to die for them.

40

Horror at Passchendaele, Heroics at Cambrai

Sometimes things went from bad to laughable. Over the next two months Seely, Warrior, Antoine and all the rest went through two seminal experiences, unique for their mix of horror, gallantry and gallows-humour absurdity. They sank in the mud at Passchendaele and attacked with the tanks at Cambrai.

Seely had been back a few weeks, Geoffrey Brooke had won the showjumping at the horse show, General Kavanagh, he of the 'Sack Seely' saga nine months before, had driven over to pin on the medals for Fisher's Crater and the 'Great Raid' and say what a cracking brigade this was. Then orders came. They contained just about the worst idea yet. That the Canadians should go north to Ypres. The cavalry would be going for the 'G' in 'Gap'. Only this time the 'Gap' would be at Passchendaele.

Warrior did not like it and he was not the only one. On the way to Ypres he suddenly stopped so sharply that Seely, his left arm still crippled, was nearly thrown from the saddle. The horse who had walked into the waves at Brooke as a two-year-old and who would stand rock steady under shell fire was not the shying kind. But he had seen something. Seely eventually persuaded him forward. Ahead appeared a long row of bedraggled Chinese labourers. They were digging graves.

Out the other side of Ypres towards the ruins of Passchendaele and the omens accumulated:

> The north west wind, and the pitiless rain beat down on us in a
> way I shall never forget as we rode through St Julien, and thence

along the corduroy road. After a time even the road seemed to disappear. There were many dead horses lying about which had foundered in the mud, and could not be extricated. All of a sudden Warrior went deep into the mud up to his belly. Antoine was just behind me with Corporal King and another orderly. It was only with immense difficulty that the four of us managed to get him back on to sounder ground. It was a narrow escape.

Seely and Antoine did the last part on foot, armed with nothing better than walking sticks. Slipping and sliding and picking their way round the edge of shell craters, it took them three hours to do the final couple of miles 'to reach the ruins of Passchendaele, a scene of mud and misery, almost impossible to describe'. Finally they found the much depleted battalion they were supposed to support. The commander roared with laughter at the idea of Seely and Antoine being there to 'recce' a cavalry attack. There would be no 'Gallop'; there certainly was no 'Gap'.

But come 20 November they were given the biggest chance they would ever have: the huge quarter-of-a-million-man assault on Cambrai, featuring for the first time a mass tank attack, 374 of them crashing through the fabled defences of the Hindenburg Line 'as if they were a bed of nettles'. This really should have created a 'Gap', and Haig had assigned no less than 27,500 cavalry, five divisions, to go through, in the hope, to quote the official order, of 'a most far reaching effect, not only on the local situation but on the course of the war'. Leading the 5th Division on the right flank were the Canadian cavalry. Seely, of course, was at the very front.

'For a few hours it was a glorious success', wrote Seely, despite low cloud and drizzling rain. 'It was fine to be cantering along just behind a tank into the village of Masnières. I am sure Warrior enjoyed every minute of it.' There is a fair degree of exaggeration in this, especially in the idea that the first tanks could move at cantering pace, but the commander's enthusiasm was certainly shared.

Along the Fort Garry line Bill Cowen was to become a major player in one of the most momentous days in his regiment's history.

Overnight he and his men had ridden a dozen miles north under cover of darkness from their own camp at Caulincourt, west of Saint-Quentin, to the collecting point at Gouzeaucourt. At eleven that morning they had trekked another five miles north-east in the wake of the tanks until they were halted, and shot at, in the long single street leading up to the bridge at Masnières, some four miles short of Cambrai.

'We were under field artillery and machine-gun fire', wrote Cowen, not for the movies but for real life,

> enemy snipers were still in Masnières picking off our men. But Brig-General Seely and his Brigade Major, Major Geoffrey Brooke, sat calmly on their horses issuing orders, scorning even to put on their steel helmets. The composure of the senior officers had a marvellous effect on the men. I saw chaps whose bravery had been questioned calmly light cigarettes and start picking up their horses' feet to look for chance stones while our farriers went down the lines as we huddled for protection against the wall, tightening a shoe wherever they found a loose one.

'Jock' Strachan was cut from very different cloth to his fellow lieutenant, but he too began the day in a very positive vein. 'Everybody was in high spirits, the squadron being a picture, up to strength with 4 officers, 129 men and 140 horses, with everything polished and burnished as if for the general's inspection.' Their own general had liked what he saw, but not up ahead. What was to happen on that bridge at Masnières would be military farce of historic dimensions.

Tanks might have been a truly terrifying thought in 1917 but even the most obligingly dumb German knew that they could not swim canals. The Canal de l'Escaut ringed the route to Cambrai. There was a bridge at Masnières. Somewhat unsportingly, if not entirely unsurprisingly, the Germans blew it up. Or blew half of it up. As Warrior champed and the farriers flexed, Second Lieutenant Farrar in the lead tank wondered whether the bridge would hold if he tried to rumble over it. Finally he did. And it didn't.

But if the tank was heavy, it was also hot – boiling hot after running its engine for four hours. As it hit the cold November water of the canal, there was an explosive hiss as the whole apparatus was enveloped in a cloud of steam. 'Mein Gott!' the Germans must have thought – was this some cunning plan? For, under cover of the steam, the driver struggled free and escaped the enemy fire almost unscathed. Almost, but not entirely – he was a man with a wig. That did not survive. He sued for damages. The Army v The Hairpiece lives in legal history yet. Second Lieutenant Farrar did the big double. He got the money – and an MC.

We may laugh, but it wouldn't seem so comic if you had been in the saddle half the night and were all psyched up, as Seely's men were, to gallop through enemy bullets past Cambrai, capture the German corps commander at Escadoeuvres three miles further on, and be part of something that would 'change the course of the war'. Seely strode forward and had words with the tank team. He wasn't into hairpieces, especially not those who were to later sneer about 'mediaeval horse soldiers'. This looked like one for 'Tiny'.

Major W. K. Walker MC from Toronto was, physically at least, by far the greatest asset in the whole maverick Seely brigade. He had somehow been accepted by the RCD as a cavalryman but one look at his monumental six foot two, seventeen-stone bulk suggested problems beyond the resources of the remount section. Tiny was put in charge of the machine-gun squadron. And of anything else that needed fixing. A canal crossing could do for now.

If only someone had known, or even looked, there was a perfectly good, albeit well-defended, bridge a mere 400 yards to the left of the collapsed one. Instead they went a thousand yards to the right to a narrow and dilapidated lock gate. Not the most obvious passage for at least four hundred men and horses but Tiny liked a challenge. He took his machine-gunners down to the lock, found some handy planks of building timber, commandeered a string of other hands including twenty German prisoners and set to work.

Using the prisoners was a wartime Judgement of Solomon. German sniping from the far bank threatened to sabotage every-thing. So Tiny told the prisoners they had a choice. They could agree to stand and work on the far side of the team and risk being shot by their friends. Or they could refuse, and be shot for certain by their enemies. They agreed. The sniping slowed, the building quickened and soon after 3 p.m. the 'bridge', some forty foot long by ten foot wide, was ready for a try.

Yet the odds were lengthening horribly. Sunset was timed for 4.03 p.m., so there was not a lot of light left of this dank winter afternoon. It was six long hours since the divisional chief General McAndrew had ridden through the Fort Garry lines and promised the German-speaking Cowen the enemy corps commander's chargers if he brought that gentleman back with him. Six hours since the general had explained how big a breakthrough this would be, how the infantry and the tanks would have cleared the field for the cavalry to take its chance. But now only a few of the infantry had crossed over and the tank hissed on the bed of the canal. At HQ they took a decision. They ordered the cavalry back.

But 'B' squadron of Fort Garrys were already crossing – and counting the cost. Those farriers had been tightening horses' shoes to handle fields and tracks, not walk over wet wooden planks on narrow locks. Several slipped over the side, taking their riders with them. The snipers had a field day. A few never made it to the bank.

Lieutenant 'Dunc' Campbell, now a DSO from his exploits in the 'Great Raid' in the summer, was in charge. He and his men drew their swords. They were 140, not Tennyson's 'six hundred'. It was November, the ground was wet and marshy. He turned and galloped the squadron northwards. The infantry had at least captured the first set of German trenches but they needed the wire to be cut. It didn't take long but 'Dunc' Campbell never saw it finished. A single bullet caught him. He slumped on his horse's neck. Suddenly he was just a body, not a rider.

'Jock' Strachan took over. The next obstacle was a mile-long camouflage screen which the Germans had set up to shield their traffic from enemy eyes. A gap was cut, troops trotted through, shells and bullets were winging but blood was still up. And as they crested the next ridge Strachan saw what he had always wanted to see.

'Every time a real cavalry man dreams of heaven,' he said later in rather un-bank manager language, 'you know what he is dreaming about? He is dreaming about coming on an unprotected battery of guns. So we got up over the hill and lo and behold, four 77 millimetre guns. They were lined up roughly with gun teams all behind and the crews all congratulating each other about the fine shooting they were doing. Boy did they know what was going to happen to them.'

The scene could go straight to Hollywood. Bill Cowen remembers it for real:

> They fired, doing no damage as we were travelling down grade at a good rate of speed. Two of the gunners stood at attention after firing their shots and were run through with the swords of our men. The drivers tried to get away with their teams. One of our corporals cut the battery telephone wires. I called on the drivers in German to halt. In reply they kicked up their ponies – they were riding little Russian horses – and I stopped the two drivers of one team with my revolver, while our men attended to the other.

They may have seemed deadly but they were doomed. Evening was coming and support was not. Colonel 'Bob' Patterson was so upset that he himself crossed over to recall them, only for his horse to go lame. This was becoming not so much 'breakthrough' as Balaclava – and with attitude. Cowen continues:

> My horse had two bullets in his flank and was beginning to weaken, when off to the right of us we saw a group of about 150 Germans with four machine guns lying in the ground in front of them. The Germans had their hands raised in token of surrender. I told Lieutenant Strachan that I was going to take a section and send it back with those prisoners. Instead of allowing this he seized my reins as I started to give the order, directing me to keep going – a serious mistake which cost many lives, for the moment we had gone by, the Germans picked up their rifles and machine guns and started firing from our rear. We took shelter in a sunken road about half a mile further on and counted up our losses.

The situation was on the extreme side of desperate. Poor Strachan had thought that the regiment's other two squadrons (almost 300 men) were following to sweep up the surrendered enemy behind him. However misguided that moment with Cowen might prove, he was now in charge of a hand no one would want to play:

'A hurried inspection was made', he records in much cooler, more clerical vein, 'and the squadron was found to have suffered severely, more so than had been anticipated. Only 43 [out of 143] men were left, all the pack horses were lost, several men had minor wounds and all the horses but seven were found to be wounded, many were exhausted and several actually dropped dead while we were going around looking for them.'

The silent suffering of the wounded horse as he stands quietly bleeding to death is an ineradicable symbol of the horror of war. But for Strachan's Canadians the slim hope of safety was all that mattered. Scouts came back to report Germans further to the east whilst to the west they could hear the ear-bruising rumble of metallic wheeled troop lorries coming up from Cambrai. Strachan sent men to cut the power lines but one of them was electrocuted. The dream had been to spearhead the greatest cavalry attack in history. The dream was dead.

To aid their return they had just two cards – invisibility and desperation. They had tried to stampede the horses as a diversion – but you don't get much of a stampede from the dying. Cowen had got a bullet in his neck but he could still talk. As they crept cautiously south it would be he who would return any German challenge and keep in conversation until they got within bayonet range. Without any confirmatory paperwork, it is the received Fort Garry wisdom that a number of their troopers were in fact Native Canadians (Red Indians). Right or wrong, the German 'scalping' fears raised at the Somme were proof of a handiness with steel that served Strachan well that night.

For him it still had a long way to run. Amongst the things you least want to find when stumbling, rain-soaked, wind-swept and exhausted through enemy lines is a mile long, twenty foot high camouflage screen. Somehow Strachan kept them going until they found the gap, but when they were through it they lost Cowen. They were so weary that when they came upon a crater they just pitched down in it and went to sleep.

Cowen had prisoners with him. He had put the bayonet blade to their necks and said that if they made a sound when a German challenged he would kill them. They had no difficulty in believing him. At last there were lights and voices ahead. Cowen threatened again and crept forward to listen:

> At first it sounded like Scotchmen talking but when I came closer I heard the East Prussian accent, and the voices complaining about being sent to the front without gas masks. Then I slipped and fell into the knife-rest fascines [wood and wire tangle] that were blocking the road they were guarding. I was caught in the wire and four Germans started towards me, so I commanded them very curtly (in German) to put down their arms and get me out of the wire. With amazing obedience, the four rifles went to the ground and they sprang to help me. It was dark and they had no way of recognizing my uniform until I was free and able to cover them with the rifle I had taken from one of our dead men. As I pointed my bayonet at them they loosened their belts and bayonets with alacrity and raised their hands over their heads.

One gathers that Bill Cowen's arguments were strangely convincing to the gaggingly terrified youths from East Prussia. With only occasional bayonet prompting he got them to guide him to the canal and they then worked their way along until another challenge came. This time it was a Canadian accent. It was from the Newfoundland Regiment. They had been through the mincer that afternoon but now held the bridge just beyond the one of the tank-and-hairpiece fiasco:

'With one of their officers acting as guide my nineteen men and eight prisoners picked our way over the dead which lay on the bridge like railway ties, and then we set out for the Canadian Brigade HQ. A mounted officer of the Lord Strathcona Horse found us along the road and led the way to Brigadier General Seely, reaching the farm house, where he was having a council with all the Brigade Officers at 8.15 pm.'

Cowen must have been a wild if welcome sight, his neck bandaged and dropping with exhaustion. But for Seely, and in particular for Patterson, his appearance begged an ever more dreadful question. What of Strachan and the twenty-two others, less than twelve hours after those shining, jingling high spirits as they had trotted into Masnières with 'changing the course of the war' at the end of their bridles? It was as bad a prospect as the brigade had ever seen.

Out the other side of the canal things were not getting any easier. When they awoke in the crater Strachan tried threading his way east alongside the camouflage screen. The first thing they discovered was 'Dunc' Campbell's already stiffened corpse. They solemnly buried it and then cut south to get to the 'bridge that Tiny built'. There was a light in the lock-keeper's cottage. After all this time they could not risk it being German and set their teeth to work back westward. It was 3 a.m. when they arrived at where all the day's troubles had begun. And the bridge was still a bastard in the dark.

But Strachan was not going to be beaten. He was to be awarded the VC for his efforts and it came at a price. The tank and the bridge were locked into some dark, post-collapsed embrace. Strachan got three-quarters of the way across the bridge and then had to step down on to the tank roof. It was not an even surface. He slipped, skidded, and ended up in the drink. Despite the warning many of the others then did just the same.

They limped on back to headquarters. Bob Patterson was there with Seely beside him. Later on they could dress this whole horror movie up with suitable heroics and pay tribute to the courage and steadfastness of so many men and horses who never came back. But for now, with Strachan standing, soaked through, in front of them, Patterson realized the enormity of the loss – and the miracle of the return. He burst into tears.

Another Bloody Winter,
1917–18

The Canadians had been lucky. Next night they were even luckier. An order came that they should cross the bridge on foot and push on, apparently unprotected, to the next village of Rumilly–Cambrésis. Even Seely, the great adventurer, admitted that he 'dreaded this one', adding, 'I was certain in my own mind that few, if any of us would survive.'

The doubts were widely shared: 'The order did not reach the regiment until 10.15 pm at which time the conference was held', wrote Luke Williams. 'All officers and NCOs of the regiment attended. I think that Colonel Docherty sensed that we all felt pretty dubious about the project because he said, "We will be all right. We'll all be there together and I'll be there with you and we will be all right."'

Those of us who have not been through a wartime experience, or even for that matter been subjected to military discipline, once again have mixed emotions: bafflement at the ingrained obedience which will carry out orders however seemingly foolhardy, and admiration for the courage that so unhesitatingly supported the communal risk. For Seely, it had become central to his being.

> In a night attack it is always best for the commander to lead. So off I went with Geoffrey Brooke and Antoine, keeping close to the southern wall of the little main street so as to avoid the continual bullets which were splintering on the pavement in the centre of the road and on the north side. I felt very lonely without my horse Warrior. The rest of the Strathconas, now commanded

by Docherty, were following in single file. We had just got to a corner where an alleyway on the right led to our little bridge over the canal when I heard galloping hoofs coming from behind. This caused a redoubled burst of enemy rifle fire from the other side of the canal and a number of my men were hit. In a moment a staff officer came running up to me, whispering breathlessly: 'Is that General Seely?' I replied: 'Yes.' He then said, 'Your attack is cancelled. Here is the message.'

A visit to Masnières today: the street and the houses are much as they were. It is not that difficult to start thinking oneself back into that unthinkable position. It would be best late on a wet and cold November day with the first snows of winter due in a week. Williams's simple verdict on the Cambrai attack which was going 'to change the course of the war' would then hit even more directly home: 'The next day we moved back to Equancourt, tired, miserable and discouraged', he wrote. 'We had gone into action with such high hopes and with the exception of "B" Squadron Fort Garrys, had accomplished nothing at all.'

Within a week Docherty's luck was to run out, and back in England the whole future of the cavalry would also be questioned. Orders had already come to send the Canadians back towards the coast to recover, re-fit and re-horse when a galloper interrupted Seely's early-morning slumber. The Germans had broken through, General McAndrew, the divisional cavalry commander, was at a crossroads three miles east and needed help at once. Within minutes Seely and Warrior were there. Within the hour, his whole brigade was with him, to go into action at first on horses and then, tragically for Docherty, on foot.

The official Strathcona war diary for 1 December 1917 merely states that the colonel lost his life from a sniper's bullet just as he was showing his sergeant the point of attack. Seely's version may well be liable to the Fred Harvey criticism of 'exaggerating a little' but it is worth taking for what it says about his pride in his Canadians and they in themselves:

'He [Docherty] arranged with his officers that the signal for attack should be when he jumped on to the little parapet at the moment when our intense covering fire began. Up he jumped. I see him now, poised there for a second while his gallant men leapt up as one man. An enemy bullet struck him in the forehead and he fell dead. Again we captured many prisoners and still more machine guns, but Docherty's death was an irreparable blow.'

There was heavy snow that week around Saint-Quentin, making conditions miserable for men and even more so for horses. Indeed, the wisdom of having cavalry at all was now an open argument. On the ground Seely and his like felt that the Strachan Squadron's exploits showed just what an effective weapon cavalry could be if deployed correctly and with appropriate support. Any failings, they claimed, stemmed from the idiocy of launching an offensive across a canal, the one obstacle that with bridges sabotaged would be absolutely impassable to tanks or horses. Back in England many were taking the opposite view.

Cambrai had been the last chance for cavalry, they argued. All five divisions and those 27,500 men and horses had been deployed to only brief effect. Churchill wrote a memorandum for the War Cabinet suggesting the cavalry be disbanded and its personnel used for armoured cars, tanks or the Royal Flying Corps. Lloyd George said in Cabinet, 'Cavalry would never be used in France.' In his definitive *History of the British Cavalry* Lord Anglesey suggests that the plan Seely's brigade and others were being asked to carry out was doomed from its conception. He quotes the brutal verdict of an American observer: 'You can't have a cavalry charge until you have captured the enemy's last machine gun.'

By any standards it was a massive disappointment. After the first day of the battle the newspapers had run headlines like, 'Greatest British victory of the War' and for the first time in the conflict church bells rang across the land. After a fortnight no territory had been gained and the two sides had lost 90,000 shared equally between them. But for Seely the challenge to his raison d'être did not come just from British politicians dubious about cavalry. It came from Canadians dubious about him.

Two and a half years earlier the Canadian premier had only

22. The officers of 'C' Squadron, Lord Strathcona's Horse: two VCs, four DSOs, four MCs and one Croix de Guerre

23. Frank Seely (1896–1917), Jack's eldest son: 'The dreadful democracy of death'

24. But the other family beckons. Seely at Brooke in August 1917 ready to return to the front. The strain shows on those around him. From left to right: Kitty, Emmy, 'Baby Lou', Evie, Jack, Patrick and Irene

25. Prince Antoine
d'Orléans-Bragance – the
ultimate ADC. A portrait
of the heir to the French
throne by Sir Alfred
Munnings

26. Lieutenant Fred
Harvey VC – 'a great
athlete, but a tiger
in action'

27. The role of Seely's Canadians in the great, but fatally flawed, tank attack on Cambrai

Thun-Leveque
Cuvillers
Eswars
Tilloy
Escaudoevres
CAMBRAI
MASNIÈRES-CANAL
ESCAUT
BEAUREVOIR LINE
Marcoing
La Targette
Rumilly
Masnières
Miles
Crèvecoeur
0 1 2 3

Rumilly
GERMAN ATTACK

Masnières
German Battery
Camouflage
Crater
Gap Screen
Broken (tank) Bridge
ST QUENTIN CANAL
Mon Plaisir Farm
Col. Walker's Bridge
Schelde Stream

—— Route out
----- Route in

Yards
0 500

ACTION OF LIEUTENANT STRACHAN'S SQUADRON, 20 NOVEMBER, 1917

28. Lieutenant Harcus 'Jock' Strachan VC and the remnants of his 'Hell for Leather Garrys'

29. Seely on Warrior. Portrait by Sir Alfred Munnings, January 1918

30. The Canadian Cavalry Brigade on the march as seen by Sir Alfred Munnings. 'The paratroopers of their day'

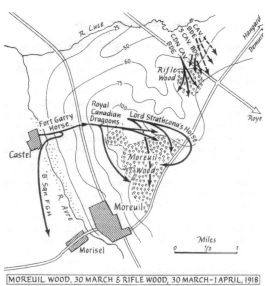

31. 'It is a splendid moment Sir, I will try not to fail you.' Lieutenant Gordon Muriel Flowerdew VC

32. The Battle of Moreuil Ridge, Easter 1918

MOREUIL WOOD, 30 MARCH & RIFLE WOOD, 30 MARCH–1 APRIL, 1918

33. The Munnings recreation of Flowerdew's charge – but the reality had been little short of slaughter

34. Sir Alfred Munnings's bleakest work – his view of the Canadian Cavalry's Easter, 1918

35. 'A sympathetic figure – one who knows what they went through, who understands how to talk to them, and someone who can stand Parliamentary badgering.' Churchill to Lloyd George, Autumn 1918

36. Seely before flying
to Westminster,
9 April 1919

37. 'The Air Under-Secretary in a seaplane: General Seely flying
through the Tower Bridge en route to Westminster'
Illustrated London News, 19 April 1919

38. Hitler and Mussolini: 'Duped by the dictators – but he was not the only one'

39. General Jack, the Lord Lieutenant of Hampshire, in full regalia

40. Lord Mottistone welcomes home the King and Queen, Southampton, June 1939

41. Sailing to the shore

grudgingly accepted Kitchener's appointment of this Englishman to take charge of Canada's mounted brigade. Canada may have been an intensely patriotic dominion but it wanted to be led by its own. It wanted its men in the field to know that Canada mattered. Seely would have been well aware of this and on the night that Docherty died, he clearly thought that they tried to make Canadian domestic affairs matter too much. It was an incident almost as ridiculous as the heliograph above Harrismith seventeen years earlier which told of Lord Roberts's visit to Queen Victoria at Cowes, and it showed just how little some things had advanced in the intervening years:

> The difficulty of maintaining communications with our forces in the rear became more and more acute. Messengers were almost always shot before they could get away with their messages. Any attempt to use flag signalling at once resulted in the shooting of the signaller. We had several helio lamps, but many of them were shot away with the men who were using them. At last we got one lamp into position in a place where it could not be, or at any rate, was not hit, and great was my joy when I was informed that I was in communication. I sent a message giving our position and numbers, saying that we had plenty of food and ammunition. I did not add that reinforcements would not be unwelcome, because I knew my friends in rear were well aware of that fact having already sent us all available help.
>
> This message got through. Then the answering helio, having acknowledged the message, winked again. I saw this and anxiously awaited the message. In a few moments a signaller crawled along and handed it to me. It ran as follows: 'Reference Canadian General Election now proceeding, please note that your signal troop will vote as a unit not with the Royal Canadian Dragoons.' I believe that although I have innumerable faults I am not a particularly blasphemous man; nevertheless Geoffrey Brooke told me that for five minutes I expressed my opinion of politics and elections in language so lurid that it almost turned the air pink.

Seely cursed the politicians because he and his Canadians had grown ever closer as they shared horror and hardship – and the shedding of blood. In the Strathconas alone, twenty were killed and another thirty-one wounded on 1 December. Seely would have heard how Fred Harvey carried his batman Private Underwood through rifle fire to the first aid post, cradling him in his big rugby-playing arms like a baby after the luckless private had been shot. How Andy Morgan, the singing Welshman of the previous Christmas, had gone out to collect the body of Rex Young, his sharpshooting fellow lieutenant from Manitoba, and returned crying like a child with the body on his shoulder.

Seely was their man and they his. One afternoon that December his horse was shot through the neck and fell stone dead on to Seely's injured left side. The pain was excruciating but when he finally got up he discovered the fall had broken down all the adhesions on his crippled left arm and he could now lift it above his head. That was a major bonus but not one fraction of the relief that he had felt almost immediately: the horse he had taken that morning was a bright bay remount called Saint-Quentin. What for both Seely and his soldiers if it had been Warrior?

A miserable snowy Christmas came and went. The brigade's band did their best and Antoine liked to pick out tunes on the piano. On New Year's Eve Williams, Harvey and a recovered Hammy Harrower (he had been wounded in the summer) went to the Fort Garrys' mess where Tiny Walker had named himself 'President of the Court Martial'. They then proceeded to 'try' Major Benson for 'not being drunk enough'. A sentence of 'hung, drawn and quartered' was passed. The hanging was mercifully forsworn but Tiny carried out the second two parts of the sentence by having the over-sober major dragged in a basket back to his quarters, and throwing his own bulk on top of the hapless victim whenever Benson tried to struggle out.

There was a brief trip home on leave. For Seely it was wonderful to see the family again but it would be an exaggeration to say that everyone was settling in well or that the finances were in good order. There were letters from John, now eighteen and with the horse artillery in Trieste. There was a return to France and another successful Bangalore Torpedo raid, the torpedo this time dragged up to the German wire by the intrepid nineteen-year-old Evan Price, last heard of galloping, sword drawn, ahead of his men at Guyencourt. There was a journey back to the Château d'Eu where Antoine got himself into a bit of trouble falling through the kitchen skylight trying to climb in late after visiting a 'Mamselle'.

But all the time twin spectres loomed for Seely: the probability of a last-ditch German offensive and the showdown with the Canadians about his replacement. The Americans had come into the war in the summer of 1917 and within months would be ready to pour thousands of 'doughboys' at the enemy. If Germany wanted victory they had to go for it now. Aerial observers in the Saint-Quentin area reported the greatest build-up ever seen. And Seely's men were right in the target zone.

But the second spectre threatened to take him first. Letters came and went. No matter the tributes, no regard to the successes and the twin VCs, the Canadian cavalry should have a Canadian commander. If ever Seely needed a diversion it was early in February 1918. And he got it. A man called Alfred Munnings came up the line.

42

Munnings and the Gathering Storm

In later life Sir Alfred Munnings won notoriety for his well-wined, 'modern art is rot' speech as President of the Royal Academy in 1949 and for his highly priced if rather gilded equestrian portraits of the richest families in the land. But at thirty-eight he was at the very height of his powers, if not yet of fame. He was a brilliant, eccentric, carousing, country-loving horse-worshipper. He was just Seely's cup of tea.

He had been assigned to the Canadian cavalry as a war artist, as significant a release and opportunity for him as it was a memorable meeting for Seely and his men. Munnings had been turned down for military service on account of a right eye blinded by a thorn twig back in 1900. He had even been refused enlistment as a farrier, and had spent the previous eleven months working as a groom at the remount depot at Basingstoke, some of whose horses would become his models with the Canadians over in France. The job at the depot had come through Cecil Aldin, the noted equestrian painter who was officer in charge. But even that connection could for a while advance him no further and Munnings ground his teeth in frustration that he could not join his friends Augustus John and William Orpen as a war artist in France.

The call eventually came via the Canadian War Memorials Scheme instituted by the young Max Aitken (later Lord Beaverbrook) to ensure a pictorial record of the Canadian forces in France. The painters were chosen by Paul Konody, art critic of the *Daily Mail* and the *Observer*, and Munnings was sufficiently grateful to compose a ballad, one of his favourite party tricks, in Paul's honour entitled 'The Great Konodian Army'. He crossed to Boulogne in late January with a light narrow box containing all his painting kit and enough canvasses to keep him going for a while. He was going to a place where ballads would be welcome.

Barney Torrance picked up Munnings at the main Canadian HQ, a small chateau in Hesdin, thirty miles south-east of Boulogne, and set off on the journey towards Saint-Quentin. The artist's words are almost as his pictures:

'I was taken by another officer in a Cadillac car to General Seely, who was then stationed with part of the brigade near the front line at a place called Small Foot Wood; but there was no sign of a wood – only charred stumps of trees standing in desolate wastes of mud with duck boards about, leading to dugouts. I was taken to the staff dugout, where I met General Seely himself and he arranged there and then that I should paint him on his horse Warrior next morning.'

Seely's recollection is that Munnings met him and Warrior as they came back from the front line caked in mud and that the painter insisted on starting the portrait immediately. One suspects that the Munnings account was a bit more reliable. Certainly the image of the first night rings true. 'In that underground dugout', he wrote, 'I had my first taste of a staff dinner, and General Seely's Irroy brand of champagne which he got out only on special occasions because he said "Irroy made you laugh."'

The general was experiencing his fourth bitter winter in the front line. He had seen plenty of troubles, and would see many more as the German build-up continued on the other side of no-man's-land. He had hassles both at home and with Dominion busybodies from overseas. But dugout or no dugout, he had not lost the ability to enjoy life whenever it was there. There was food and wine and a game of bridge; Brooke and Antoine and Torrance and a neck-bandaged Cowen who had been moved to HQ. The first war was full of misery and Munnings's life-size study for a never finished mural depicting the shattered Canadians that Easter is as harsh as Picasso's *Guernica*. But he could also bear witness to the lighter side.

The next morning I saw the General wandering about in a thick, tan-coloured sort of camel-hair suit of pyjamas. He warned me that the sitting would be short, and after breakfast in the brilliant light of a low January sun, with a frost on the ground, myself standing on a duck board so that I should not sink into the mud, the General posing on Warrior ten yards away in the right light I began my portrait.

After the first quarter of an hour my sitter looked at his wrist watch and said, 'Quarter of an hour gone!' I said, 'Yes, sir,' and worked away, using a little copal varnish in a small dipper to set the paint as I worked on that red countenance glistening in the sun. General Seely for some reason or other always made me think of the Peninsular War – he belonged to the Wellington period. Sitting there on his charger, in general's uniform, on a cold, still day, with a long brown, woollen muffler thrown once round his neck, Jack Seely was a picture. He sat on no wooden horse, as many of my sitters had done in civilian life – he was on the patient Warrior, who as the minutes went on, sank deeper and deeper into the mud, until his fetlocks were covered.

Artist and sitter hit it off. Munnings's father was a miller just as Seely's ancestors had been. Like Seely he put the horse first above all animals, above quite a few humans too. The sweeping sky of Munnings's already renowned set of pictures of gypsy horses at a Norfolk fair had a wildness about them that appealed to Seely's Islander heart. Besides, the team in the dugout liked the portrait of Seely on Warrior. They broke open the best claret. Munnings was one of them. So much so that Seely gave him a free ticket. He took a horse, sometimes even Warrior, a paint box, a sheaf of pencils and a portable easel and wandered around to sketch where he liked. It has to be said that kitted out in cloth cap and gaiters the future President of the Royal Academy did not look the absolute military type. Cue the entry of General Kavanagh – the old Seely-bashing martinet himself.

'What on earth', spluttered the general through the most indignant of moustaches, 'do you think you are?'

Munnings was a whimsical soul, but a sharp one. 'Well I don't really know what I am,' he replied with what seemed to Kavanagh a blood-boiling lack of deference, 'but when they sent me out here they told me I was a genius.'

Munnings stayed barely five weeks with the cavalry but they were five of the most productive as well as the most dramatic of his whole life. With Barney Torrance as his guide he visited the reserve as well as the front line of a brigade which at this stage, prior to the great German offensive, was at full strength, some 2,500 strong in both men and horses. Besides the three regiments there were another 500 men in the Royal Canadian Horse Artillery with their two batteries of four thirteen-pounder guns. There was a 24-man signal troop. There was Tiny Walker's 230-man machine-gun squadron with their six Vickers .303s. There were 200 men in the No. 7 Field Ambulance, another 100 in the brigade supply column, and twenty-seven in the mobile veterinary section whose Captain, Joe Duhault, was to become a particular companion to Munnings on the march.

Forty-five of Munnings's pictures from this period were exhibited at the Royal Academy in 1919 and have since been much reproduced. But the reproductions are apt to miss the war-time edge beneath the pastoral scenes in khaki that are on the surface. One summer afternoon in 2001 my son and I were taken into an air-conditioned vault in Ottawa where picture after picture was slid out down its hanging rails for our inspection. There, almost as if the oil was still fresh, were Seely and Antoine and Brooke and Connolly and Patterson. There were the Fort Garrys on the march, the Strathconas at the water pool, the RCD in their stables made from farmhouse rubble. Look closely and one sees the faces of men and horses ready to face a threat. They knew and he knew that the storm was about to break.

They were horsemen and so was he; 'the finest and best fellows that I ever met', he said of them. But caring for horses the way he did meant that the compliment could equally be applied to his four-legged friends. When the much dreaded, long-awaited opening bombardment began in the distance on Thursday 21 March, the thought of what would happen to the horses was very hard to take.

> The Brigade had a band, and during the fine days that preceded the German attack in March 1918, morning after morning I would be painting in the horse lines to the dreamy strains of old tunes of the last generation. On that particular morning with the band playing, I was finishing a picture of the horses as they stood with their heads out, basking in the sun, between tattered camouflage hanging over roughly-built rows of stabling. I had been painting each patient head, with eyes blinking in the sun, and was working on the sixth, which might have been somewhere to the right of the middle of the picture, when suddenly something was happening – men were running; a sergeant came along saying: 'Hurry up, lads! Saddle up and stand to!'
>
> The order went along the lines, and soon those patient horses were saddled up in full marching order, mounted and the whole brigade rode away. I still have a drawing in a sketch-book of one of the horses standing ready in full marching order to go – where? And what was his end?

That dreamy feeling had been evident earlier at the top. Having regrouped and re-horsed back at Cramont just ten miles east of Abbeville at the beginning of March, the Canadians had then marched again towards Saint-Quentin, stopping off for four days around Davenescourt near Montdidier. 'Exercise rides and re-fitting parades were the order of the day while here', records Luke Williams in his diary. But in these final days there was a bit of relaxation too. For headquarters Prince Antoine had excelled himself: the Marquis de Bargemont would invite them to his chateau. Von Kluck had used it for his headquarters in 1914. Seely and his team would be welcome, and his painters too.

'The host of this Chateau, at Davenescourt somewhere on the Somme, was in residence', remembered Munnings.

> During that short stay the brigade band played in the outer hall whilst the staff dined with the Vicomte in the larger hall at a big

circular table. Sir William Orpen who had been painting Marshal Foch, was at the chateau and joined us at dinner.

This pleasant interlude was the lull before the storm. One morning after breakfast whilst General Seely, Brigade Major Geoffrey Brooke and myself were reclining in the sun on the sloping lawn, Seely remarked 'This is my Ecole des Beaux Arts,' for Orpen was painting him in a large upstairs bedroom each morning whilst below I was painting Prince Antoine on a black horse in the sunlight.

It could not last. And for Seely both storms broke at once. On the 15th the brigade had begun to gather around the ruins of Ennemain and Athies, just east of the Omignon River and five miles due west of Saint-Quentin. 'In this place', recalls Munnings, 'we were living in dug-outs or Nissen Huts.' He also remembered Seely coming back from dinner with General Harman, the divisional commander, who had told him that two enemy deserters had said that the German attack was to be on the 21st. On the 19th the Marquis de Bargemont, 'a pleasant black-bearded host', invited them all back for a farewell dinner. It was a splendid occasion; Antoine played the piano, Munnings did one of his ballads, and they toasted the Marquis and all their futures as best they could.

Seely thought he had two days. He didn't. Next morning at 10 a.m. he had a cable from the Canadian authorities summoning him to London. So the bastards were going to insist on replacing him after all. Seely remained too ludicrously patriotic to complain publicly. But they knew how to hurt.

V. THE ULTIMATE EASTER

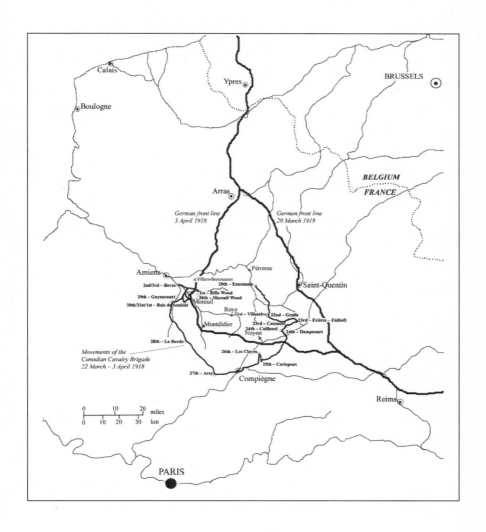

Calais

Ypres

BRUSSELS

Boulogne

BELGIUM

FRANCE

Arras

German front line
3 April 1918

German front line
20 March 1918

Péronne

Amiens

Villers-Bretonneux

20th – Ennemain

Saint-Quentin

2nd/3rd – Boves

1st – Rifle Wood
30th – Moreuil Wood

29th – Guyencourt

30th/31st/1st – Bois de Sénécat

Moreuil

Roye

21st – Villeselve

22nd – Genlis

23rd – Frières – Faillöel

23rd – Caumont

24th – Caillouel

24th – Dampcourt

Montdidier

Noyon

28th – La Borde

Movements of the
Canadian Cavalry Brigade
22 March – 3 April 1918

26th – Les Cloyes

25th – Carlepont

27th – Arsy

Compiègne

Reims

| | 0 | 10 | | 20 | miles |
| 0 | 10 | 20 | 30 | km | |

PARIS

43

London, Lloyd George and the Road back to Hell

Of all the days to choose, Wednesday 20 March 1918 – Seely's brigade and the whole Allied army were threatened as never before, and yet the Canadian authorities wanted to have a conference back in London. Nowadays there would be a 'forget it or I quit' phone call. But these were telegram times. Seely had his orders and he followed them. He and General Currie, who was still commanding all the Canadian forces in France, boarded the boat together at Boulogne. Seely and Currie got on well with each other despite, or probably because of, the 'stud duck in this puddle' incident with 'Foghorn' Macdonald back in 1916. Seely respected Currie's efforts to protect his men wherever possible. Since his early experiences in the Boer War Seely had been convinced that better thinking could save lives. He needed that thinking now more than ever before. But he was on the boat.

Once summoned, Seely had cabled Evie to ask Maurice Hankey round for dinner. Hankey was a good listener and Seely had a lot to tell. How he had got a pilot to fly him behind the German lines last week and just how huge all those German stockpiles were becoming now that the Bolsheviks had signed for peace at Brest-Litovsk, freeing up much German force and supplies from the Eastern Front for the Western. He would talk of Gough, not to revisit the old sores of the Curragh incident, for the two men were well reconciled now, but to tell of a dinner a week earlier when Gough explained that his Fifth Army front was now stretched to forty-two miles and he had a mere twelve divisions to defend it with. He would be in trouble if the German wave were to break.

It did on that Thursday, 21 March 1918, 8,000 guns opening up at 4.40 a.m. with what was then the greatest bombardment in history. 'So this is it', Hugh Tripp muttered across the Nissen hut he and Luke Williams were sharing at Ennemain. It was a feeling shared. Winston Churchill was reporting for Lloyd George on the front line near Saint-Quentin. 'And then,' he wrote, 'exactly as a pianist runs his hands across the keyboard from treble to bass, there rose in less than one minute the most tremendous cannonade I shall ever hear.' The storm had struck. And Seely was in an office in London.

The Canadians were unhappy, not just with Seely but with themselves. The huge casualties in the field had changed the mood back home. The overwhelming flags-and-bunting enthusiasm of 1914 had been replaced by open hostility to the idea of war. There had been protests against enlistment in 1917 and now feelings against the Conscription Act were running so high that armed mobs attacked the registration offices in Quebec. The authorities needed Canadian praises to sing. They wanted a Canadian to command their cavalry.

In vain Seely would have told them that with Geoffrey Brooke having become the colonel commanding the 16th Lancers, 'Con' Connolly had been appointed the brigade major, meaning that all the principal posts except his own were now occupied by Canadian-based officers. To no avail would he have reminded the room of the VCs for Harvey and Strachan, of acclaim for the 'Great Raid' in 1917, of the success of the second Bangalore Torpedo raid hardly a month ago. They would agree with him that the Canadian cavalry was a crack team. But they wanted a Canadian to lead it.

The best he could hope for was to nominate his successor. Bob Patterson had been a perfect deputy when Seely had been home injured last year. Bob was in charge now. The men liked him and their unique special-unit morale would be in good hands. But that was agreed for next month. What mattered was now. The last four years, maybe in Seely's case the last forty-nine years, had been leading to this hour. He needed to be with his Canadians, to try to keep them together, to help them do their duty for the cause for which so many including his own son had already died. He left the room.

That had been in the afternoon of that fateful Thursday, 21 March. A couple of hours earlier Lester Piggott's grandfather Ernie had ridden Poethlyn to win the Grand National at Gatwick Racecourse (Aintree having been commandeered as a prison camp). The four-and-a-half-miles distance was the same but the Gatwick fences were no match for Bechers Brook and the rest of the real thing. In peacetime, for those of us who have ridden in it, the Grand National beckons as the ultimate challenge. For my grandfather that evening, even the idea of it would not have merited a passing thought.

Hankey had brought Lloyd George with him to Chester Square for supper. 'But', Seely recorded, 'it must have been one of the shortest dinners on record.' First reports from France were very depressing. It looked as if the Fifth Army was giving way just where Seely's force was likely to be involved. The Prime Minister was under pressure. His host knew his hour was nigh.

Seely and Currie and Antoine were at Victoria Station next morning. There was hassle enough getting the boat across to Calais and then the altercation when Antoine sorted out the Crossley car. It had been wet but now the real challenge was raining from the skies. Seely and Antoine and Smith and Anthony were coming into Boulogne in the Calais-borrowed Crossley, a huge storm was brewing and not just from the weather. The place was ablitz with the biggest air raid Seely had ever seen.

Today's TV viewers will have seen pictures of conflagrations a hundred times worse, of bombers a whole space age more sophisticated. But Seely and Antoine were adults before the Wright brothers ever flew. As far as they were concerned, this was an inferno from a sky-centred Hades: the German planes droning in like devil's disciples to drop their incendiaries on the beleaguered city. In London he had heard of the air raids that had killed a dozen people in Maida Vale on 4 March, had been told of the ninety bombs dropped on Paris four days later leading to a 200,000-strong evacuation.

On Friday 22nd the Germans would have flown a hundred miles up from airstrips by Saint-Quentin to bomb the docks and supply lines at the Channel ports. These were biplanes, not the stealth bombers of today; they hand-dropped canisters of methane rather than launching computer-programmed missiles. But it was all part of Germany's Operation Michael. For anyone under it or near it, this would have been very terrible indeed.

Seely had hoped to find a hotel to snatch a few hours' sleep in Boulogne. But the only repose his little team looked like getting that Friday evening was of the 'shut your eyes forever' variety. The car was working all right, although the hood at the back was beginning to leak a little and the more exposed Corporal Anthony at the wheel could not drive forever. They would have to stop a bit further down the way.

Up above them the German planes continued to swoop past with only a few Allied aircraft making fruitless attempts to chase them off. Seely looked out and grimaced. The need to develop aircraft had been one of his passions at Westminster. He remembered that windy afternoon at Croydon in 1910 when he became the first Cabinet Minister to fly, recalled all those hours as chairman of the Air Committee, thought of that miraculous petrol-soaked escape in 1914, shook his head now at the pettiness of those Commons debates when he had been attacked by the Tories for not having enough aircraft whilst knowing that his fellow Liberals were anxious not to budget for too many.

By the time the war broke out he had realized that we were still a fair way short of the Germans in air strength. Three and a half years later he was staring skywards twenty-four hours after Lloyd George had been assuring him that the British now had record numbers in the air. Looking out at those deadly fireworks in the Boulogne night he was entitled to wonder just where they were. It would have hurt but not surprised him to know that his own Canadians would be sharing the same thoughts the very next day – and in their case with a very bloody form of bitterness as the Germans crossed the Saint-Quentin Canal and broke the line at Frières-Failloël without any challenge from the air.

It was going to be a long and difficult eighty miles to Amiens and then a further twenty-five to Noyon, where the Fifth Army HQ ought to give him news of his men. 'Boulogne was in complete darkness,' he recalls, 'with an air raid of exceptional violence going on. But I managed to get some food, fill up with petrol and stores and resume my journey.' The problem, he was to find, was that a large number of luckless ones were making their way in the other direction.

'Towards daybreak I met a concourse of people the like of which I had never seen. Not only the French civilian population with carts and wagons of all descriptions, but crowds of men of every race and colour, all fleeing from the wrath to come. I was told by a staff officer whom I found coolly but vainly endeavouring to direct this strange crowd that eleven races were represented.'

They were all part of the whole army of workers that had come in to service the needs of millions of men locked for the last three and a half years into the static lines of the Western Front. With the line broken, everyone had to get out, be they barbers, builders or women euphemistically referred to in some old-time reference books as 'brothel technicians'. The road to Amiens had not been very good in the first place. It was slow going now.

They finally made it to the Noyon HQ late on that Saturday, 24 March, and could only then begin to appreciate the true magnitude of the disaster. Seely wanted to know and he wanted to tell – to tell of the uncharitable jibes in London at the competence of Gough and the Fifth Army. He didn't get much of a hearing. General Beddington had just laid down to sleep for the first time in forty-eight hours. He bawled Seely out.

General Butler was more sympathetic. He explained how the Front had been bust open at Saint-Quentin, how the Germans had advanced over four miles and taken 20,000 prisoners on the very first day, how they were now over the Somme, across the Saint-Quentin Canal and coming at Noyon itself. He told how Seely's brigade had been split up on the 22nd, half had been kept mounted to 'fire-brigade' for other regiments on the retreat, the other half had been drafted into the now broken front line beyond Villequier-Aumont which had been formerly guarded by the banks of the canal.

It sounded as if that dismounted section had been almost

overrun by the Germans. What was left of them should have got back to bunk up at Caumont. He should try to meet them further east at Caillouel. What's more, he had better take command of any other cavalry units in the area and take a message putting them at the disposal of the French commander General Diebold as they fought to save the position at Noyon.

It was a grim, if not totally unexpected, briefing. The brigade's remaining horses were across the Oise at Carlepont, a couple of miles to the south. Warrior was with them. Seely would be more than pleased to see him. It would then be a ten-mile ride, first east, then north across the river to get to Caillouel. Together he and Warrior had a job to do.

44

Picking up the Bits: Caillouel to Dampcourt

There were still some 800 of them together that Palm Sunday morning, 24 March 1918. The dismounted remnants of the Canadian cavalry were sore-eyed and exhausted as they marched into Caillouel at 8.30 a.m. Seely on Warrior was just the sight they needed. What a start to Easter week.

They hadn't slept much. They had been up at 5 a.m. and marched five miles westward to try to buy space from the German advance. Up till now all the villages had just been ruins, but turning up the hill into the one long, straight street that is Caillouel they were at last in a place as yet unravaged by the whirlwind of the Germans' Operation Michael. All the occupants had left, but a most important presence had returned. Seely and Warrior stood resplendent and unbowed in front of the *mairie* (village hall). The troops looked at the red ribbon of the general's cap and the cocked ears of the thoroughbred. It was a statement that they were all in this together.

They had taken a pounding. Connolly was a tough guy from Calgary and County Limerick. Seely was sure that making him brigade major earlier in the month had been a good idea – 'the best choice I ever made', he said later. But even Connolly looked as if he had been through the mincer.

On that first night of the retreat Luke Williams had found Connolly at 2 a.m. still at work in his temporary HQ in the village of Villeselve, now deep in German hands. As a first job Connolly was set the task Seely had always tried to avoid. He had been ordered to split up the brigade: to send one half mounted under the pike-shooting Colonel Stevenson to support the retreat, and the other half dismounted into the line to prop up the already depleted forces, which in some cases included other regiments' cooks, servants, bottle-washers and assorted unlikely not to say unwilling combatants.

Stevenson's 200 included both Harvey and Flowerdew and they were about to start a dizzy and dangerous five days. But they would have horses and the Germans wouldn't, as Operation Michael had no cavalry in its ranks, something which would have allowed them to harry the Allied retreat. By contrast, Harvey and company would have a chance to show once again that in mobile warfare the cavalry could still count. They would have a whole lot better time than their brothers on foot. The separation had come on the Friday after the whole brigade had trekked down through thick black fog from Villeselve to the abbey-flanked village of Villequier-Aumont where the spare horses and their main supplies, not to mention a now strangely uniformed and tin-helmeted Alfred Munnings, were taken off westward to safety.

The 200 then went to join General Harman while the dismounted men were marching up to wooden huts in the Bois de Frières to stare danger in the face. But these were no cooks and bottle-washers. These were Canadians like Jack Cooper, the former Mountie whose revolver shooting had been a star turn at the horse shows. Men like him did not scare easily.

Saturday had been a living nightmare. When everyone had broken for a rudimentary breakfast in Caillouel on the Sunday morning, Connolly's deep Limerick brogue would have carefully told his general the story and Seely would have listened with mounting concern. But for us to understand not just the chaos and the exhaustion, but also the continued combative commitment of the 800 men who tramped into Caillouel, there can be no better way than taking the diary of Stewart Chambers, another young Strathcona lieutenant:

> Saturday, March 23 – Got up at 2.30 a.m. to relieve Luke Williams
> and deal with any despatches coming in. Slept again from 5.30

a.m. until about 8.00 a.m. Order arrived about 9.30 a.m. to proceed to Faillouël and place ourselves at the disposal of 54th Infantry Brigade – Enemy advancing – Took up position behind our own line at right edge of Faillouël village – Our infantry being driven in – Batteries have to withdraw after being heavily shelled – Many wounded coming in to our Dressing Station – Hundreds of our infantry straggling back. Officers apparently have lost control – We try to round them up and put them back in the front line but they won't remain. We are now the front line – Bosche planes doing as they please – Have not yet seen one of ours – Enemy guns unlimbering in the open 1500 yards away – Our guns are all gone – Can see Huns advancing – Machine-gun fire very heavy but our line holds. Jackie Tatlow shot through the heart – Our casualties pretty heavy – Salmon wounded – Our flanks are in the air – Infantry have fallen away – Bosche now around both sides of the wood – We have to retire – French troops come up and hold line behind wood – Gwynn badly wounded – Have to march back to the Bois de Caumont where we stay the night – Very tired and hungry – It is maddening to think that we could have held the Bosche had the infantry hung on.

That last line is crucial. What Seely now had before him was a battered but definitely not defeated bunch of men. More than that, Connolly had already heard of several instances where the Germans, when challenged, could be rolled back. It was the sheer numbers flooding around and the lack of support on the ground, not to mention in the air, that had made the day impossible. But give them the chance, above all give them their horses, and they could stop the tide. 'It has been a terrible mistake to dismount us', continues Chambers with his entry next day. 'Could have done much more mounted. Have now lost most of our kit.'

Seely had to get them mounted and kitted up. As Connolly took him through the whole harsh reality of the last three days, there was no time for recriminations about the unhelpfulness of that call summoning him back to London. Now that the Germans had crossed the Saint-Quentin Canal there was no natural protection for the Allies as the enemy swept west towards Noyon. He would need to get his men down off this plateau to where the Oise and its canal could provide a formidable barrier to the enemy's attempt to push south. Once that was secured, he needed to get back along the far bank to Carlepont where their wagons, their horses, not to mention Munnings, their horse artist, were waiting. Chambers was right: if these men were to be of any use beyond cannon fodder, they would need to be operating on four legs not two.

Caillouel was empty but untouched. On a normal morning it is the prettiest and most tranquil of spots. The troops set down to wash up and breakfast. All the cooks and most of the supply wagons had gone with the horses, so any chickens or rabbits left behind by the villagers made a welcome addition to the rations of bully beef and hard tack. In one barn somebody found a young calf. It would taste good on the barbecue.

Connolly set up his headquarters unit in the main hall of the *mairie*. Seely wrote out despatches to tell General Diebold and the Noyon HQ what he proposed to do and sent the gallopers off with them. No phones, not even any helios at this moment, communication was utterly basic. The fog of the morning was lifting, but not the fog of war.

A couple of hours' recovery was as long as they could risk. Trumpeter Reg Longley stood outside the *mairie* and called the force together. The little road south from Caillouel slides quite steeply down off the plateau. There was space ahead of them. They crossed the main Noyon–Caugny road and went on to the few cottages of the village of Dampcourt with the bridge across the canal and the river just a quarter of a mile beyond. There were some troop huts set beside the village. It was not luxury but there would be roofs over their heads. There was a touch of security creeping in.

But not for long. In the afternoon Luke Williams borrowed Colonel Macdonald's horse and rode back up to the Noyon–Caugny road, then continuing east up towards Abbecourt. He looked across to where they had been. It was happening already:

'I could see the Germans marching into Neuflieux, just marching along in column of route quite unconcerned. It made me mad to see them so saucy, but there was nothing I could do about it. I could see one of their observation balloons too, apparently on the road east of Caillouel, sitting up there bold and saucy as you please.'

One may smile at words like 'saucy', but this was the endgame and there was safety in aggression. They had to be ready to fight, their lives depended on it. On Saturday they had been reminded just how deadly the game could be. Back in Dampcourt, Seely and Connolly and Macdonald were counting the cost – and telling the tales.

Poor Jackie Tatlow. That Saturday, 23 March, Macdonald had told him to take the safer long route round to the troops in the Bois de Frières. But he wanted to get back quick. He chanced it across the open field. He had hardly gone 400 yards when a sniper got him. Private Morgan found a wheelbarrow, put the body in it, and pushed Jackie a couple of miles towards Villequier-Aumont. Things were getting rough, so when they saw the abbey gates on their left they put the body inside in some hope of safe keeping.

Wheelbarrows had also been used for the wounded. Lieutenant Reg Timmis of the RCD had been through the very worst of things that day. In the morning he had been sent with 240 men and part of the machine-gun section to hold the line along the railway embankment east of Mennessis a mile north-east of Frières. Beyond the embankment was the Saint-Quentin Canal with a bridge over it which the French promised to blow if the Germans broke through. The French for 'blow up' is *'faire sauter'* (make jump). The Germans broke through and the bridge didn't jump. Timmis had the enemy all over him.

It was a deeply traumatizing experience. He lost half of his 240 men. The fighting became hand-to-hand and very ugly. 'The Boche came up,' he recalled later, 'and as we advanced to the edge of the wood we got a rather heavy knock-out and the Boche came up and bayoneted a lot of our wounded. I saw that. We got away a great number in wheel barrows but we could not help a lot of them being bayoneted.' He held on as long as he could, got back as many as he could and that night tried to make light of things by saying that losing half his men meant the rest got double rations. But he looked in shock. Connolly was worried about him.

Yet there was one point about which Timmis was insistent. 'The Germans attacked in a very funny way', he said. 'They seemed to be probing for weak spots rather than just attacking straight. If you could fight back hard they would back off.' It confirmed what Connolly had been told by others. Reports coming back from the high ground they had left were gloomier than ever. Even defending Noyon was beginning to look unlikely. Churchill had a bucket-of-water metaphor about offensives: they make a big splash when they hit the ground but the further they spread the weaker they get unless another follows. Seely had to believe that he could put theory into practice. That his men could still make a difference yet, if they got clear of this opening splash.

'But the German observation balloon had not been up for the air', records Williams.

> Shortly before dusk they had got a line on the Canadian huts at Dampcourt. The first shell landed in a field about 500 yards away. A second one was only about 250 yards from our huts and the third was only about 100 yards away. When the third landed we felt that it was about time for us to be moving out. We started gathering up our kits and getting out. Colonel Macdonald had just gone out of the door when the fourth shell arrived and landed smack on the hut next to the one we were in.
>
> Why we didn't get a number of casualties is beyond me as there were lots of men around. Trumpeter Reg Longley was in the hut that was hit by the shell as was Private Goddard who got a tiny splinter in his thumb which Captain McCullough [the medical officer] dressed and that was that. By this time it was too dark for the balloon to do any more observing and that was the end of the shelling.

They were too close and there wasn't much comfort. The night before they had found a hay barn to collapse in, if only briefly. Now there were just the bare boards of the hut. But they were still alive. Seely had told them that they would be moving in the morning. There was hope in the slumber.

45

Getting Together: Dampcourt to Arsy

They were the last across the river. From Dampcourt that Monday morning, 25 March, they had marched a mile downstream to cross at Appilly. The very last detachment of the whole Allied retreat over that bridge was in the charge of Hugh Tripp, that same Hugh Tripp who had sat up that Thursday morning and said, 'So this is it.' It was now. This was desperate retreat, the main German forces might still seem a few miles away but their snipers could be much closer than that.

Seely and Warrior had come too far to start worrying now. The bridge needed crossing but danger lurked in the rushes. As the troops filed over, Seely and Macdonald stood together, their horses' noses touching. Suddenly there was a flash from along the bank 200 yards away. Macdonald's horse crashed down, a bullet through its neck. What overworked guardian angel made that shot miss Warrior and the red-capped general on his back?

The south bank may have been clear of individual snipers, but it was well within range of German artillery back on the hills to the north. The roads were narrow and clogged with all sorts of traffic, the adjoining fields were little more than water meadows. The long serpentine of carts and refugees and trucks and leg-weary troops made a good target. For Williams and the others it became another long day.

'It seemed our march that afternoon never would end. It did come to an end however and we found our horses waiting for us. We arrived at Carlepont quite late in the afternoon [Monday 25th] and had hardly finished getting sorted out and reorganized before night was upon us. I am sure that if the horses could have talked they would have said that they were as glad to see us as we were to see them.'

It was the horses that made them special. They could be a proud unit of fighting centaurs again, not cannon fodder to be pushed up to the line. Carlepont is set on a slight hill above the forest about seven miles south of Noyon. It has a large main square flanked by the high walls and splendid main gate of its chateau. There was shelter for horses – and for men too. 'My first good sleep', wrote Stewart Chambers, 'since the offensive started.'

As Seely tried urgently to regroup next morning, Williams went north on reconnaissance. 'I took Sergeant Fred Wooster with me on this occasion. We rode up to a spot not far from the village of Sempigny which is just across the Oise river from Noyon. The Germans seemed to be doing their best to blow it up and burn it down.'

Throughout that day Seely continued to try to make some sense of the confusion, not to say catastrophe, that appeared to be happening across the river. There were stories that the offensive had pushed on past Noyon almost to Roye, which would make over twenty-five miles in five days. Williams's report the previous Friday that all were agreed 'that a major disaster was in the making' seemed to be corroborated by the hour. The Germans seemed to be pushing for Amiens; if they got there the British and French armies would be split, the war could be into meltdown. But the offensive was ragged at its edges, and the Germans had no cavalry. A year earlier Seely had seen how effective his brigade had been at picking off small enemy pockets when they were at the head of an advance. Now he wanted to muster his full strength to do the same thing on retreat.

Harvey, Stevenson and Flowerdew were already at it on horseback: shooing the Germans back over the Canal du Nord by moonlight on Monday night, breaking back some enemy gains on Tuesday whilst tired infantry withdrew. When they finally met up with Seely on Wednesday evening Harvey in particular would be full of what was possible. But as the shells continued to fall you could never be sure that you would make the next rendezvous. On Tuesday Seely had moved his HQ just a couple of miles to Les Cloyes. Come Wednesday morning it looked like curtains for Warrior. Even Seely thought that the horse's number was up.

> I had stabled Warrior the night before in the drawing room of a little French villa which was still completely intact – so much so that I remember giving him his corn on a small ormolu table.
>
> At dawn next morning I stood in the square of the little village dictating orders to my brigade major. The Germans, who were not far off, perceived that the village was occupied, and opened fire with a big naval gun. Almost the first shell that came over our heads hit the little villa fair and square and exploded inside, knocking it completely down except for one corner.
>
> I said to Connolly: 'I am afraid that is the end of Warrior.' But no, there was his head poking out from the few bricks still standing with the joist of the ceiling resting on his back.
>
> We started to try to pull the bricks away, but before we had got very far with it, Warrior made a supreme effort and bounded out. As he emerged the joist fell, and the whole remaining corner of the house collapsed in a heap. Except for a little lameness from having carried most of the weight of the top storey, Warrior was none the worse, and I rode him all that day.

Which was quite something. They slogged twenty miles down through the forest across the river at Compiègne and out east to another long low village called Arsy. At Compiègne Seely saw Munnings, who had spent the previous night in a hay loft close to the river at Choisy-au-Bac. It had been a disturbed rest as German bombers had been trying to take out the bridge. The afternoon boded no better when a French gendarme came up to this suspicious figure sketching away in a tin hat, dodgy would-be officer's uniform, Sam Browne belt and cloth gaiters. 'Qui est-il?' said the gendarme, pointing at Munnings. Seely gave a mischievous shrug, took a drag of his cigarette and answered, 'C'est un Boche.'

In fact, that evening had to be Munnings's final one with the cavalry. He had avoided trouble this far, but everyone sensed that the showdown was coming. Much as they liked their artist friend, this had to be a fighting force. Next day Seely gave him a case of despatches and put him in the brigade Cadillac to head for the main Canadian HQ at Hesdin with Anthony at the wheel. Munnings had loved the company and the feeling had been reciprocated. But that Wednesday night their minds were hardening. Patterson, Stevenson and Harvey were back. They confirmed a catastrophe. But they insisted it could be fought.

On the face of it the situation was truly terrible. They were now a full week on from the gigantic opening barrage which had signalled the start of Operation Michael. Politicians and generals and indeed Marshal Foch, who was put in overall charge of the Allied forces on the Wednesday, could well make remarks like, 'We must not retire a single centimetre', and claim that the German advance was slowing as their support systems failed, but most of the Canadians had seen only death, devastation and retreat.

That Wednesday the Canadians had marched through Compiègne, now an abandoned city whose streets were a fine powder of broken glass, and that evening the gallopers were reporting that the Germans were threatening Montdidier, that ancient town whose cliff-like escarpment dominates the western approaches south of Amiens. The Kaiser's 'we have won' dance on Berlin station the previous Sunday might have been a bit premature but it didn't seem by much.

Harvey had been in action. In his own words he had 'had some nice little scraps'. Operation Michael might have bust a big hole in the Fifth Army and taken over 100,000 prisoners, but these Germans did not frighten Harvey a bit. To put it extremely bluntly – or rather sharply: 'they did not like it up 'em'. In Britain, as a defence mechanism against the true horror of the reality, this phrase and others such as the 'taste of cold steel' have been wrapped up in sit-com humour. Fred Harvey was a fine upstanding rector's son originally from County Meath, but as March 1918 drew to a close he was neither sweet nor anything related to harmless. The 'cold steel' of cavalry sword or bayonet was not a joke. It was a life-taker. And therefore a life-saver.

We are talking about killing. In these times when the killing machines are high-tech and war is something that happens at a distance, even discussing killing can be uncomfortable. But to understand how Seely and his team handled their war experience in general and the Easter weekend of 1918 in particular, it is essential to get our heads round how important killing had become. Every single one of the 1,200 who were to ride out north from Arsy on that Thursday morning would know that there was likely to be no escape. That they were likely to be presented with a moment when the most mortal danger threatened, and when the best hope would be to take out the nearest threat: 'kill or be killed'.

That is why Harvey is important. For he was the rugby-match metaphor come to life – and death. At Guyencourt in March 1917 and then again on that Tuesday of Easter week 1918, he had shown that by attacking with complete commitment you had more chance of success, less chance of injury. His individual exploit, taking out the machine gun at Guyencourt, had won him world renown and the VC. What had happened on Tuesday 26 March at the Bois des Essarts with his 58-man squadron was only just being told to Seely, Williams, Connolly, Antoine and the others gathered in that abandoned house in Arsy which had been requisitioned as an officers' mess.

This exploit was different from that at Guyencourt, but there was one crucial similarity – it took out a machine gun. Later commentators can nod sagely at the much quoted maxim, 'You can't have a cavalry charge until you have taken the enemy's last machine gun.' But what if cavalry is your only weapon? And what if you are a machine-gunner suddenly confronted with twenty or thirty or fifty men galloping at you from several directions with swords drawn and every intention of taking you out? True, if you got enough warning, and you kept your nerve, you couldn't miss the horses. But you would not stop them all – and plenty keep galloping despite a deadly bullet through them. If you stayed at your gun you were going to die.

This was not the heavily fortified trench-system stalemate that is the First World War's traditional image. Easter week for the

Allies around Noyon was a rolling, slipping retreat. The Germans were clawing, handhold by handhold, ever forward. But they were pushing infantry back, they were not ready for sudden paratroop-style assault along their flanks. A cavalry attack under Harvey, fast, split up and utterly ruthless would hurt enough to make them pull that handhold off. Harvey lost just three men in the Bois des Essarts but the machine gun was taken, Sergeant Hodgson got the DCM, and the whole squadron got the renewed belief that this was an enemy they could beat.

Imagine that music to Seely's ears. He may have been a mere brigadier waiting for orders, but by Wednesday night he had his heroes back together. True, they had been through a traumatic experience on Saturday 23 March, but since Monday they had been reunited with their horses. They had their bodies and their minds back in shape. They had travelled far enough west to get round the side of the German assault. They were ready for the call.

46

Maundy Thursday and the Long Good Friday: Arsy to Guyencourt

The news came early. At 4.15 a.m. on Thursday 28 March there was the putter-putter of a motorbike, the challenge of the sentry, the hurried little conference, the signing-off of the despatches and then the acceptance that the unfolding disaster to the north of them had an inexorability about it. The Germans were in Montdidier.

A four-year-old child looking at the map could see what was happening. The German offensive was continuing, with arrowheads of attack prodding west and south-west. They had found the weak points where the British and French armies were supposed to join. The latest breakthrough was in the French section at Montdidier. There were no infantry left to call on. So the orders went out to the cavalry to get up there and plug the gap like the horse-borne paratroopers that they were trained to be.

The countryside between Compiègne and Montdidier was wide open – no rivers, no canals, no forests to make a defensive battlement. Just a few scattered villages and the odd little hillock to give you the blessing of elevation – and the distant view of Montdidier on its cliff top to the north. The locals knew what to expect, they were expecting the worst. For Luke Williams riding through Estrées-Saint-Denis, Rouvillers and Pronleroy with the Strathconas en route to Montigny, the landscape was a surreal sight.

> When we left Arsy it was a beautiful spring morning, the kind of morning when it was a joy just to be alive. The larks were singing up in the sky and everything was perfect and lovely. There was not a sound of firing of any kind to be had and the only thing that

told of war was that on the western horizon long lines of refugees could be seen hurrying their way to safety. All the towns and villages we passed were quite empty, all the inhabitants having been evacuated. We rode through one fairly large village. Not a soul was to be seen except one poor lonely looking French soldier who had come home on leave, only to find all his family gone.

Thursday 28 March 1918 was a day of message and counter-message. Stewart Chambers was attached to headquarters, which may have sounded quite grand but in reality meant a truck, some portable tables, assorted boxes of files and a stand-up typewriter. He was a young lieutenant somewhat dazzled by his flush-faced, ever optimistic commander and the maverick gang he had around him: Prince Antoine who knew every village and certainly every chateau for miles around; Connolly, the brigade-major, gruff and correct but strong on every detail of his new responsibilities; and of course Bill Cowen, the joker, who could swear in seven languages and whose speciality was getting German prisoners to tell the tale.

For Stewart Chambers, for everyone, it was a day of confusion. 'Move from place to place all day', he notes. 'Order follows order until we wonder what really is happening.' Seely shared in the frustration but he had been through critical crises before. In March 1914 he had been embroiled in the throes of the Curragh crisis and General Gough had been crowing about his part in bringing Seely down. This Thursday Gough was a forlorn figure in Amiens being shouted at by Seely's friend Foch. It had been his overstretched Fifth Army that had caved in west of Saint-Quentin and now he was being used as a scapegoat by Lloyd George and had been replaced by Rawlinson. Seely was sympathetic, but he had his own part to play.

A message came from the French at Welles-Pérenne, a small farm village five miles south-west of Montdidier. Seely sent the Strathconas up there. German detachments were seen moving in on the right. Flowerdew took most of 'C' squadron out to stop them. The Germans didn't fancy it. The Germans backed off.

Gordon Flowerdew had been the smallest but a long way from

the least figure in that now historic team photo of 'C' squadron officers taken a year earlier at Yzengremer. In his Suffolk school days he had gone to the same Framlingham College none too happily endured by Alfred Munnings ten years before. 'Flowers' was a neat little man and his second name was Muriel. But at thirty-two he had done eight years' ranching in Canada. He understood men and horses and hard work. Connolly had just recommended his promotion to captain. He was as tough as old boots.

Yet like everyone else he was in awe of the long tall Irishman who was his fellow, and indeed junior, lieutenant. At this stage Fred Harvey was an unstoppable force. That Thursday afternoon he had a patrol out on the Montdidier–Breteuil road of the French line. He saw German activity in Fontaine, a village that clung to the side of a short dip off the plain a mile away. In a couple of minutes Harvey was down on them like a wolf on the fold. For a German it would not have been a pretty sight.

Meanwhile, to misquote the Duke of Wellington, 'If he scared the hell out of the Germans, he was putting the wind up the French as well.' As Harvey came back out of Fontaine he met the French belatedly moving in. He explained to them what he had done and how he was a Canadian officer. They were much too wise to fall for that one. They knew nobody spoke English like that. Spies disguised in Allied uniform were everywhere (that was true). They arrested Harvey and locked him up.

In Seely's book the best way to get a commendation was to start with official disapproval. It had worked for the man himself in the sun of South Africa and the snows near Péronne. It worked now for Harvey. Seely got word that his star man had been arrested and sent a galloper with a protest. Harvey didn't just get his freedom. By next morning Seely received an official apology from the French commander and Harvey a citation for the Croix de Guerre.

Before that there was the not insignificant matter of getting a bed for the night. The losses in killed, sick and wounded during the eight days of the offensive had reduced the three Canadian cavalry regiments to half their full strength, averaging no more than 250 men each. But with supply wagons, veterinary trucks, the machine-gun squadron (the horse artillery were currently seconded to the infantry), cyclists and signal troops, there were still well over a thousand mouths to feed, both on two legs and on four. What's worse, it was coming on to rain.

For Williams and his Strathconas it was no problem. At six o'clock they were ordered to billet at Sains-Morainvillers, a couple of miles south of Welles-Pérenne. They found the village empty, the roofs intact and a good dry night was had by men and horses. Life was not so easy for Timmis and his dragoons. He lost the way in the dark, was forced to bivouac in the open and the situation, and his own continuing trauma after the events of the previous Saturday, was only partly improved by the finding of a large pig to put on the spit.

For Seely's HQ and his assorted attachments, Thursday night was nothing if not a Prince Antoine special. A mile to the north-east of Sains-Morainvillers lies the chateau home and wild-boar forest of the Comte de La Borde. Of course the Comte would entertain them and duly did, but not before poor Stewart Chambers had failed to turn the key. It cannot have been easy trying to handle the demands of your eccentric commander, his royal ADC, and 24-carat heroes like Harvey, but the diary entry of the young lieutenant for Maundy Thursday evening 1918 is a classic of the greenhorn kind:

> General Seely sent me to locate Brigade Headquarters in chateau at Sains Morainvillers. Now raining, no chateau to be found in village. Rode around in the dark until finally located chateau in wood near there. French sentry at door with orders to allow no one inside. Had to ride back to Welles-Pérenne to notify General Seely. My horse too much all in to return at once. Had some grilled chicken and French fried potatoes with Harvey, who had been arrested by the French and released several hours later. Returned to chateau about 2 a.m. It was a beautiful place and I was certainly glad of a comfortable bed there.

The next morning was as deceptively peaceful as the larks in the sky had been the morning before. Reveille was at six o'clock, rather than five, and there were no orders to move until 2.30 p.m., so the whole morning could be spent cleaning and grooming and polishing and parading as if they were having an easy day on the sands near Ault.

And what a place. To this day the Chateau de La Borde has a red-brick, early-Edwardian pride about it, with its gates, its gravel drive, the avenue in the forest, the little statue of the goddess Diana, the farm, even a chapel where the family used to worship. Some of the outbuildings are a bit overgrown, some rooms inside are a bit old and cold as if they were indeed aristocrats in their nineties. The comte himself is some twenty years younger, a mild, unpretentious man with photos in the kitchen of his sons and grandchildren at last winter's wild-boar shoot, complete with the fallen quarry laid out in all their porcine goriness. But he is also proud of the photo of himself flanked by uniformed and be-ribboned officials at the unveiling of a plaque on the chateau wall. It was in honour of a haven.

Not just in the First War, but in the Second. When France was overrun in 1940 the chateau was requisitioned as a rest home for German officers, a fate with which the comte's parents had to comply. They were correct in their dealings with their conquerors, gave them meals on time, gave them their own space in the large salon downstairs and in the many bedrooms upstairs and across the courtyard above the stables. In return the Germans gave them respect. And did not suspect.

They did not suspect that with quite astonishing daring the comte and his wife had fugitive Allied airmen hidden away in the attic. The present comte remembers being sworn into the secret as a small boy. The penalty for discovery was death. But there was no discovery. Scores of lives were saved. And on the kitchen table is a folder of letters and cuttings from British and American airmen, some of whom returned grey-haired but still grateful, for the unveiling of the plaque.

The chateau was certainly a haven for the Canadian cavalry as Maundy Thursday gave way to Good Friday in 1918. After a week of barns and ruins and bivouacs, here were beds and a proper roof over their heads. Antoine fetched up the best wine from the cellar, he opened the piano, they all sang sentimental songs, ending with 'Roses of Picardy'. For those few brief hours, in that odd way in which people bond when Armageddon lurks round the corner, they were happy there. Next morning, during a break from supervising all the grooming and cleaning and checking of 'C' squadron, Gordon Flowerdew wrote a letter to his mother, the farmer's wife from Suffolk, the rearer of fourteen children. As recommended by the censor it was in pencil on the official brown letter form. Its postage date was 31 March 1918. It would be read posthumously:

> My dearest Mother.
> Have been a bit busy lately, so haven't been able to write, I managed to borrow this card. Haven't had any mail for some days, so we are very keen to see the papers. The weather is still very good, but very keen at night. Have had the most wonderful experiences lately. I wouldn't have missed it for anything. Best love to all.
>   Your affectionate son,
>   Gordon

By March 1918 four years of war had broken morale all over Europe. The year 1917 had seen the Bolshevik revolution in Russia, an outbreak of mutiny amongst the French at Verdun and Siegfried Sassoon and Wilfred Owen giving voice to the suffering in the Allied trenches. Nine days into Operation Michael parts of the British and French forces were in freefall, and the Germans themselves were foundering as starved troops fed and drank themselves senseless on captured drink and supplies.

But through luck, origin and inspiration, Seely's force was different. As his extraordinary three-quarter-mile caravan trailed its way northwards to an ever more uncertain destination, he could look down the line and marvel at the team he had built around him. There was Antoine, Connolly, Macdonald, Patterson, Harvey, Flowerdew, Strachan, Cowen, Williams, the Nordheimer cousins, 'Big Nick' Nicol, Reg Timmis, Munnings's friend Joe Duhault the vet, young Evan Price who had dragged that torpedo, Reg Longley the trumpeter, Fred Wooster and his fellow sergeant Harry

Hooker, both originally from England and who had both joined up in Winnipeg on the same day a full three and a half years ago. And of course Seely's own men: Anthony driving the staff car, Smith keeping the kit in place, Thompson with the horses and Corporal King by his side. They had all been a long time together.

He rode Akbar that day. He would take Warrior tomorrow. The troops liked them both. For the troops liked horses. That's what made them different – as soldiers and as people. As soldiers it meant that the twenty-odd-mile trek they were embarked upon could be accomplished without the morale-sapping exhaustion suffered by the infantry. As people it meant that they had something beside their own discomfort to think about.

Anyone who has ever been through an ordeal with their horse knows the courage you can draw on to deal with your four-legged friend's predicament. Conditions, in snow and fog and mud, had often been bad for these Canadians, but never as bad as for their horses. They were at risk, but not a quarter as great as their partners. That's what made their morning care that Good Friday so special. They were not to know it, but they could suspect it. For many, many of them, it would be their last full day together.

As they travelled, the news was once again not good. Ludendorff's final throw was becoming obvious. He had split the British and French armies and was going for broke for Amiens. Reports had it that several German divisions were now pushing forward on the high ground between Roye and Moreuil. The brutal truth was that there was not much left to put in front of them. A thousand still comparatively fresh cavalrymen could get around this left flank and do their duty. It was likely to need every man.

'The Brigade moved off shortly after 3 pm', notes Williams who was riding his much loved Spider for this fateful trek.

> Late in the afternoon a motorcycle despatch rider caught up with us bearing fresh orders. We grew to hate the sound of a motorcycle as they meant despatches, usually 'Move at once.' We crossed over the west bank of the Noye river at Ailly sur Noye and bivouacked for the night in Guyencourt Wood at 11.00 pm,

after having watered in the Noye River. Of course we had to put up our horse lines, take the saddles off and feed the horses before there was any sleeping, which meant it was about midnight by the time we were ready for sleep.

It had been a long Good Friday. On the morrow their Calvary would come.

47

30 March: All My Life Had Led to This

Seely was asleep when it started. Not exactly tucked up in bed, but sat down dozing next to a wall with Warrior tethered beside him. Over the next three days it was almost the only sleep he was to get. He was dozing because he was ready and waiting. The brigade had been up at 4.30 in preparation for a move at 6.30. At 6.15 a motorbike came down from Boves with a two-hour postponement. Girths were loosed, cigarettes smoked. It was dark and misty. There was not a lot to talk about. You had to take whatever came.

At 8.30 they heard the sound of the staff car. This Guyencourt was quite different from the place of the same name where Harvey had won his VC. It was a village set below a wooded ridge, and just west of the swampy bed of the river Noye four miles south of Boves from where General Pitman, the new commander of the 2nd Cavalry Division would have now driven. On the way he had stopped to brief General Bell-Smyth, commanding the division's nearest other brigade, which included Geoffrey Brooke's 16th Lancers. Even Seely, no wilting violet in the face of danger, considered Pitman 'a cool card if ever there was one'. But the commander had wanted to come down and brief Seely in person. The situation over the hill 'was grave in the extreme'.

The Germans were now on Moreuil ridge, five miles due east of Guyencourt. They were in the large triangular wood dominating the ridge and were threatening the town of Moreuil and therefore the crossing of the river Avre. If they crossed they could take the next ridge between Moreuil and where Seely and Pitman now stood. There were some French infantry defending Moreuil, but not many. After ten days of Operation Michael, that now was the front line. Seely would have to get his Canadians over there and see what he could do.

The trumpets sounded even before Pitman's car had left Guyencourt. Within minutes the brigade was on the march. The RCD were at the head of things, followed by the Strathconas, then the machine-gun squadron, then the Fort Garrys, with the ambulance and veterinary wagons following on, a three-quarters of a mile caravan in all. It took half an hour for them all to cross the river at Remiencourt, as the horses needed to drink and the men to fill their water bottles. Then over the railway line, up the steep south-east climb to Rouvrel, left for a couple of miles on the sheltered west side of the big Bois de Senécat before turning back south again towards Castel. By then Seely, Antoine and Connolly had been there for forty minutes. By then the die was cast.

Seely had cantered across country from Rouvrel. Despite the mist he had begun to see the implications of the Germans crossing the Avre and reaching here. Along with him he had Antoine, and Connolly and Cowen and Corporal King and a twelve-man signal troop. Bullets were already whizzing in to Castel from over the river. Above the clatter of hooves you could hear the drone of planes as the Royal Flying Corps harassed the Saxon regiment of 101 Grenadiers in Moreuil Wood, which ran triangular shaped, north–south, roughly one mile long by one mile wide, on the ridge beyond. The RFC orders had said, 'It is of the utmost importance that the enemy should be held on his present line for at least another day.' Yes delay; delay was essential until regrouping and hoped-for reinforcement could happen. But here, sheltering under that big red barn wall that still flanks the little crossroads at the head of the farm, church and cottages that is Castel, was the French commander. He was about to retreat.

Seely's stories are not characterized by understatement and at this moment there were other last-ditch attempts to block the enemy arrow-head push for Amiens, most notably the heroic Australian defence of Villers-Bretonneux, six miles to the north. But this time one has to forgive the purple passage. Because for Jack

Seely and for those who rode behind him, this was just as bad as it
could get.

> I saw at once that the position was desperate, if not fatal. If the
> enemy captured the ridge I had just left, the main line from
> Amiens to Paris would be definitely broken, and I knew already
> that when that happened the two armies – the French and the
> British – would be compelled to retire; the French to Paris, and
> our army to the Channel ports. All our sea power, even the great
> host of determined soldiers now crossing from the United States
> would not avail to save the Allied cause. All that we had fought
> for, and bled for, for nearly four years, would be lost.

But that was all written with hindsight. On Saturday 30 March 1918
Seely was absolutely in the present. He and Connolly and Antoine
had Cowen with them as they tried to stiffen the French commander's back. Beyond them was one of the strange mechanized
monsters that had done such good work for the motor machine-
gun squadron. None of them had ever been to Moreuil. They got
out their one map. They needed a plan – a simple plan.

They would re-take the wood. When the demoralized Frenchman pointed out that a mere brigade hadn't much hope against an
enemy division rapidly amassing on the ridge, Seely seized him with
one of those trademark assertions that had saved his bacon with
that Basuto chieftain eighteen years before. With him he had not
just the 1,000-strong brigade queuing up on the hill behind them,
but the Hussars and the Lancers (true) and the whole new British
cavalry offensive, 'le grand push Foch' (if only).

The French commander reluctantly agreed to keep defending
the west bank of the Avre down to Moreuil. Seely and Connolly
briefed Roy Nordheimer, in charge of the leading squadron of the
RCD. The attack would start by the signal troop galloping up
the slope ahead and placing a red pennant as a gathering point at the
edge of a little coppice jutting out on to the north-western edge of
Moreuil Wood.

The RCD had three squadrons. Nordheimer with his 'A'
squadron would be the first to follow the signal troop across the

river, come to the gathering point, turn right there and take the wood head-on. Then 'C' squadron led by Terry Newcomen would cross the river, turning right below the wood to cover and then attack the western flank. Finally Timmis's 'B' squadron would come past the pennant and encircle Moreuil Wood to assault the eastern side. Any questions?

For a moment Nordheimer thought to ask who would be leading the signal troop on the crucial opening gallop. Who would be taking them and Corporal King and his red pennant up what looked like at least half a mile of dangerously open, bullet-whistling ground before gaining the shelter of that coppice called the Bois de la Corne? But Seely was already in the saddle. Warrior was jerking his bridle and circling round as only a lit-up thoroughbred could. Antoine's horse was jigging and ready. It was 9.30 by the church clock. There would be no questions.

Seely did not need to do it but his nature said he must. The orthodox wisdom would be to risk a subordinate with the signal troop while the general briefed the men coming through. Orthodoxy? Seely called to Antoine, Corporal King and the signal troop and led from the front. 'I knew', wrote Seely later, and nothing ever altered his opinion, 'that moment to be the supreme event of my life.'

Warrior was wild for it. He had cocked his jaw and was pulling Seely's arms out as they clattered down the street and over the humpback river bridge. The general got a hold on him as they steadied at the apology for a trench which was the French front line. 'We are going to re-take the ridge', he shouted at the bewildered carabineers. 'Fire on both sides. We are going up.' The ground suddenly stretched much longer and emptier than they had expected. The bullets were starting. He let Warrior run.

Seventy seconds would be record time for six furlongs. But this was uphill, on rain-softened ground and there were fourteen men trying to keep together. It was three full minutes before the red pennant, with that black 'C' on a white star, beckoned the Canadians up toward it with as clear a message as Nelson ever sent at Trafalgar. Corporal King and Antoine made it, five of the signal troop did not. Seely hauled the heaving Warrior round to stand and look back at Nordheimer's eighty-strong squadron thundering up, all steel-helmeted and ready for combat. Behind him came galloping squadron after galloping squadron, a whole hillside pounding towards the fight with some already somersaulting to their doom. These were his 'paras'. And they were coming in.

Roy Nordheimer's 'A' squadron struck first, and straight away it was brutal. The wood was not thick and being the end of March the beeches were not in leaf, so for the opening few moments the defenders could not miss the horsemen however apocalyptic their appearance. But the wood still provided some cover for cavalrymen once dismounted. And bayonets fixed to rifles were a fearsome weapon not yet encountered by many of the young Saxons now braced before their foe. There would, in the very harshest sense, be no quarter asked for nor given.

No quarter for Timmis either, and after his Saint-Quentin trauma his was the unhappiest of situations. He aimed the eighty men of 'B' squadron towards what he thought was the wood's far north-eastern corner. But it proved to be a false tip and being so close to the enemy meant he was shipping a terrible range of punishment. In his recollection there were even machine guns in the trees. He couldn't continue as ordered. He wheeled right on his attackers. Inside the wood it was even worse. He wheeled out left to try to save his men, only for many more, including Roy Nordheimer's cousin Victor, to get a bullet in the back. They had tried but the squadron had lost it. Seely and Connolly would see the stragglers and have to think again.

Down on the western flank Newcomen's 'C' squadron took an almost equal hammering. As planned, he had galloped hard south towards the French position at Moreuil intent on harrying the enemy from the rear. But nobody plans for a combined assault from machine and field guns. Inside the wood Leutnant Gottschid, the battery commander of the Feldartillerie-Regiment could not believe his luck.

'Then, in peace so often practised,' runs the German regimental report with a degree of celebration, 'and in war so rarely used, command "attacking cavalry to the right" could now be used. As if electrified, the gun trails flew to the left, and with lightning-like quickfire, the two guns opened fire at a range of 400 yards. In a few minutes one could only see a few rider-less horses heading towards our gun lines. The greater part of the riders lay dead or wounded on the ground. A few lucky ones were able to escape this fate through quick retreat.'

So all three dragoon squadrons were up against it. The only communication on this still misty morning was through distant images or by the bullet-dodging testimony of the gallopers from the signal troop. Up by the red pennant, Seely and Connolly were getting only some of the picture. Now they had to throw in their second wave.

Big Donald Macdonald at the head of Strathconas was just the man they needed. They wanted him to dismount his first two ('A' and 'B') squadrons, fix bayonets and take up what Nordheimer had begun. That black moustache did not plan to take a backward step.

Flowerdew, newly promoted to captain, was preparing to do the same with 'C' squadron, but Seely stopped him. The stragglers from Timmis's group were limping in as battered proof of a plan that had failed. But that original encircling attack on the eastern side still needed trying. It was from there that the enemy were reinforcing, and pressure there would make defenders in the wood uncertain. It was time to call on the men from the west.

It was a long time since Flowerdew had hunted down bandits in British Columbia but he had not lost his eye for a country. He saw now that he could profit from Timmis's mistake. He would not go across to the far side as an open target, but would circle off north-east to connect with a narrow cutting which should give his men a shielded passage right round to their target. He got trumpeter Reg Longley to call the squadron up behind him. He sent Harvey on with the advance guard, and then suddenly Seely and Warrior were alongside, supportively saying that this was the toughest, most important call of all. 'I know sir,' replied Flowerdew, neat and direct and fearless. 'I know it is a splendid moment. I will try not to fail.'

Down in the cutting, half a dozen Germans paid a high price for carelessness. Ten days surviving on what had become little short of starvation rations meant that the sight of an untended supply wagon was an irresistible temptation wherever it might be. But they needed to keep a lookout. Especially for fifteen westerners with their blood running high. 'The patrol dealt with them', is Harvey's neatly typed report to which he has added in his surprisingly small, spidery writing, 'using their swords.'

While this little fracas was pursuing its brief and bloody course, Harvey spotted a large number of apparently unaware and unprepared Germans in the corner of the wood. By now Flowerdew was with him. The new captain had great faith in his deputy. 'Dismount your men, Harv', he said decisively. 'Get into those Bosch from this end. And I will take the rest of the squadron and have a go on the other side.'

It was a decision that would buy him a place in history – but at the ultimate price.

48

It's a Charge, Boys

Flowerdew was prepared for trouble. He had seen what had happened to Timmis. He knew he had to go in hard. He had his seventy-five men ready with swords drawn. But he was about to gallop into an armoury on alert.

He was quite hidden in the hollow. He planned to come up out of the mist and attack down the Démuin–Moreuil road on the east face of the wood. That should knock out any of the Germans that Harvey had forced into the open and then threaten the enemy positions at the southern end. But waiting at the top of the slope were rather more than the odd defensive position and a few refugees from Harvey's bayonet. In fact there was a six-gun artillery battery and the combined rifle and machine-gun strength of five infantry companies. They were not expecting seventy-five horsemen from 'C' squadron of Lord Strathcona's Horse. These Germans were ready for a tank attack.

It had been those reports of the motor machine-gun monsters in the morning mist which had done it. To a jumpy German scout they had looked much too like tanks for comfort. Captain Jungnickel had got a warning message. He had a howitzer unlimbered off the Villers-aux-Erables road and aligned facing north-west. An artillery company and a machine section were also primed for tanks coming round the wood. Then Flowerdew and his Strathconas rode up out of the dip. It became a slaughter by another name.

Flowerdew's charge was originally immortalized through his posthumous VC, the Canadian cavalry brigade war diaries, Alfred Munnings's romantically recreated painting and Seely's own 'greatest battle in history' report. The VC citation says that the squadron 'passed over both lines [of defences] killing many of the enemy with the sword; and wheeling about galloped on them again'. The regimental diary (written by Connolly) has Flowerdew then galloping into the wood to join Harvey and the rest. Munnings depicts two massed ranks of cavalry at the charge with Flowerdew, sword aloft, at their front. Seely claims that seventy Germans were killed by sword thrust alone.

These pictures don't square with either the survivors' reports or the German analysis. The splendidly named Freiherr von Falken- stein avows that 'the attack was bloodily repulsed, the last rider falling dead from his saddle two hundred yards from the rifle muzzles of No 8 Company'. While the Grenadier-Regiment 101's official account details the exact gunnery and says, 'the last horses collapsed 200 metres in front of the Company, only one horse and two wounded troopers reached our line'.

Sadly, the now received wisdom, as excellently chronicled by John Grodzinski and Mike McNorgan in their part of *Fighting for Canada* (published by Ensign Heritage, Ontario, in 2000), is that the Grenadiers' report is the nearest to the truth. They call on the two most telling witnesses, Albert Dale, who was shot down early on in the charge, and Luke Williams, who spent a while afterwards picking up the bits. Albert's testimony is not entirely foolproof as he thinks his day started in Amiens! But he has a vividly believable picture of the opening moments when the squadron breasted the rise and not a quarter of a mile away the most bristling of enemy defences lay ahead.

'Flowerdew half turned in his saddle and shouted, "It's a charge, boys, it's a charge." The boy trumpeter [Reg Longley], riding behind Flowerdew and in front of me, raised the trumpet to blow the call, but the trumpet never spoke. For the boy and the horse went down. My horse jumped over them in passing.'

In later, debunking, post-Empire years, the whole idea of a cavalry lieutenant shouting 'it's a charge' is riddled with ridicule. But this was not a chinless wonder playing soldier games. This was a 32-year-old former bandit hunter from British Columbia having to make the only call the circumstances allowed. Seventy-five men on horses suddenly confronted by machine guns can't either turn round or lie down. Their one chance was to throw everything into attack. 'It's a charge, boys', was not just a brave shout. It was a command. And it was the right one.

It was carnage from the very first. If Warrior had got lit up down in Castel, it was hardly surprising that some of these horses' minds flipped completely as the shells and bullets smashed home. At least three horses hooked wildly off to the left, and another poor sergeant bolted clean into enemy land. Albert Dale went straight, but not for long:

'There's not much I can tell of the actual charge because everything happened with such speed and fury. I have a hazy recollection of Flowerdew and his horse falling as we swept by. Everything seemed unreal – the shouting of men, the moans of the wounded, the pitiful crying of the wounded and dying horses. When I woke up I was pinned under my horse which was mercifully dead.'

The survivors, both two-legged and four-legged, were a shocking sight. Sergeant Watson, 'C' company's farrier, somehow made it back into the wood, where he found big Donald Macdonald rallying his men to drive at the enemy. Watson was on foot but his horse, despite walking soundly, had its flesh hanging in tatters. Seeing his commander Watson's military reflexes were still triggered. 'Sir,' he said to Macdonald, 'the boys is all gone.'

Twenty-four of the seventy-five men had died on the battlefield, fifteen more died later, almost everyone was wounded. The horses suffered even more severely and the Germans continued to shell those who got away. 'Some of them went calmly on with their grazing', is Luke Williams's graphic recall, 'and paid no attention whatever to the shelling, while I saw others lay down and scream when a shell came particularly close to them.' By next morning over 500 horses were no more.

Luke Williams's brother George had been in the charge. Luke eventually found him, leg smashed, propped against a tree. George could speak and lived out the war, but Harvey found Tripp against another tree too far gone for words. Flowerdew was in the open. Hammy Harrower went out to him and was machine-gunned in the foot. 'You had better get under cover, "Hammy",' said Flowerdew, hit hard but still conscious, 'or they will shoot your head off next.' Harvey saw him later, weak but still cheerful, on the way to the clearing station. But Flowerdew would not see Easter through.

Flowerdew's charge became a martyrdom, but it also had a vital military as well as symbolic value. For the assault, although repulsed, both broke the balance of the German defence inside the wood and stopped them continuing, for fear of more attacks, their stream of reinforcements up the Villers-aux-Erables road from the east. Down to the west the successful opening artillery barrage of the Fusiliers against Terry Newcomen's dragoons faltered as first the Fort Garrys then the 4th Hussars from General Bell-Smyth's 3rd Brigade came in as support. Oberstleutnant von Alberti was still preparing to launch his 2nd Battalion into the town of Moreuil and across the river around the Allied flank. Then a frantic runner brought the first news of Flowerdew's attack. 'Enemy in the rear', he shouted. Von Alberti drew his men back.

It's important to recognize the scale of things and the difficulty of communication. Moreuil Wood was a full mile long on each of three sides and was now being attacked from three different directions. What's more, it was being hammered from the air from tree-top height by the Royal Flying Corps. In all they dropped 109 bombs and fired 17,000 rounds into the melee. 'One bomb dropped from a negligible height', records the fusiliers' official history excitedly, 'places the whole staff of the 1st Battalion "Hors de Combat". Moreuil Wood is a hell!'

It certainly was in that northern to north-eastern corner. A lot of the Grenadiers up there were very new to action and especially to mad Canadians with the bayonet. Fred Harvey had seen what had happened to his friend Flowerdew. When the artillery couldn't deal with the German field gun in the open, he got his sharpshooters to sort it out. Now the business was hand-to-hand and was up ahead of him. If he had 'lost his temper' at Guyencourt a year earlier, it was nothing to what happened next. He never ever wrote a word about it. But at a regimental dinner many years later, he said quietly, 'I don't know about Guyencourt. But I think I did a VC's worth at Moreuil.' He took a bullet through the shoulder but fought on into the afternoon, when he was taken off to the same clearing station as Flowerdew.

The battle raged on, but one utterly shattered Strathcona worked his way back to try to find Seely at headquarters. It was Fred Wooster. He and his horse had been the only pair in 'C' squadron to gallop unscathed across both sets of enemy defences. He had run his sabre through the first German, clubbed the head of the second, but as he wheeled around he realized the scale of the slaughter. So many of his friends back there dead and dying. Guns or no guns, he had to see if Harry Hooker still had a chance.

Miraculously Fred found him. Harry and his horse had been hit early but he was alive, and boy, was his mate pleased to see him. Fred got Harry upright to help him into the saddle. Another shell landed and the shrapnel took Harry. He looked Fred in the face one last time and asked him to speak well to his mother. 'This is it', said Harry. Then he was gone.

Hooker and Wooster, both originally from the south of England, had joined up together that Manitoban summer day in June 1914. They had crossed back to England together a year later and both landed in France on 1 December 1915. For two and a half years they were inseparable. They took their leaves together. They visited their families in Southend and Guildford. Now for Fred Wooster the whole thing seemed to be a wipe-out. He needed to see the general to tell him about the horror, about Harry. Seely saw him coming. Quietly he took Fred by the shoulder. He made him lie down.

It was coming up to 11.30 and the wood was spangled with mocking spring sunshine. Even generals need friends in battle and Seely now found one. All his reserves were committed, but there had clearly been a disaster for Flowerdew and the wood was still not clear. But who were these lancers riding up to the pennant? It was the 16th with Geoffrey Brooke at their head. 'We looked', records the usually laconic 'Con' Connolly, 'upon this gallant officer as one of ourselves.'

Brooke had new ideas as well as fresh cavalrymen. He got the now Anglo-Canadian forces into a line and organized what he called a 'rabbit-shoot'. They walked fifty yards forward, fired 'five rounds rapid' into the bush and tree glades ahead, paused and did it again and again. It cleared the Germans almost to the southern point of the wood. But they kept reinforcing, and they kept shelling the wood.

It was going to be tough, but Seely was sure he could at least hold the line until nightfall. That was key information for the beleaguered Australians being besieged and bombarded five miles north at Villers-Bretonneux. Messages had to be sent but messengers were special targets. There was a slow safe route in the shelter out to the left, and then there was the straighter quicker one. But that was within rifle-range. Seely had an each-way bet; Colonel Young of the RCD and Prince Antoine of the 'sang royale'.

> Young was to go to the west of Hangard. Antoine, on his very fast horse, was to try and get through direct. Antoine had only gone 300 yards when his horse was shot dead. He jumped up unhurt, waving his hand for another horse. My orderly, Corporal King, galloped up to him and gave him his horse, also a very fast animal. It was wonderful to see Antoine swing himself into the saddle completely unconcerned and gallop off again. This time he got through, and gave the message to both the Australian and British commanders in Villers-Bretonneux. It is a most precious recollection to me that for his gallant action on this day Marshal Foch himself invested him in my presence with the Chevalier Légion d'Honneur.

Antoine was a star. But in the afternoon it began to rain. Until then the day had been lucky for Luke Williams and his horse Spider. But that changed with the weather:

> All throughout the rest of the day the Germans kept dropping shells in the wood from one end to the other. Sometime during the late afternoon they finally got lucky and a couple of big shells landed fairly amongst the party of us who were in the middle of

the wood, causing quite a few casualties and stampeding the horses, Joe Yans had been sitting down holding 'Spider' and his own horse. Both horses were hit, but Joe was not touched. Evidently one of the shells must have landed right under Joe's horse as it was blown all to pieces. My horse 'Spider' had one hind leg blown off and he ran away on three legs. I afterward learned that someone had shot him down near Brigade Headquarters.

It was getting dark. The wretched Spider had stumbled down the hill, searching, as stricken horses do, for the route back to where his last safety had been. As he came down to the road he checked at a row of three official, tricolour-crested staff cars. Ahead of the first was a white-haired, grey-suited figure looking up the hill with excitement. It was Georges Clemenceau, the indomitable 77-year-old Prime Minister of France. Beside him, thirty years younger and with a face lit for battle, was Lloyd George's special envoy. Winston Churchill was at Moreuil Wood.

49

The Minister at Moreuil

Somehow the fates must have intended it. The greatest war reporter, as well as the greatest war leader, that the world has ever seen had arrived at the point of his old friend's as well as his country's most terrible hour. Churchill had already had quite a day.

He had met the French premier and his cavalcade outside the Ministry of War in the Rue Saint-Dominique at 8 a.m. on that Easter Saturday, 30 March. But his trip had begun at the same time two days earlier when he had met the British Prime Minister in Downing Street. Lloyd George had been in bed – 'a grey figure amid a litter of reports and telegrams'. There was too much conflicting information, he needed first-hand evidence of how bad the situation was, how strong would be the French support. Churchill was to use the PM's authority and see Clemenceau and Foch at once.

A special train was run from Charing Cross. By midday Churchill and Bend Or Westminster, that ever faithful travelling companion, had boarded a destroyer at Folkestone bound for Boulogne. By mid-afternoon they had motored down through pouring rain to British General Headquarters in the old walled city of Montreuil. Haig was out for his daily ride but his chief of staff, Sir Herbert Lawrence, had 'the presence of a man who knew he was in the hands of fate'.

'Already', continued Churchill as they studied the charts, 'we had lost totally more than a hundred thousand men killed or captured and more than a thousand guns, while scores of thousands of wounded were streaming through the hospitals of England

straining even that gigantic organization to its utmost capacity.'
While they talked, Sir Herbert was handed a telegram saying that
the French had lost Montdidier. 'No doubt they are doing their
best', he said with doleful resignation.

Churchill and Bend Or hurried on to Paris and the luxuries of an
almost empty Ritz Hotel. 'Now all doubts were cast away', he
wrote later. 'No longer was it a question of fighting to impose hard
terms upon the enemy. Actual defeat seemed to stare the Allies in
the face; and defeat before the weight of the United States could be
brought to bear.'

Next day, as Britain's Minister of Munitions, Churchill checked
out developments in the city and saw the long-range shells coming
in, one of which hit a church killing eighty of the Good Friday
congregation. So on that Saturday morning, just at the time when
Seely and Warrior were cantering over the hill towards Castel, the
Tiger was greeting his former colleague at the French Ministry of
War enthusiastically if somewhat idiosyncratically: 'I am delighted
Mr Wilson (*sic*) Churchill that you have come,' said Clemenceau.
'We shall show you everything.'

A couple of hours later they were marching quickly up a stone
staircase to a big room on the first floor of the town hall in Beauvais.
'The double doors were opened,' wrote Churchill, 'and before us
was Foch, newly created Generalissimo of the Allied Armies.' On
the wall there was a two-yard-square map of the German advance.
'General Foch seized a large pencil as if it were a weapon and without the slightest preliminary advanced upon the map and proceeded to describe the situation.' The performance had begun.

Foch must have been one of the most arresting lecturers of all
time. He wanted to show Clemenceau and Churchill that victory
could still be theirs. He did it by charting the nine days of invasion,
beginning with lots of 'Ah's and 'Oh's and 'Aiee's as he showed
huge gains for the enemy, pausing for an 'Oho, Oho' as he
suggested things were more in the balance after four days, and
concluding with a theatrical dismissal of the spent force of the
advance. 'His whole attitude and manner', wrote Churchill,
'flowed out in pity for this poor weak miserable little zone of

invasion which was all that had been achieved by the enemy on the last day.'

It had been a bravura performance and Churchill's image of the finale is too good a scene not to share:

> The worst was over. Such was the irresistible impression made upon every mind by his astonishing demonstration during which every muscle and fibre of the General's being seemed to vibrate with the excitement and passion of a great actor on the stage.
>
> And then suddenly in a loud voice 'Stabilization! Sure, certain, soon. And afterwards. Ah afterwards. That is my affair.'
>
> He stopped. Everyone was silent. Then Clemenceau advancing 'Alors, Général, il faut que je vous embrasse.' They both clasped each other tightly without even their English companions being conscious of anything in the slightest degree incongruous or inappropriate.

Quite how Foch's upbeat message would have sounded amongst the desperate cries and shouts and sounds in Moreuil Wood is not hard to imagine. It certainly found no echo in Rawlinson's British HQ, which was in a small house some ten miles south of Amiens with large shell holes in the surrounding fields showing how real was the enemy threat. Inside, the normally imperturbable Rawlinson was as near as he ever got to despair. Lunch of meat and bread and pickles as well as Clemenceau's 'chicken and sandwiches of the most superior type' was put on the table. Haig arrived and took the French premier into the next room to plead for instant reinforcements. Rawlinson let Churchill know the score.

'We have had a success', he said. 'Jack Seely with the Canadian Cavalry Brigade has just stormed the Bois de Moreuil.' Any pleasure Churchill might have taken at the news of his old friend's achievement was quickly tempered by Rawlinson's response as to whether the Allies could now make a front. 'No one can tell', came the reply. 'We have hardly anything between us and the enemy except utterly exhausted, disorganized troops.'

Lloyd George had asked Churchill to hear the situation first hand. Here it was and it was bad. 'The cavalry are doing their best to keep a line', said Rawlinson. 'We have a few batteries scattered about. All the Fifth Army infantry are dead to the world from want of sleep and rest. Nearly all the formations are mixed or dissolved. The men are just crawling slowly backwards. They are completely worn out.'

It did indeed sound desperate. Finally Rawlinson was asked if he would be still in position next day. 'He made a grimace,' Churchill records with majestic understatement, 'the dominant effect of which was not encouraging to my mind.'

Haig and Clemenceau then reappeared. The Tiger had promised to send reinforcements at once and was soon lit up by the thought of the battle, and possibly by the taste of the whisky and soda on the table. He told Rawlinson, 'I want to claim my reward.' He wished to be taken across the river and down to the front line.

Wearily the commander replied that the events beyond the river were too uncertain. That nobody was sure what the situation was.

'"Good," cried Clemenceau. "We will re-establish it. After coming all this way and sending you two divisions, I shall not go back without crossing the river. You come with me Mr Winston Churchill [this time he got it right]; and you, Loucheur. A few shells will do the General good," pointing gaily to his military Chef de Cabinet.'

'So we all got into our cars again,' records Churchill in wonderment,

> and set off towards the river and the cannonade. We soon began to pass long trickles and streams of British infantry in the last stages of fatigue; officers and men sometimes in formation but more often mingled. Many of these walked as if they were in a dream, and took no notice of our file of brightly flagged cars. Others, again, recognizing me, gave me a wave or a grin, even sometimes a fitful cheer as they would no doubt have done to George Robey or Harry Lauder, or any other well known figure which carried their minds back to vanished England and the dear days of peace and party politics.

They would cross the Avre at Boves. It was where Pitman had driven down from that morning. It was just five miles from Moreuil.

> At length we reached the river. The Artillery fire was now fairly close. Near the bridge was a large inn. A French Brigadier, pushing on in front of his troops had already established himself in some of its rooms. The rest of the place was filled with British officers from twenty different units for the most part prostrated with exhaustion and stunned with sleep. A Provost Marshal, I think, was serving out whisky to enable them to get up and crawl onwards as soon as possible.

Clemenceau talked to the brigadier and then came back to his line of cars and called Churchill over. They were now in British lines. He, as a Briton, should lead them. Churchill got out the map and this unlikely procession crossed over the bridge and turned right, going on through Thennes towards Moreuil. Things were getting hot up ahead, and to think Jack Seely was somewhere in the midst of it.

'The guns were firing now from every quarter. The flashes of the British and the French batteries concealed in wooded heights behind the river were every moment more numerous. The projectiles whined to and fro overhead. On our left towards the enemy was a low ridge crowned with trees about three hundred yards away. Among these trees a few dark figures moved about.'

They had reached the line. Up in the wood Seely and Brooke and Bell-Smyth would be checking on how the problems were developing in the southern tip, and in the middle of it Williams and Joe Yans were going to somehow survive the shell that blew up one horse and sent a bloodied and now three-legged Spider galloping dementedly out of the wood and down the hill.

'The Bois de Moreuil or its neighbouring woodlands lay before us at no great distance', says Churchill of the spot where the motorcade had halted.

> The intervening ground was dotted with stragglers, and here and there groups of led horses – presumably of Seely's Brigade – were

standing motionless. Shrapnel continued to burst over the plain
by twos and threes, and high explosive made black bulges here
and there. The Tiger descended from his automobile and climbed
a small eminence by the roadside. From here you could see as
much as you can ever see of a modern engagement without being
actually in the firing line, that is to say, very little indeed.

For ten minutes their eyes drank in the picture while shells came
crashing in as close as a hundred yards away. Eventually Churchill
persuaded the French premier that being blown up would not help
either his country or the Allied cause and began to lead him back
towards the cars. That is when Spider, or some equally battered
companion, came upon the scene.

'A wounded and rider-less horse came in a staggering trot along
the road toward us. The poor animal was streaming with blood.
The Tiger, aged seventy four advanced towards it and with great
quickness, seized its bridle bringing it to a standstill. The blood
accumulated in a pool upon the road. The French General expostu-
lated with him and he reluctantly turned towards his car. As he did
so, he gave me a sidelong glance and observed in an undertone,
"Quel moment délicieux."'

The cars withdrew for a date with the French commander
General Debeney to the south. The rain continued into the miserable night and finally, at 9.30, the infantry came as relief. At last the
remnants of the Canadians could take whatever horses and kit they
could find and trail back over the river to Castel to bivouac up by
the Bois de Senecat a mile beyond. Seely and Connolly waited up at
the front line. His contact with Elkins's batteries down towards
Thennes meant he still had artillery support, but the centre of the
wood was now getting heavy shelling from the Germans, much of
it gas. If they were sending over gas, it meant they were not
intending immediately to return.

It was 2 a.m. by the time Seely and Connolly thought it right to
leave the line. By then Churchill was back in the Ritz writing his
telegram to Lloyd George. He had met with Debeney and dropped
in on General Pétain's railway carriage HQ at Beauvais station for

dinner in 'the sumptuous saloons of this travelling military palace'. He had an awful lot to tell and his letter to his wife next morning concluded, 'a most formidable, prolonged tremendous struggle is before us – if we are to save our souls alive . . .'

It had been four years to the day since Seely's resignation over the Curragh crisis. It was Easter Sunday. He and Connolly came over the bridge into Castel and dossed wearily down in the old barn that Antoine had organized as headquarters. There had been deeds of great valour but so many had died. There seemed little hope of resurrection.

50

Easter in Extremis

Seely was asleep again. He was dozing next to Warrior after giving him his afternoon feed. It had been a difficult day trying to put the bits of the brigade together. There had been a simple Sunday service with heads bowed for so many comrades fallen. There were renewed sounds of shelling above Moreuil. Now there was a hand shaking his shoulder. General Pitman wanted him for a conference about an attack in the morning. Would there be no end to this Easter sacrifice?

That long-standing sense of certainty must have been tested like never before. The images of the previous day reeled across the mind. The crumping menace of the shelling, the deadly sweep of the machine gun, the noise and bestial ferocity of the bayonet fighting in the wood. Bits of tree being used as stretchers, bits of flesh on the ground, great bodies of beasts left to the crows. The misery of the rain, and the blood, and the dark. 'Who rests in God's mean flattery now?' the poet Isaac Rosenberg, serving in the trenches up at Arras had written. He was killed on that Easter Monday. His last letter, written on the Thursday, had been to Eddie Marsh, private secretary to Winston Churchill, late of Moreuil Wood.

But Seely and his Canadians were in a fight, a fight to the death which was not over yet. They tried to rejoice in the achievements, not reel from the blows. Already the Flowerdew charge was taking on mythic proportions. Harvey had gone beyond myth long ago and was on the wounded list that Sunday. One had to be just as untiring to friends as unrelenting to foe. There was the story of Roy

Nordheimer riding back through the wood to tend the badly hit Private Harrison who had been the Nordheimer family coachman in another life. There was the heartbreakingly brief reunion of Hooker and Wooster after the failed charge. Even the fierceness of the enemy was seen as something to marvel at. Freiherr von Falkenstein says of the Canadians (we think with exaggeration): 'Not one of them allowed himself to be taken prisoner – each man had kept the last round in his pistol for himself', and Seely returns the sentiment as he tells about the Germans:

> Not one single man surrendered. As I rode through the wood on Warrior with the dismounted squadrons of the Strathcona's I saw a handsome young Bavarian twenty yards in front of me miss an approaching Strathcona, and as a consequence, receive a bayonet thrust through the neck. He sank down with his back against a tree, the blood pouring from his throat. As I came close up to him I shouted out in German, 'Lie still, a stretcher bearer will look after you.' His eyes in his ashen-grey face seemed to blaze fire as he snatched up his rifle and fired his last shot at me, saying loudly 'Nein, nein. Ich will ungefangen sterben.' (I will fight to the last drop.) Then he collapsed in a heap.

The Germans would have had their own Easter service up over the hill. They would have bowed their heads and prayed for victory. And the Bible speaks of a 'Jealous God'?

So much blood had been shed. And now there was to be a conference for yet another counter-attack. And it was to be neither close nor early – eight miles north at Gentelles at 2 a.m. There wouldn't be much banter as Seely, and Connolly and Antoine and Corporal King and the signallers, set off from Castel at midnight. Just before Gentelles, Warrior slid, slipping and laming himself. It would prevent him being ridden the next day. It would save his life.

Pitman's news was a nightmare. The Germans had reoccupied Moreuil Wood and had pressed northwards to take the neighbouring Rifle Wood (Bois de Hourges), which meant that the arrowhead of their assault was now only seven miles from Amiens itself. Pitman had received orders to have Rifle Wood retaken. He had just three depleted brigades of cavalry (the 4th, the 5th and the Canadians) with which to do it. And Seely, as he would later joke, was the only commander still awake. The plan was anything but a joking matter. The German position was well defended and its contours and the sheer lack of Allied horses meant that a mounted assault was not an option. So Seely's troops would have to march on Rifle Wood. For him it was back to worse than basics. They were going to walk towards machine guns.

Seely and his group sent messengers to prime their forces, and at 4 a.m., sore-eyed and accompanied by a limping Warrior, they set off back down to Domart to plot their doom. Even today Domart is little more than a square, an *auberge* and a crossroads. Seely had called his meeting for 7 a.m. and he received some unexpected guests. 'As the officers gathered around a billiard table in the inn,' records the RCD's Mike McNorgan, 'they were joined by three cows who entered through a hole that had been blasted in the wall by a shell. From all reports the cows behaved admirably. Following the meeting Seely moved to Hourges to establish his headquarters.'

Gallows humour could not cloak what lay ahead. 'I explained the plan to the commanding officers,' says Seely, 'ending up by telling them that it was a good plan and certain to succeed. I do not think that one of them believed in success, for indeed it seemed to be an almost hopeless enterprise, but not one of them made the least demur.' And as the clock ticks on he allows us an unusual peep of naked nervousness in his normally so robust report: 'So I waited at the doorway of my headquarters for our barrage to begin. Those were the most anxious moments of my entire life.'

It had been 4 a.m. when the Canadians left their camp that morning. Under cover of darkness they had ridden over the bridge at Castel and threaded their way round to Domart, where they left their horses and rested along a bank. One man could lead no more than four horses, so in having to dismount the brigade was at a stroke reducing its strength by a quarter. The Canadian cavalry was now going to war with less than 500 souls. Luke Williams was one of just twelve officers waiting for the day to come and watching the first battle – in the skies.

'We still had about two more hours to wait', he wrote. 'We lay on the cut bank and watched the morning coming into being. It was a wonderful spring morning, bright and clear. We had a wonderful view of the aeroplanes above us trying to gain the mastery of the air.' Just nine years after Blériot had first creaked across the Channel it now seemed that the whole heaven was filled with men with wings – and guns.

'There were at least fifty or sixty of them and all so mixed up with each other that we found it hard for us to tell which was friend and which was foe. It was a welcome sight to see our planes in the air again and to see them telling the Bosche that they were not going to have things all their own way any longer. Watching the airplane fight helped to pass the time and to take our mind off the impending attack.'

But it was hard not to think. 'Big Nick' Nicol came along for a chat. He had done the same thing at stand-to yesterday, when he had amused himself by trimming Williams's moustache. Now he was quieter, as if he sensed he had used up his luck. If either of them didn't make it, they could have the other's horse. It was 1 April but not a day for April Fools, not quite the dashing cavalry picture that the press so loved to paint.

Williams and Nicol had ridden through Castel in the darkness. Sir Philip Gibbs, the legendary war correspondent, had looked out of his window and gone back to bed. A week later Williams got a copy of the continental edition of the *Daily Mail*: 'We swept up the slope', he read of the Canadian attack on Rifle Wood, 'with our sabres flashing in the sunlight, swept through the wood and on beyond to take a battery of guns.'

Luke Williams was unimpressed. 'All very lovely,' he wrote, 'but not at all what actually happened. We trudged up the slope on our own two feet, being under machine-gun fire the whole of the way. And as for the enemy batteries beyond the wood, we should have had many fewer casualties if those batteries had been put out of action.'

So to the actual assault, which was cruel in its simplicity. The attack would be timed for 8.55 a.m. Half an hour earlier a 'softening-up' artillery barrage would begin. At zero hour four squadrons of machine guns would begin a barrage in support. On the ground the dismounted cavalry would march in three waves, first the 4th Brigade to the left, then the 5th Brigade in the centre and finally the Canadians, under Bob Patterson, on the right.

In that first wave was Trooper H. Ward of 'A' squadron, Queen's Own Oxfordshire Hussars:

> We were near a road that went up a slight incline to the top. Funnily enough we took pack-horses up with us at that time. I was No1 on the machine-gun and we had a pack-horse with the gun and the ammunition. The officer was in front of me, just a few yards and he was shouting 'Come on. Come on.' And there was a machine gun firing at us just at the side of the road, about thirty or forty yards in front, and of course the horses were scared. You could hear the 'pwhht, pwhht' of these bullets going past and the horses were hanging back. So I went behind the horse and gave it a smack to make it go forward. The officer was killed by that machine-gun; Second Lieutenant Dove he was – hadn't been with us very long, and down he went.

Seely, commander of the entire attack, was a connoisseur of courage in its many forms. Luke Williams was not the most flamboyant of his officers and in later life settled for a steady job with Eaton's, the Harrods of Canadian department stores. But the general would have been proud of the calm way he rationalized and described the ordeal that the third wave now began:

> It is very interesting to conjecture what a man thinks about when he has to advance under enemy fire. I figured that as we couldn't do anything about it the best thing to do was to ignore it. My job was simply to keep the line going forward at a steady even pace and to pay no attention to the enemy fire. I was quite conscious of the fire just the same. We had about a thousand yards to go up the hill all the way before we reached the edge of the wood. Three times the machine gun swept along our line. The first time it was too low and I could see the bullets hitting the ground just

in front of our feet. The next time it swept along the line the man on my left went down and the next time it was the man on my right. I didn't see who either of them were, nor how badly they were hit, as our job was to keep going. Those coming behind us could look after the wounded.

Somehow they got through, but the anxious Seely back in the ruined farmhouse on the edge of Hourges village, three-quarters of a mile away, would have hated to see what happened next: 'Just as we were starting down the cut bank of the first side of the road,' continues Williams, 'a shell whizzed past my ear and exploded among a bunch of Fort Garry's who were going up the other bank of the road. It was a frightful mess. Heads, arms, and legs were all over the place. Just then I received a message saying that Lieutenant Atwood had been wounded and that I was in charge of the Strathcona's.'

It was a success, yet at quite a cost. Once their opening machine-gun barrage had been weathered the Germans were noticeably less determined than at Moreuil Wood. But being able to drive right through this much smaller ridge-top glade, as Williams and his Strathconas did, meant that you were then a sucker for a well-targeted shell and machine-gun attack from across the dip.

Poor 'Big Nick' took a high explosive direct. News of his death included a report that Lieutenant Barnett was wounded. Luke Williams was now the only Strathcona officer in the field. But he was an officer backed by heroes: Jack Maley, the Hotchkiss gunner who was knocked out when a shell blew up the rest of his crew and came round to find himself staggering into a trench full of Germans; Private James who lost several fingers to a machine-gun burst, bound his hand up and put the Hotchkiss gun back to work; and Fred Wooster who worked tirelessly for Williams as if the Harry Hooker trauma had never happened. Then there was Lieutenant Bennett of the Fort Garrys.

A piece of shell caught him just below the crotch. He was lying there sobbing while Captain Hutchinson tried to comfort him. He thought that he had lost his manhood completely. He was saying to Captain Hutchinson between sobs, 'Hutch,' sob, sob, 'The dirty bastards,' sob, sob, 'Have shot my balls off.' There was not a happier man in the whole hospital the following day than Bennett when a more careful and complete examination showed him to be still a complete man.

Seely was never happy as a mere spectator and twice this day that almost cost him dear. Within the hour he could contain himself no longer, he left his farmhouse headquarters and took the path to the wood.

'As I walked up the road I met the first bunch of prisoners, a party of seventy Germans, headed by an officer marching sullenly along. I told the officer to walk straight down the road and surrender to the first party he met. It so happened that I was all alone, and I wondered whether temptation to these enemies to crack me over the head would be irresistible. But the officer dutifully saluted and said "Yes."'

When this first trip was over Seely returned to the hubbub of messages and decisions that were needed in that farmhouse HQ. But within a while he was back at the wood. This time he was on horseback but the risks proved even greater. As he toured the top of the ridge with Brigade Commander Bob Patterson, the general's horse was shot from under him. Warrior's lameness had proved his salvation. As Seely walked home, there was danger in his path:

On my way back down the road for the purpose of sending a further report to Pitman I saw a sergeant of Strathcona's whom I knew well, lying in a fresh shell hole with much foam flecked with blood coming out of his mouth. Then, on the spur of the moment I did an incredibly foolish thing for a man of my long experience. Instead of holding my breath and running on, I went up to the man to say I would send stretcher-bearers for him. As I drew breath to speak I had an intense pain in my throat exactly as if someone had plunged a dagger down. Indeed, for a second I thought that a bullet had traversed my gullet.

It was gas. His chest never really recovered, but he still had a long day and a night to run. 'Have communication by wire, visual and despatch runner,' reports Stewart Chambers who had been seconded as signal officer, adding, 'every building in vicinity hit except the one we are using. Only hit once by a piece of shell which does not penetrate my clothing.' The horses tied up in the courtyard were not so lucky. A shell landed right on them and killed all three. The cost was becoming almost too dear to count.

General Pitman wrote:

> Our casualties were very heavy but when one considers the issue that was at stake, and the result gained, no price could have been called too high.
>
> The Germans had been advancing steadily at an average of about five miles a day since March 21, and were within 12 miles of Amiens. Our action at Moreuil Wood on the 30th had steadied them, but the action of April 1st settled them once and for all.

Hindsight can adopt the most conclusive of tones. Things hadn't seemed that steady to Luke Williams. He was one of only nine officers left in the whole brigade. He had started the day with 488 Canadians. Now he was one of just 363. One-quarter had gone. Williams had been in deeper than ever before. And come evening he had a long march home.

'I don't think I was ever more tired in my whole life than I was on the way back to our bivouac in the Bois de Senecat. We had about 7 or 8 miles to go and it took us about three and a half hours. We would walk for a mile and then sit down and rest for ten or fifteen minutes. We were grateful to have no alarms that night and to have a good night's sleep.'

There was less rest for his general as he struggled with his breathing and with the endless and often contradictory messages that came in. It was hard going. It was turning 5 a.m. on 2 April before Seely was able to hand the position over to officers from the 14th Division.

General Seely was a wreck. He had barely slept for seventy-two hours. He was utterly exhausted. Over the last few days his men had taken the 'big hit' that he had always feared. His breathing was ragged from the gas he had inhaled. Warrior was safe. Yesterday's horses were gone. Seely could not walk, but he had Corporal King. He was being led home – on a stray mule.

That famous all-conquering certainty – oh, where was it now?

VI. THE END OF CERTAINTY

51

Bittersweet Return

He should have died that Easter, that Easter of '18.

That may sound a ludicrous thing to say of someone who continued in varied and distinguished public service for another twenty-seven years, and it's downright uncharitable to my Uncle David who was not born until December 1920. But if Seely's luck had finally run out on 1 April 1918, his inspirational gallantry at the head of his Canadians would have been hailed across the Empire, Churchill would have given a funeral oration of Ciceronian proportions and Seely's name would have lived in history. Instead a coughing, retching figure was slumped across a stray mule. 'The dead', wrote Robert Graves, 'are the lucky ones. For they are complete.'

Come the dawn on 2 April Seely's little band had become extremely incomplete. As they stopped to eat at midday they became more so. Eight or ten shells suddenly dropped where they were sheltering at the Bois de Senécat, killing half a dozen men and fifteen horses. What was left of the brigade struck camp, and headed north-west to Boves from where General Pitman had motored that fateful Saturday morning just three days before.

The Seely command which had left Ennemain on 21 March, the first evening of Operation Michael, at a full strength of 2,700, had been reduced to a thousand active men by the morning of 30 March. When General Rawlinson came to praise them at Boves on Wednesday 3 April they were down to half that number, individual regiments scarcely mustering a hundred men. Rawlinson gathered each group around him. He said that without them Amiens, even the whole Allied cause, might have gone.

'Speeches to soldiers', wrote Seely, who ought to know, 'are seldom a success. This one was an exception. We knew that Rawlinson was a great soldier, we knew that he meant what he said, and his praise put heart in us all.' Redemption too for Seely: the official Canadian congratulations included the news that he could, after all, keep command of the brigade.

When the medals came in twenty went to the Strathconas alone. Luke Williams got an MC for his heroics in Rifle Wood, Harvey was given the same for Moreuil, Macdonald a bar for his MC, both Antoine and Patterson received the Croix de Guerre, and for his ultimate sacrifice in that brief, unexpected, but battle-turning slaughter alley on the Démuin road, Gordon Flowerdew was awarded the VC. On 29 June 1918 it was presented to his mother by King George V at Buckingham Palace. That little pencilled 'wouldn't have missed it for the world' note was not all that Gordon had sent her from the grave.

By that time Seely was back across the Channel. He was still breathing certainty, but he was not breathing well. He and Bob Patterson, also a gas victim, had been treated at the Duchess of Westminster Hospital in Etaples. He had ridden a now recovered Warrior on a long, weary trek north to Béthune in readiness for a rumoured German attack, but by the middle of May the Canadians felt politically unable to honour their promise of continuance. A Canadian would have to command their cavalry. Seely would have to go.

In four years of war Seely had been made a Commander of the Order of the Bath for his services in 1916, was to be given the CMG (Commander of the Order of St Michael and St George) for 1918, as well as being honoured with the Croix de Guerre and the Légion d'Honneur by the French Government. Characteristically his memoirs breathe no word of rancour. Publicly his farewell message talks only of being 'summoned to other duty'. Privately, cough or no cough, he was angry and determined to get back into the fray. He wrote a letter to Maurice Hankey, passionately stressing the need to tell Westminster that we were now ready to push for victory. And to his greatest ally he turned again.

But Churchill could not help him with the military. 'They were quite civil about you,' he wrote on 6 June, telling of his enquiries about getting Seely, still tainted by being of yeomanry and political origins, a division to command, 'but evidently they do not think anybody but a professional competent to train a division even though he could fight it well.'

Other enquiries came to nothing, so Seely reluctantly returned to what some observers had unkindly dubbed his natural place – he went where Churchill placed him, joining Winston at the Ministry of Munitions as Under-Secretary. He had left Warrior in France with his successor Patterson but he brought Prince Antoine over. Seely and Antoine may have had only four months left to work with, yet the pair attacked the job with characteristic gusto. Memoranda on everything from delayed-action shells to dazzling lights to better propaganda poured from the new assistant minister. Only two weeks before the Armistice he was negotiating for extra men to work night shifts and Sundays at Morecambe's Munitions Factory.

It was work for the cause but it could never replace that 'in the saddle', front-line, band-of-brothers feel he had with his Canadians, and just two days into peace there was another dreadful blow. Antoine crashed and was killed in a flying accident in Hampshire. For Seely and the others he had been a prince in much more than name. Prince Antoine now lies buried alongside his Bourbon ancestors in the Chapelle Royale at Dreux.

In peacetime Seely the inveterate flyer was not to be daunted. When his job with the Ministry of Munitions ended in January 1919 he switched to join Churchill at the War Office as Under-Secretary of State for Air. In March, flying to attend the Versailles Peace Conference, he flew from Folkestone to Paris in sixty-three minutes, a new record at the then unheard-of speed of 157 miles an hour. A somewhat less successful achievement was Seely's attempt to travel airborne with F.E. Smith, then Lord Chancellor, to see the King at Windsor Castle. The transport chosen was a little airship anchored at Wormwood Scrubs. After an hour into a headwind they had only managed to go backwards. F.E. looked down and muttered drily, 'I always did want to see Epping Forest.'

With Seely the daring never flagged. In April, flying from Medway to land on the Thames at Westminster before answering air-ministry questions in the Commons, his seaplane dived above the omnibuses but below the superstructure of Tower Bridge. The Lord Mayor was very shaken and cabled the air ministry to track down the as yet unknown fliers. Seely responded officially 'that I had administered a severe reprimand to the person in the aeroplane who was responsible'. A couple of months later Seely was to be on the receiving end of another reprimand. This time by his oldest colleague: Seely and Churchill, Mars and Neptune of that pre-war zenith, were to fall out.

Looking back it was inevitable, although their friendship seemed as strong as ever. Before the December 1918 election Seely had left his Ilkeston constituency to campaign for Churchill in Dundee when Winston returned to London to tend Clementine and the Churchills' new baby daughter. But Seely was not a natural subordinate and Churchill had himself predicted the problem in a memo to Lloyd George on the make-up of the new Cabinet.

He proposed Seely as Minister of Pensions. 'Its execution', Churchill wrote, 'requires a sympathetic figure – "one who knows what they went through", who understands how to talk to them, and someone who can stand Parliamentary badgering. It involves dealing with a mass of detail in a humane and warm hearted spirit – not entirely without knowledge of politics.' It is a revealing list of Seely's virtues, but it came with a caveat about offering him a lesser post. 'I do not think', added Churchill, 'he will take an under-Secretaryship now that peace has come . . .'

But Seely did accept Under-Secretary of State for Air under Churchill for want of better, was ridiculed by Beaverbrook as 'peeping out from his [Churchill's] coat tails' and when in July he altered some Churchill arrangements, the War Minister wrote a note of censure: 'I very much regret that you should treat me in the way you do.' Despite a full explanation from Seely, Churchill later responded huffily, 'you countermanded my instructions and took some other action which you had thought better, without even informing me of the changes you had made'.

Churchill's earlier thoughts had proved prophetic. After all that Seely had been through, he wasn't made for the hassle of the underling's role. Besides, he was so committed to the idea of a separate air ministry that he was prepared to put his job on the line. 'Winston's impossible', he wrote to Hugh Trenchard, the RAF chief of staff in November 1919. 'I'm going to force his hand and the government's. Either they agree to a separate Air Ministry or I go.'

He forced. They didn't agree. He went. On 19 November 1919 Jack Seely resigned as Under-Secretary of State for Air. He was to remain an MP until 1924, but his official role within mainstream politics was now over. He wrote a generous note to Churchill: 'Although we part company officially, you will know that you always have in me a firm friend. May all good fortune attend you now and always.'

Winston Churchill's response, whilst acknowledging the changed state of their official relationship, is also a testimony as to just how committed he remained to those within that famous 'stronghold' of his friendship. The letter, complete with spelling abbreviations is worth taking direct:

> I am grieved to receive yr letter; but after our numerous talks I feel there is nothing more to be said.
>
> I did whatever was in my power wh sincere and old friendship suggested to assist yr return from the military to the political arena. Had greater offices been in my sphere of influence, I wd have found one for you. As it was I was able only to secure for you the best in my power. That after trial and consn you do not find it possible to retain this will always be a deep source of regret for me.
>
> I cannot accuse myself in any way, but that does not at all lessen the disappt wh I feel at the course you have taken or my own conviction that your own interests wd have pointed differently.

So Seely walked away from the big stage at Westminster, but his exit gave him the chance to concentrate on more local duties. He had been made Lord Lieutenant of Hampshire in 1917, was elected an alderman of the Isle of Wight County Council in 1919 and was soon devoting much recovered energy to helping the (growing) unemployed, the Territorial Army, the Boy Scout movement, and of course the Lifeboat Service, to which he remained as devoted as before.

His own family and finances would need attention, but first he took the chance to visit his own band of brothers across the sea. In September 1920 'Seely's Canadians' got to see their general one more time.

52

Canada, Adventure *and the* National Government

It was little short of a State visit, but Evie stayed at home because she was expecting what was to be David Seely that December. So when Jack went to Ottawa at the invitation of the Canadian Government in September 1920 he took his twenty-year-old son John with him. Their royal progress took them all the way to the Rockies.

The observation coach of the Canadian Pacific Railway across the prairies remains one of the greatest of travelling experiences. For Seely and his son, it was more than that. It was a voyage to the heartlands, to honour and be honoured in return. When they got to Calgary, Connolly and Harvey were there on the platform to meet them. Harvey's right arm was in a sling. He had played the end of Saturday's match with a broken collarbone. Heroes don't change their attitude.

At Calgary, Winnipeg (where he stayed and shot duck with Bob Patterson) and Ottawa, Seely had a very clear agenda. It was not self-aggrandizement, although shrinking violet he was not, so much as a wish to make sure Canada realized the valour of 'his Canadians'. The official arbiters would never shift from a stance of refusing 'battle' status to the events around Moreuil Wood in Easter 1918. So Seely vowed to elevate them past dull officialdom to deeds by which even Homer would be challenged.

To packed halls and prolonged ovations he told them that Moreuil Wood was 'the battle that changed the course of history', that Flowerdew was 'one of the great heroes of all time'. It was grand to be with old comrades; he met Macdonald, Wilkins, the artillery commander, and in Calgary he was introduced to the former Strathcona trumpeter who was now the bandmaster in the station hotel. Macdonald, Connolly and Harvey would all become distinguished senior soldiers, but at times Seely was hit by the realization of how many others had never returned. He went to Lake Louise, walked on the slopes above its chateau and wrote in his diary, 'quite sad'.

He remembered how close they had all been. He recalled those letters, from Patterson, from Connolly, from Harvey after he had stayed at Brooke. Most moving of all, the note in May 1919 from Sergeant Aisthorpe saying, 'that night at Twin Crater you told me that we were all your boys and friends, and well we know it. During three and a half years you were our leader, guide, and friend, and shall stay father to us all.'

By the time he got back to Ottawa he had a more pressing worry: the mail had not arrived. Back in England eighteen months earlier he had given a grand dinner at the Savoy Hotel in London, before 'his' cavalrymen left the shores. But he had not then had the letter which he now hoped would arrive before the Ottawa lunch he was being given in return. It arrived right on cue that morning. It was a message from France's Marshal Foch.

At lunch Seely could give them his own oration, could tell them that any honours of his own 'were as dust in the balance in comparison with the knowledge that my Canadian comrades trusted and cared for me even as I cared for and trusted them'. But here was a trump card he had long awaited. Foch, the Supreme Commander, had been a friend ever since those distant 1912 Cambridge manoeuvres when Seely's horse had bitten the King's foot. They had talked at the Versailles Peace Conference and now his written tribute did not disappoint.

'Je n'oublie pas l'héroisme de la vaillant Brigade de Cavalerie Canadienne', wrote the gallant marshal as he talked of the Canadians at that 1918 Easter in phrases that sound best in the tongue in which they were written. 'Elle réussit', he says of the cavalry's success, 'par son magnifique entrain et son élan offensif à tenir l'ennemi en échec et à briser définitivement son élan. En grande partie, grace à elle, la situation, angoissante au début de la bataille était rétablie.' Officialdom might not have termed it a 'bataille' but here was the statement from the man who knew. The house rose and cheered until the candelabra swung.

In a perfect world Warrior would have been on the train, would have become Canadian Pacific's favourite horse. Instead he had to confine himself to a canter across Hyde Park at the victory parade to greet 'his' Canadians (including Casey, the horse trained by its owner General Archie Macdonnell to lie down, leaping up only when the word 'Kaiser' was whispered in its ear). Warrior also journeyed with Seely to Bramshott for a farewell before embarkation. He hunted with F.E. Smith and his family when in winter 1920 the great lawyer rented Brooke Hill House from Seely. Sitting incongruously above the church, the house had been commissioned by Jack's father from the architect Aston Webb as a miniature Dartmouth Naval College but never lived in. Warrior would canter past on the Downs above and by 1921 had been given a new ambition, to become a racehorse and win the Isle of Wight point-to-point as his father Straybit had in 1908.

The first attempt, truth be told, was a cock-up. Seely, typically, had his own special in-the-ear whistle without which Warrior would not really run. Jim Seely, his dashing amateur jockey nephew, came down from Nottingham to ride Warrior but was too grand to try such whistling nonsense until too late. Once requested, Warrior sprinted, but the four-legged birds had flown. 'He was snorting with rage', wrote Seely as anthropomorphically as ever.

Next spring Jim Jolliffe, Warrior's original trainer, was given the mount, knew how to whistle, and everything went according to plan. The date was 30 March 1922, eight years to the day since Seely resigned over the Curragh crisis, four years exactly since he and Warrior had braved the bullets in that first red-pennant gallop at Moreuil Wood. After the point-to-point Seely himself took Warrior from the winner's circle and he and his horse rode back over the Downs to Brooke together. Four years since their date with destiny Warrior was a victor once again.

In politics things were not quite so simple. In the general

election of October 1922 Seely lost his seat at Ilkeston. Wartime
coalitions were over. Labour now topped the poll. Fourteen
months later another election was called by Prime Minister
Baldwin, for whom Seely had fagged at Harrow all those years
before. At the last minute Seely rushed in to run for the Isle of
Wight Liberals and won a narrow majority after the official
candidate stood aside. But a year later a third election saw him way
down the poll. The Conservatives had attacked him as a 'Free
Trade' diehard, and they ridiculed his changes of place by cari-
caturing him as a weather vane. For Seely, party politics was not the
game.

It was to a national movement he went, the National Savings
Movement, to which his energy, advocacy and war-hero fame
added such success that in 1933 he received a peerage for his efforts.
He took his title from the village he had made his home, and so
became Lord Mottistone. But it was a post for which his own spendthrift lifestyle made him privately, if not publicly, ill-equipped. It
was in 1926 that Jack Seely became the Chairman of the National
Savings Movement. He toured the country gathering support. In
1933 he presented the one millionth one-pound savings bond to
King George V.

His own family knew that Seely and savings definitely did not
go together. What Evie had spotted when she arrived in 1917 had
only got worse, £3,000 worse (some £60,000 in today's terms) after
Seely walked away from his ministerial office. In 1924 she and Jack
attempted a big tribal reshuffle. Jack's brother Charles, whose own
son Charlie had been killed three days after Frank in 1917, made a
deal to buy the Brooke estate. In turn Jack would keep the manor
house at Mottistone, to be converted by John's emerging architect
talent, and its part of the estate.

It was a transfusion of capital, but income was still way short of
the lifestyle in which a gilded, gifted gentleman like Seely had
always turned. True, he became a director of Thomas Cook and the
first chairman of Wembley Stadium but these were posts whose
stipend scored less than their prestige. For all Sir Charles Seely's
generous millions, his family now regretted his refusal of an offer

made to him back in 1905. A Mr Player had come to dinner and had suggested that Sir Charles took a share in his tobacco business. Sir Charles, himself a three-a-day man, saw fit to turn him down.

In 1928 Jack Seely would be sixty, but he still had vigour to burn. In 1926 he had dived off Sir Mortimer Singer's big yacht *Lulworth* in the Solent to rescue a deckhand who had been knocked overboard from another boat. Sir Mortimer, the sewing-machine millionaire, thought it unnecessary – the chap had a lifejacket, didn't he? It was time for Seely to write his story down. F.E. Smith was happy to pen the foreword and, truth be told, his tales were not losing much in the telling. Seely had already led a life beyond imagining, the Imperial War Museum lent maps and support as befitted an institution of which he was a committee member. In October 1929 *Adventure*, his autobiography, was published by Heinemann and serialized in the *Daily Telegraph* to much acclaim.

Perhaps the most perceptive, most accurate public comment came from L.P. Hartley in the *Sketch*, who wrote, 'The phrase "The Happy Warrior" in the light of the European War became first a cliché then a cruel paradox; reading General Seely's autobiography we catch a glimpse of its original meaning.' Whilst across the Atlantic, Professor Allison, writing in the *Hamilton Herald* said that Seely's name 'should be remembered by all Canadians. He was one of the really big men in the war and although he writes modestly of his own achievements he was one of those who shaped the future both in his work in politics and in the trenches.'

Privately the acknowledgements varied from the pithy 'my friend, you are the goods' from the author Arnold Bennett to a quite superb piece of pomposity from Buckingham Palace:

> The King will be delighted to accept your book.
> The King is, I am delighted to say, in excellent health and shot over 200 pheasants to his own gun a week ago.

More significant in view of subsequent events were two letters from London addresses. The first was from Downing Street:

My dear Jack

I was so glad when I opened a parcel addressed to me to find your book bound in the most loyal colours of the Social Revolution. I shall take the very earliest opportunity of reading it and know I will enjoy it.

    Ramsay MacDonald

The second from 113 Eaton Square:

My dear Jack.

Thank you so much for sending me a copy of your delightful book, & for all the charming things you say in it about me.

    Your sincere friend,

      Winston C.

Anyone who has ever had a good review or a nice word of acknowledgement about a book knows just what a boost it gives to the confidence. If Seely's had been lacking (which has to be in some doubt), it was bursting again now. Britain's economic position was getting desperate, unemployment had risen to 1.5 million in March and to over two million in August. Seely was sure this was time for a National Government. He, as a long-standing opponent of purely party politics, and as someone whose National Savings tours had canvassed practically every corner of the country, was the man to get the idea on the road. At the Athenaeum Club on 29 October 1930, he asked the great and good to dine.

The guests included Ramsay MacDonald, Lloyd George, Winston Churchill, the former Chancellor of the Exchequer Sir Robert Horne, the future Foreign Secretary Lord Reading, and Lord Southborough, described as 'an exceptionally close friend of the King'. The discussions went on for three hours and Seely continued to canvas until on 3 December 1930 he wrote a letter to *The Times* putting the idea forward, claiming that in his role with National Savings he had met 'not hundreds but thousands of men and women of every class and shade of opinion' and that most of them agreed that 'an all party Government is essential if we are to cure our troubles'.

He concluded by asking *The Times* to support the idea so that 'this great act of statesmanship may be achieved before it is too late'. The 'Thunderer' duly answered the call, running an editorial approving Seely's non-party credentials to raise the issue, pointing out that 100,000 Scottish miners had been laid off the day before and urging the Prime Minister to talk with the Opposition.

Of course, many others were involved in the evolution of the idea and it was not until August 1931, with the German mark in total collapse and the British pound looking in danger of following it, that Prime Minister Ramsay MacDonald announced that Conservative leader Stanley Baldwin would be joining him in the formation of an all-party 'Government of Co-operation'. But there was more than a grain of truth in Lloyd George's calling Seely the 'Father of the National Government'.

Acclamation and influence – those were the two horses which Seely once again felt pulling him. Forget petty things like finance, he was someone who had always followed his instincts. He shooed up the horses. He never realized where that would lead him. He was trotting into a trap.

53

Appeasement

They were good intentions, but we all know what road they pave. Only much later did Seely realize his folly, for the great patriot met Hitler and Mussolini, fell for the great dictators and told the world of their fine achievements. There is a bit of explaining to do.

It began with Benito. Seely's own funds might have been running out, but his friends had a bob or two. The Broughtons had a 1,400-ton steam yacht called the *Sapphire*. On 14 March 1929 they were moored in Sardinia. Seely wrote in his diary how surprisingly smart the whole place looked. He asked the local agent what was the key. 'Before Mussolini came,' the agent responded dutifully, 'dirty street, dirty house, dirty people; now clean street, clean house, clean people. Then rough people never get out of the way, now everybody obey policeman.'

That was much too interesting an answer for someone like Seely to leave alone. Back at the Athenaeum Club he had become friends with the Italian Ambassador, Count Dino Grandi. He believed in Anglo-Italian friendship, just as he did in Anglo-French and Anglo-German. He would get to meet Mussolini, no doubt failing to see what Ernest Hemingway had told his *Toronto Star* readers as early as 1923: 'There is something wrong with a man who wears white spats with a black shirt.' For Seely, flattery from Il Duce, 'the man who made the trains run on time', lay warm and comfortable on an old-style hero with an autobiography published and a rekindled sense of mission about restoring a national sense of pride.

Austen Chamberlain, Lloyd George and Churchill had preceded

him to Italy and also been impressed. Seely was captivated by Il Duce, put his signed photograph on his desk at Mottistone and used his name at the start of his latest volume. The first, *Adventure*, had been followed in 1931 by a more deliberately anecdotal set of memoirs called *Fear and Be Slain*. A year later Seely embarked on *Forever England*, a more whimsical work extolling the virtues of the finest type of Englishman, especially of the village and therefore Brooke variety, be he fisherman, farmer, blacksmith or lifeboatman.

'It was Mussolini who first set me thinking of writing this book', said Seely somewhat grandiosely in the introduction, 'when I saw him in Rome a year and a half ago. He said to me in English which he speaks slowly but accurately: "You have had an interesting life in peace and in war and I understand that you have seen much of your fellow-countrymen. I will tell you what I think: the English are a wonderful people, they have the three great Roman virtues with some of the Christian virtues added, the three great Roman virtues, self-control, self-discipline and self respect."'

Forever England is dedicated to 'The Boys of England'. It contains none of the harsh overtones of the Mosleyites. It is sincere but at times idealistic and self-deluding. But then that, in his mid-sixties and still energetic enough to cox the Brooke Lifeboat and to gallop with the Isle of Wight Hunt, is what Seely had become. For him and thousands like him, Bolshevism was the menace. The red flag had flown over the Clyde, the East End and South Wales in 1918, and Seely's fears are best illustrated in his memory of a Paris trip with Foch in August 1920. The former Allied supremo took him to the station to see General Weygand off to defend Warsaw from the Russians.

'Certain it is', wrote Seely in 1931, 'that had the Foch and Weygand plan failed, Bolshevism would have swept through Poland and might have spread over a great part of Europe with consequences almost too awful to contemplate. In backward Russia tens of millions of people died as a direct consequence of this plague, either by execution, murder, disease or starvation. In the complex civilisation of Europe it is reasonable to assume that the consequences would have been far worse.'

With Bolshevism perceived as the big threat, and with Hitler pledged firmly against it, Seely would have no difficulty with the old maxim that 'my enemy's enemy is my friend'. Besides, he was an admirer of his former foe, had discussed the great German 1918 offensive with Prince Ruprecht of Bavaria of the other side, and he was sympathetic towards the privations endured by Germany due to the harshness of the Treaty of Versailles. The newly ennobled Lord Mottistone was a sucker for an invitation when von Ribbentrop came to call.

It was as Chairman of the Executive Committee of the Air League that Seely was asked to visit Berlin and see Germany for himself. 'Comrades of the Air' was always an evocative call and Seely was an enthusiastic guest. He was introduced to Hitler and was soon in the Führer's thrall. 'Hitler told him how honoured he was to meet such a brave soldier', said my Aunt Emily, who at that stage acted as Seely's secretary. 'Daddy said that Hitler was very respectful and had wonderfully polished brown boots. At the time he thought he was marvellous.'

Von Ribbentrop, like Count Grandi, already knew Seely as a member of the Athenaeum Club. He put him up in the Adlon Hotel, took him to the theatre with Hitler, hosted a lunch with von Blomberg, a First World War general. A fellow guest was the English tour operator Brian Lunn. 'Lord Mottistone', he reported, 'glowed with affability as he said, "In the next war, General, we shall perhaps march side by side."'

In hindsight the picture grates harshly on the eye, and for a grandson the revelations sit heavy in the gut: the names, the uniforms, the images, the whole Nazi ethos of the scene. But if Seely was duped by Hitler, he was in the company of Lloyd George, who in 1936 told the Chancellor that this was 'the greatest German of the Age', and what of Toynbee, Lansbury, Halifax, Chamberlain and all the rest?

Looking past that shaming central delusion, a continuing humanity shines through. Brian Lunn was in Berlin in 1935 to try to protect the Oberammergau passion play from being emblazoned with Nazi swastikas. Seely immediately contacted the British

Ambassador, Sir Eric Phipps, on his behalf. A year earlier he and Sir Alfred Munnings had been in the German spa town of Bad Ems taking the cure and each afternoon would sit out in the square listening to the band with tears running down their cheeks. It must have been close to the scene from *Cabaret*, where all the diners join in the refrain 'Tomorrow belongs to me'. In the film the sinister overtones become obvious. In 1934 Seely was still too proudly committed to his own one-eyed, anti-war nationalism to understand.

Quite the contrary, in fact. In April 1935 Winston Churchill included him in a list of notables to whom he sent an article he had written for the *Daily Telegraph* about the need for rearmament to counter the German threat. But when the House of Lords held a defence debate in May, Seely remained unconvinced by his old friend's arguments. 'It seems to me,' he said of heavy rearmament, 'if that is all you are going to do, it is bound sooner or later to result in another desolating war, more desolating than that which we embarked on in 1914. The other plan is the plan of agreement.' And when it came to trusting Hitler? Well, no one can accuse Seely of hiding behind his hands. 'All the people who have met this remarkable man', he added in a passage which rings none too happily down the years, 'will agree with me on one thing – however much we may disagree about other things – that he is absolutely truthful, sincere and unselfish. However wrong-headed people may think him to be, they are all agreed on that point.'

A month after that debate Seely, still ludicrously vigorous at sixty-seven, was stung into action. Winston and other friends kept insisting that Hitler and the Nazis were evil, but that was not Seely's own experience. Somehow blind to the obvious illiberality of the Hitler personality cult, the Nuremberg rallies and the growing anti-Semitism, he fastened on to what the Germans were doing for their youth and the apparent drop in unemployment. He would go and see for himself. And this time he would go by sea. He bought a small, fifteen-ton cutter called the *Mayflower*, got Uffa Fox (then a young Cowes boat designer, later famous as the Duke of Edinburgh's sailing partner) to refit it, found a crew of three and on 15 June weighed anchor for the Baltic.

It was typically gallant and well intentioned, but he acted as a proud patriot, allowing past glories to cloud his judgement. In the Royal Yacht Squadron at Cowes (to which he was elected by fellow-member Lord Albemarle in 1917) there is a caricature from this time. It is of a flush-faced, uniformed Seely standing next to a large bloody sword and surrounded by dead Germans obviously killed during the course of one of his innumerable 'how I won the war' tales. There is a one-line caption, which is clearly the story's punch line: 'And that's that.' The baron could become a bore.

That said, the interests which launched the *Mayflower* were both sincere and long-standing. He had shown particular concern for young people and unemployment in his duties as Lord Lieutenant of Hampshire (also since 1917) and as an alderman of the Isle of Wight County Council (since 1919) and the citation granting him the freedom of the City of Portsmouth (in 1927) especially mentioned his work to acquire playing fields for the people. When at Winchester as Lord Lieutenant Seely met a Dr Budding, the president of West Prussia, and heard him listing the advances back home, he could not resist the chance of having a look.

Yet this was the summer of 1935, quite a bit of the Nazis' totalitarian excess was already above the line, and how Seely imagined that he would get anything but an incredibly indoctrinating tour is a mystery we will never solve. He was not into anti-Semitism, he was a liberal as well as a democrat, he was an extremely experienced and well-travelled public figure, he had family and friends openly questioning his wisdom if not his sanity. But he felt he had more first-hand experience both of war and of the public than anyone around. Avoiding another conflict at almost any cost had become another Seely certainty. Hitler and Mussolini had been friendly, not to mention flattering, to him. He fancied himself to build on this friendship. He would not be denied.

The details of the Baltic trip make me wince just to write them down. When Seely arrived at Kiel, Admiral Albrecht was there with a schedule which included seeing a cruiser, a cadet training ship, a visit to a labour camp and lunch at the yacht club. At Swinemunde it was an Admiral Schroeder who was the guide and who took him to the local Hitler Youth Camp about which Seely was somehow able to write, 'There was no difference between what is done in our Boy Scout and Girl Guide Movement' (of which he was a great supporter). Talk about being taken in by the 'outward visible sign'.

It gets worse. He went to see Hitler and told him how 'little things such as knots and ties were exactly the same and the rules of camp life were similar to those with which I was familiar in England'. The Führer lapped this up, assured the gullible old general that the Hitler Youth was of course entirely involved in toggles, canoeing, camping and other such wholesome non-militaristic pursuits. And when Seely queried every child attending such camps Hitler won him over by saying, 'Yes, but why not? They go to school to improve their brains, then why should they not go to camp to improve their bodies? Good things should be universal.'

In his final book, *Paths of Happiness*, Seely somehow manages to use this exchange to validate something much kinder and more truly socialist than the Nazi youth camps when he says, 'there are many good things which should and could be universal, but which in our country are partial', and lists as an example 'universal summer holidays in the fresh air for our children'. Cathleen Cooper, whose tireless research has unearthed the full story of the *Mayflower*, draws a generous conclusion: 'Seely was a kindly, family man and his vision of the Hitler Youth was tinged with a romantic ideal of achieving good for all young people.' Maybe, but as a grandson I can only breathe a sigh of relief that Hodder and Stoughton never actually published one item on their 1938 book list, a book due to be titled, '*Mayflower* Seeks the Truth'.

A German version, *Auf der Suche nach der Wahreit* came out in 1937. Luckily, great chunks of it are such obvious products of the Goebbels propaganda machine (long tracts of speeches by assorted 'camp leaders') that what is down as Seely opinion appears to be surprisingly un-incriminating. The book even allows Seely to say that the idea of a chosen race was anathema to him, that he didn't believe in National Socialism and that England (note how it is still almost always England rather than Britain) would never accept dictatorship.

Nonetheless, Seely had again travelled to Germany as an honoured guest. He was an English war hero the German public were allowed to read. *Auf der Suche nach der Wahreit* appeared in 1937. *My Horse Warrior*, the very touching, and of course beautifully illustrated, book he did with Munnings in Britain in 1934, was published in Berlin as *Mein Pferd Warrior* in 1938. To almost the outbreak of war Seely insisted that Germany should be made a friend not an enemy. Despite his later condemnations, despite his long-standing humanity and good nature, it is hardly surprising that at least one historian has labelled him 'a considerable apologist for Nazi Germany'.

Of course he was not alone in this. The Anglo-German Fellowship of which he had become a member in the 1930s was chaired by Louis Mountbatten's father-in-law Lord Mount Temple, and included the likes of the Duke of Wellington, the Duke of Westminster (Churchill's long-term ally), the Earl of Airlie (the Lord Chamberlain), Lord Redesdale (father of the Mitfords) and the tycoons Lord Nuffield, Lord McGowan (chairman of ICI) and Lord Kindersley (chairman of National Savings). But Seely was under pressure from family and friends not to support appeasement, not to mention a continued exoneration of Italy in Abyssinia, an extremely difficult row to hoe.

Churchill and his wife came to stay at Mottistone as late as 1936. Clementine signed the visitors' book, Winston's omission may have been oversight but grandfilial speculation likes to imagine a Winston protest at having to write beneath the huge flashing black calligraphy of Freidrich Prinz von Staufe-Coburg-Gotha, one of several German aristocrats who had also been wined and dined. As had Lord Astor at an earlier date, and with echoes of the film *The Remains of the Day* the children and servants had been sent away for the evening. Seely was never a member of the 'Cliveden Set', but it is unlikely that the two lords were talking about pheasant shooting.

If Churchill, as an old friend, was exasperated, even more so was my Aunt Lou, who by now was working for British Intelligence. 'He just wouldn't listen', she told me a couple of years before she died in 1998. 'By now we knew a lot about the Nazi nastiness but he still wanted to be reasonable. "Daddy, you must accept that you have got it wrong." But no, he said he had met these people. That anything was better than another war. I think it was quite difficult for him when war finally started.'

Today most of us look back at appeasement with contempt, imagining all those who signed up for it to be wimps or Nazi sympathizers. But when Neville Chamberlain waved that piece of paper at Heston Aerodrome on 30 September 1938 on his return from Munich and said the doomed words, 'peace in our time', the public rejoicing was well nigh universal. When he got back to London he was invited to do the same trick from the balcony at Buckingham Palace. The royal family were publicly keen to seek peace rather than risk the horrors of global conflict.

But not as keen as Seely. He had convinced himself that war and all the slaughter it would entail should not be the country's choice. The House of Lords had given him the platform and he was not shy about using it. Not just in October 1938 after Chamberlain's return from Munich, but right up until June 1939 when once again he stood up to be counted on appeasement.

Lord Cecil had called him an 'untouchable' and claimed that nobody any longer believed in appeasement. 'I do,' said Seely, adding, 'but I am quite unrepentant. I am quite sure that a conference is better than war at any time.' That House of Lords speech was on 12 June. Hitler invaded Poland on 1 September. Neville Chamberlain's haunting, hesitating broadcast: '. . . I have to tell you now that . . . this country is at war with Germany. God save the King,' was on 3 September.

Seely had sparkled through six decades by being an idealistic optimist. But in the 1930s he became a cock-eyed one. This time his certainty had led him seriously astray.

54

War, Peace and Death

Great must have been the chastening. Seely was seventy-one. He had humiliated himself and the memory of so much that had gone before. He set about his own form of reparation.

By August 1939 he had sent Neville Chamberlain a copy of correspondence he had had with Count Dino Grandi, the former Italian Ambassador, and with it an assurance of loyalty. 'I am always ready to go anywhere and do anything at your request.' By 12 September he was going direct to Maurice Hankey with details of the 'Peace Manifesto' being discussed by a group convened by the Duke of Westminster, old Bend Or of France and Bentley fame.

'Lord Mottistone called on me this afternoon,' Hankey wrote to the Foreign Secretary, Lord Halifax, 'having come straight from a meeting which had been summoned by the Duke of Westminster to discuss the position which will arise if and when the Germans offer peace terms to Poland.' The group included such notables as the Duke of Buccleuch, Lord Rushcliffe and the former war correspondent Sir Philip Gibbs, but by now Seely had clearly turned informer, bringing a copy of the manifesto with him. Westminster circulated the document to the Cabinet and received from Churchill the most withering of replies. 'When a country is fighting a war,' wrote Winston to what had been one of his closest companions, 'very hard experiences lie before those who preach defeatism and set themselves against the main will of the Nation.'

Seely had turned just in time. He may have been an appeaser but he was never going to be a pacifist, and there is a rather pathetic gallantry in his now desperate determination to show that he still had the stomach for the fight. In January 1940 there is a letter from Princess Beatrice, the Governor of the Isle of Wight, responding to his wish for front-line action but quietly suggesting that he had much good work to do at home. Four months later he set off on an even more poignant mission. He went to London to pledge himself to Churchill.

With France about to fall and British forces encircled at Dunkirk, the arrival in full be-medalled splendour of an ageing ex-general must have been about as welcome to the Cabinet team as another hole in the roof. But Seely was insistent in sending his message. He was flushed and emotional. 'Prime Minister,' he said, 'I just want to let you know, that Hampshire's right behind you.' Then he burst into tears. One version has it that Churchill did too.

It is easy to knock the image of an old hero blundering around way past his sell-by date but there was a method in all this full regalia madness. Seely wanted to put absolute clear water between him and other more extreme former members of the Anglo-German Fellowship. More than one thousand people were detained, Lord Rothermere went abroad in exile, Seely put on his uniform and toured the Isle of Wight. Scaffolding was going up on the beaches but the south of the Island, beset by rumour that this was the Germans' first intended landing point, had its morale running very low. Seely travelled from place to place full of Home Guard reassurance. Even at seventy-two there was a dynamic indomitability about him.

Early in 1941 he had to make a very personal sacrifice. Warrior was now thirty-three and living at Mottistone. He was in good health and his place as a national hero had been sealed with an appearance at Olympia's war-horse tribute in 1930. But he needed oats every day to keep his strength up. As rationing of all provisions bit across the country, the idea of an old horse getting preference was not well received. Mutterings on the Island were communicated to Seely, doing Lord Lieutenant duty in Winchester. Bitter as it was, there had only to be one answer. Warrior would have to go.

It was in every sense a heartbreak. Warrior had been Seely's equine fantasy made flesh, what impossible memories he evoked.

Born in his beloved Island, reared by the devoted Cinderella, a star from those very first two-year-old days when he screwed up his courage to face the waves crashing around his feet just as later he stood rock steady under shell fire. Warrior was a wonder: athletic, bold, kind, intelligent and unbelievably tough. In his other books Seely's writing style can be a bit over-creamed with self-glorification, but in *My Horse Warrior* the simple devotion to another is touching in its sincerity. And the illustrations by Alfred Munnings, for which Seely paid, being as ever impossibly short of cash, with that trip to Bad Ems, are a comparable delight.

Of course there are times when the whole thing goes hopelessly sentimental – 'I have never seen Warrior so angry', writes Seely after that first point-to-point defeat – but man and horse were certainly blood brothers. The old horse calling to Seely whenever he saw him, the pair hacking over the Downs with the turf beneath their feet almost to the end. When it came, Seely wrote instructions to have Warrior put down but that it should not be done until he was next in London, a good distance from the deed. On Good Friday 1941 he wrote an obituary line which remains amongst his Nuffield papers. 'I do not believe, to quote Byron about his dog Boatswain "that he is denied in heaven the soul he held on earth".'

Other writings for the *Sunday Times* and the *Evening Standard* reveal the totality of Seely's conversion in the harsher, wider world. In 'A Call to Youth and a Call to Action' he instructs us about those 'scout camps' he so admired in Germany and Italy: 'Now we see that the whole force of this Youth Movement in both countries has been enlisted in the cause of cruelty, faithlessness and wrong.' In a piece entitled 'Duty to Serve' he extols the strength of the British constitution and its principle of equality under the law: 'The whole doctrine is the negation of Hitlerism and that accursed theory of "Herrenvolk" which the German tyrant has taught the growing youth of Germany the last fifteen years. The effect of that teaching on the young German Soldiers and members of the Gestapo is seen in the almost incredible horrors perpetrated by them against their prisoners and especially against the Jews.' The scales had dropped from the eyes.

But optimism would always out. By the middle of 1941, with France occupied and Hitler invading Russia, you would not think there was much to be optimistic about. But from somewhere, perhaps the capture of Damascus, the surrender of the Italians in Abyssinia, the growing pledges from the USA, Seely was beginning to warm his hands again on hope.

He kept a sporadic diary at this time. Note the entry for 22 July:

> Dinner at the Other Club. Sat close to Winston. He was ever so much better than when I saw him last and his happy natural self. HG Wells was there bubbling over with the way things had gone.
>
> Next day Privy Council with the King. It was really good to see the King so fit and well. Incidentally all trace of stammer had vanished completely. So now I know that the Head of State and the Prime Minister are both of them confident and robust.

Diaries are notoriously unreliable, but three days later the change of mood from the appeasement years becomes quite ludicrously evident when he writes of an imagined scenario that caused Rudolf Hess to set out on his recent parachute mission to Scotland: 'Hitler then flew into a passion and marched up and down the room screaming just as he did at our last interview when I told him to stop persecuting the Jews.' True recollection or not, his condemnation of Hitler was completed that winter when he wrote, 'History acclaims the code Napoleon. There is no code Hitler. The man and his regime has no redeeming feature. No, not one.'

His own health was beginning to fade, his lungs were getting worse, but some things still got the old gander up. In 1942 it was a Civil Service leaflet on how to deal with an enemy paratrooper or suspected spy. The cautious advice was that any civilian should stay inside until help came. This did not square with the experience of the boy who had defeated the bully at Hawtreys, the youth who had swum out to the *Henri et Léontine*, the general who had galloped Warrior through the bullets to the Bois de la Corne. 'Of course what he must do if he has the least prospect of success', snorted Seely about the would-be cautious civilian, 'is to hit him over the head, disarm him and hand him over to the police. How the cloistered Civil Service came to issue such a fantastic defeatist document passes my comprehension.'

There was still some fire left. He toured Hampshire and the Island when he could, but there was now the odd note in the diary about being checked by the doctors, about choosing not to walk up the hill to a service at Windsor. There was also a sensitive touch of concern as well as reconciliation in a diary note for 29 September 1944, just after Churchill had sailed back from talks with Roosevelt in Quebec: 'Dinner at the Savoy. Sat next to Winston. He was cordial, even affectionate to me – after all we had been intimate friends for 48 years. He looked and was very well. Every time he travels by sea it does him good. Long journeys by air do him harm.'

In truth Seely was a much more sensitive soul than the fire-eating 'And That's That' caricature his later stories cultivated. He remained a liberal for the rest of his life and, for all his own privilege, was open and honest in his affections, be they farm-hand or family. When my parents were in Uruguay in the 1930s calls from my mother to her father quickly became incomprehensible as both parties dissolved into tears. But he had set himself on this duty-first 'Fear and Be Slain' adventure and right to the end tried to stick to the old Empire certainties with which he had been raised.

In the *Sunday Times* of 27 May 1945 he wrote, 'Let us now show that this Empire which has served not only ourselves but mankind so well, shall be fostered in its full vigour.' It was a gallant call but the tide was running out on the Empire deal just as his own reserves were running down. The lungs got worse. Sometimes he was still strong enough to rekindle the old glories, as in early 1947 when Bill Cowen, now a Hollywood veteran, brought his young son Garry across from America to call. But often he needed the oxygen cylinder. After all these chapters, that image of the old man in the dressing gown still remains the only direct memory I can conjure up.

He was like that in October 1947 when my sister took her baby son to see him. It was his first great-grandchild. He was not well enough to hold him in his arms but the rheumy eye was proud in what it saw. He was seventy-nine. Jack Seely had given it quite a go.

'The cares of office and the carelessness of freedom', he wrote at the beginning of *Adventure*, 'have taught me that neither things nor people are ever as bad as they may seem; that no venture is so forlorn that it cannot be carried through, no emotion so great that it cannot be borne, that good fortune seldom deserts the resolute; that no man, even if he be a politician or a priest is as devious or devout as the world supposes.'

His was a spirit that should never die. But on 7 November 1947 the old chest was finally beaten. No more great adventure now.

Epilogue

To end this voyage I need to ride the breakers to the shore. To land at Brooke where the lifeboat used to launch, where 150 million years ago the dinosaurs left their mark. For the story is locked on to an Island and it is to this special coast that I must return.

Seely footprints are everywhere, and for a grandson they evoke smiles and tears by turn. Ben Jacobs's cottage stands thatched and weatherworn at the end of the green. Much more cliff-top erosion and wags will call it 'Beach Cottage' soon. The old lifeboat house lost its roof long ago, but close the eyes and conjure up those ten great carthorses heaving the 'whale-on-rollers' lifeboat to the slipway path.

David Hookey, the blacksmith, would be with them. His grandson farms here, a living symbol of continuity that only the sea and the downland and a few of the buildings carry now. Imagining Brooke House at its zenith is not easy. Bungalows where once was lawn, not even a sapling left of the Garibaldi Oak. Best to go to the lodge and recall the curtseying gatekeeper's daughter and my mother tossing a sixpence into the outspread skirt in thanks. Just one part of a whole interlocking rural workforce based on the comically doomed Belloc couplet: 'It is the duty of the wealthy man / to give employment to the artisan.'

Mum's bedroom, too, has gone to the builder's hammer, but there is enough of the great house's eighteenth-century frontage to spin the time machine back to 1906 and think of her looking down at her father, and he gazing back with the wistful adoration so beautifully caught by Sassoon:

The brave March day; and you not four years old
Up in your nursery world all heaven to me
Remember this – the happiness I hold
In far off springs I shall not live to see.

Walk on up towards the church and a touch of sadness clings. Stand below the graveyard and see Nim's cross, Charles Seely's cenotaph and Harry Gore-Brown's russet-crusted memorial stretch up the hill, three crosses in a row. Next to Uncle Harry is a stone slab topped by a carved midshipman's cap. His grandson Geoffrey was just fifteen when he was sunk in September 1914.

In the church Frank Seely's name is on the altar window, so too that of his cousin Charlie and of carpenter's son Ernest Newberry, killed at Arras just three days before the squire's boy met his fate. The lifeboat's honours board lists the rescues, but coxswain Reuben Cooper has a plaque all his own. He perished in the *Sirenia* storm of 1880. He was sixty-six. The sea has taken them young and old.

Walk back out of the porch and the vitality comes flooding in. It was from here that my parents walked after their wedding in the summer of 1924; it was here I held my second son after his christening in 1979. This view was one of Seely's inspirations. Look down west and the ocean awaits you, swing the eye north and the high ridge of Brooke Down and its Bronze Age Five Barrows beckon. Four thousand years ago earlier Islanders had built them. Already they would have known the place's virtues even if it was the Norsemen who gave it the name of 'Wight'. It translates as 'Island of the Brave'.

Up on Five Barrows Warrior and Seely loved to gallop, but the old horse had other tricks. The village school stood next to the Sun Inn at Hulverstone. The general liked to ride by and give the children sweets. If Warrior dipped that white-starred face cutely, the kids were bound to share.

It was at Hulverstone that I first found euphemism. Questioning my mother as to why our 'cheery' Uncle Patrick went to the Sun Inn of an evening, she told me he was 'getting a box of matches'. On up Hulverstone Chute to Mottistone, and there on the left wall of the graveyard one stone stands alone. It is for my sparkling, red-haired young cousin Penelope, tragically electrocuted playing sardines one November evening in 1955. She was eight. She was my first acquaintance with grief.

Across from her are Aunt Emmy's and Aunt Kitty's headstones. To the right Uncle John Nicholson and Aunt Vivian. And up the top, the stone white and resplendent, is that of Harry Smith and his wife Rose, the cook. Trust a butler to still keep things spruce and elegant fifty years beyond the grave.

The blossom is out and in the church porch the swallows are nesting. Inside the magic soon takes thrall. A notice reads that the first, twelfth-century church was built by someone called Brian de Insula. Man was an island even then.

The roof of the nave is made of shipwreck timbers, and candles hang by the lectern where my dad sometimes read the lesson, looking very serious behind the glasses, that naval blazer ready for a sherry soon.

Jack Seely's ashes are in the Cheke Chapel alongside those of Evie and of his sons John and Patrick. It's a four-pew pool of contemplation on the northern side of the choir. John had designed it in his guise as architect, an eight-poster parclose linking it to the chapel altar, slender carved oak pillars supporting a wooden frieze around which is carved a Latin inscription penned by the second Lord Birkenhead, son of F.E. It is a place fit for heroes and if you sit and allow the mind to wander it won't be long before the shades of Seely's special legends gather in the air:

William Gladstone – Ben Jacobs, the coxswain – Louis Botha – Winston Churchill – F.E. Smith – Prince Antoine – Alfred Munnings – and of course Warrior, a horse for any heaven. Then a taller, younger presence is emerging. The others shift as older men do for sporting tyros. Fred Harvey is with them. Celebrations can begin.

The place seems a-swirl with a whole Valhalla of applauding heroes. Give it a minute and Antoine will have ordered up the wine.

But praise is a dangerous liquor and now two other shapes are moving. The church goes cold. A jackboot sounds in the aisle.

Il Duce is big-faced and gleaming, claiming Garibaldi's mantle and much more. The Führer, shiny-booted, is eager to lay on his 'great soldier' flattery with a trowel. Yes, Hitler and Mussolini would like to share the feast.

But there is a frisson amongst the heroes. Winston's jaw clenches like a bulldog's, Harvey's great shoulders begin to square. Seely turns, nods and stiffens. The dictators slink away.

The eye shifts to see what made them vanish, and you remember this is a chapel after all. In the stained glass of the east window a gilded angel kneels, hands clasped, beside an open scroll. As the words begin to register the other shades melt back towards the door.

The words are from St Paul: 'Whatsoever things are true, whatsoever things are honest, whatsoever things are just, whatsoever things are pure, whatsoever things are lovely, whatsoever things are of good report; if there be any virtue, and if there be any praise, think on these things.'

As I began these pages, ending them in a church was an agnostic's unlikely destination. But if you put your faith in heroes, you have to note where their own trust lies. 'Fear and be slain' can be more than a fire-eating motto. Its second half is 'Believe and live.'

For seventy-nine years it sustained this happy, sometimes heedless hero on a voyage without compare. Maybe spreading the story will pass lessons, as well as laughter, down the years.

And that Seely grandson who has now lived the old man's journey?

Ah yes – he seeks some certainty still.

Index